MIMESIS
INTERNATIONAL

ATMOSPHERIC SPACES
n. 8

ATMOSPHERIC SPACES

Directed by Tonino Griffero

What is an "Atmosphere"?

According to an aesthetic, phenomenological and ontological view, such a notion can be understood as a sensorial and affective quality widespread in space. It is the particular tone that determines the way one experiences her surroundings.

Air, ambiance, aura, climate, environment, genius loci, milieu, mood, numinous, lived space, Stimmung, but also Umwelt, ki, aida, Zwischen, in-between – all these words are names hiding, in fact, the founding idea of atmospheres: a vague ens or power, without visible and discrete boundaries, which we find around us and, resonating in our lived body, even involves us.

Studying atmospheres means, thus, a parte subjecti, to analyse (above all) the range of unintentional or involuntary experiences and, in particular, those experiences which emotionally "tonalise" our everyday life. A parte objecti, it means however to learn how atmospheres are intentionally (e.g. artistically, politically, socially, etc.) produced and how we can critically evaluate them, thus avoiding being easily manipulated by such feelings.

Atmospheric Spaces is a new book series whose aim is to become a point of reference for a community that works together on this philosophical and transdisciplinary subject and for all those whose research, more broadly, is involved in the so-called "affective turn" of the Social Sciences and Humanities.

Otto Friedrich Bollnow

HUMAN SPACE

First English edition published by Hyphen Press, London, in 2011
Translated from *Mensch und Raum* © 1963 W. Kohlhammer GmbH, Stuttgart, 11. Auflage 2010

Translated by Christine Shuttleworth
Edited by Joseph Kohlmaier

www.mimesisinternational.com
e-mail: info@mimesisinternational.com

Book series: *Atmospheric Spaces*, n. 8

Isbn: 9788869772832

P.I. C.F. 0241937030

Contents

II
THE WIDE WORLD

III
THE SECURITY OF THE HOUSE

IV
ASPECTS OF SPACE

Otto Friedrich Bollnow and Lived Space

by Tonino Griffero

1. It's really incredible. Over the last sixty years we have gone through the Vietnam War and the landing on the Moon, the sexual revolution and the events of 1968, the fall of the Wall and fundamentalist terrorism. In the humanities we have witnessed first structuralism and hermeneutics, then deconstructionism, cognitivism and, more recently, neuroscience; intellectuals and even ordinary people have long transformed nomadism (physical, touristic and intellectual) into a veritable myth, soon reinforced by globalisation and the digital age. And there have also been massive developments in studies on space and the environment - hence the so-called "spatial turn" in many disciplinary fields, corroborated by increasingly sophisticated reflections on landscape and ambiance (or atmosphere, in my lexicon), as well as on the "place" as both a descriptive and normative concept. In short, a lot of water has gone under the bridge, and yet the 1963 German book by Otto Friedrich Bollnow dedicated to lived or experienced space (*Mensch und Raum*) - whose English translation (*Human Space*) I am happy to present here as part of a series explicitly dedicated to the concept of "atmosphere" - is still fully relevant. Indeed, it has reached its eleventh edition in Germany. It is therefore no overstatement to say that it has become a twentieth-century classic on the topic.

Yet, this book features a understated style, devoid both of the theoretical harshness of orthodox phenomenology and of the vertiginous ontological incursions typical of Heideggerianism, both of the fascinating poetic-pantheistic (Bachelard) or existentialist (Sartre, Merleau-Ponty) French explorations of our being-in-the-world (also in a spatial sense) and of the (alleged) scientific precision claimed by academic geography and anthropology. Despite being a bit old-fashioned (or perhaps even because of that), it deserves to be read again, and in a more widely spoken language. The research presented here by the philosopher and pedagogist Otto Friedrich Bollnow (Stettin 1903-Tübingen 1991)[1] – a representative figure of the

1 For some introductory information and a complete bibliography see https://bollnow-gesellschaft.de/ The recent *Studienausgabe* includes 12 volumes: 1: *Das*

convergence among the (understated) philosophy of life and philosophy of culture, hermeneutics and (soft) existentialism – must, of course, be historicized. How was he supposed to know about the transformation of the perceptual space induced by cell phones and GPS, Internet and videogames, etc.? Still, this is a book that can be read with extreme pleasure and is sometimes even surprising. In fact, anyone who wants to learn something more about the philosophical but also multidisciplinary notion of "lived space" cannot do without looking at this text.[2] To be clear: many more brilliant thinkers have devoted themselves to this topic in the last century, especially after Bollnow. If, however, one should point to a single book for a balanced introduction to the concept of lived space, I think one would end up recommending Bollnow's *Mensch und Raum.*

Now, this easy-to-read and sufficiently anti-academic book does not present great interpretative difficulties, nor is it necessary to know the personality of its author to better understand it. However, perhaps it might be useful in this brief introduction to quickly outline how the issue of the lived space reached Bollnow's ears and attracted his (and our) attention.

2. In Kabbalah it is said that God "is the place of every place and this place does not take place". This is certainly not a prediction of the postmodern discourse on non-places or of the modern dissolution of space "in a stream of currents of information, goods and money".[3] Instead, it reflects, in its own way, the millenary discussion (which was first and foremost phenomenological in the last century) on a spatial dimension that is more original than the measurable one.

Wesen der Stimmungen (2009); 2: *Die Ehrfurcht; Wesen und Wandel der Tugenden* (2009); 3: *Einfache Sittlichkeit; Maß und Vermessenheit des Menschen* (2009); 4: *Lebensphilosophie und Existenzphilosophie* (2009); 5: *Neue Geborgenheit – Das Problem einer Überwindung des Existentialismus* (2011); 6: *Mensch und Raum* (2011); 7: *Anthropologische Pädagogik* (2013); 8: *Existenzphilosophie und Pädagogik; Krise und neuer Anfang* (2014); 9: *Sprache und Erziehung; Das Verhältnis zur Zeit; Vom Geist des Übens* (2017); 10: *Dilthey; Hermeneutische Logik von Georg Misch und Hans Lipps*; 11: *Studien zur Hermeneutik*; 12: *Philosophie der Erkenntnis; Hermeneutische Philosophie.*

2 The same can be said for at least another book by Bollnow, which is still the best introduction to the philosophical question of *Stimmungen* (basic moods): *Das Wesen der Stimmungen* (Frankfurt: 1941, 1956), not yet translated into English. Bollnow is also the author of the first book focusing on pedagogical atmospheres: *Die pädagogische Atmosphäre. Untersuchungen über die gefühlsmäßigen zwischenmenschlichen Voraussetzungen der Erziehung* (Heidelberg: 1964).

3 Martina Löw, *Raumsoziologie* (Frankfurt a. M.: 2001), p. 106.

It is a fact that in most of our spatial experiences flat geometry proves inadequate. For example, it is unable to justify the (not only metaphorical) voluminousness of the Sunday silence or the distressing narrowness of a living room (perhaps metrically identical to another which is yet perceived as more spacious), the huge difference between the space full of directional saliences in which a dancer moves and the anodyne space of one who crosses the same dance floor for no particular reason, the different length of a journey for someone who strolls casually and someone with a precise destination in mind. A flat geometry is also unable to account for the fact that the outward leg of a trip always seems longer than the return, or that the plan of an apartment tells us very little about the functional but above all emotional and bodily qualities that it could have if it were "our home". In these and other cases, the usual anesthetization of spatial perception gives way to a "sense of space" that, as if it were the topological anti-epistemic correlate of "common sense", imposes itself as something irreducible to metric dimensions. It follows that "the spectrum of spatiality is [...] much more extensive than its classical conceptualization in the philosophical and scientific field".[4] Therefore, no Occam's razor can cut out lived space and thus reduce space to something strictly physical – a panorama to look at with detachment and in which to draw arbitrary lines at will.

The founder of proxemics Edward Twitchell Hall is certainly right: "A room that can be traversed in one or two steps gives an entirely different experience from a room requiring fifteen or twenty steps. A room with a ceiling you can touch is quite different from one with a ceiling eleven feet high".[5] It is only because humans have such a (lived) space that it makes sense to say that there is not enough or too much space, that we want our own space, that we need space, or that we can make space (thus creating a void that was not there before). The genesis and effects of lived space are clearly psychosocial and relatively independent from physical ontology. It could also be said that "man is never a subject deprived of space, [...] he always finds himself in some lived and experienced relationship with space, a relationship that determines it and gives it an imprint".[6] It follows that human beings are not "in" space as if in a big container (i.e. in an invariable and pragmatically useful reference system for things and places, mutually

4 Hermann Schmitz, *System der Philosophie*. III.1. *Der Raum* (Bonn: 1967), p. XVI.

5 Edward Twitchell Hall, *The Hidden Dimension* (New York: 1966), p. 54.

6 Friedemann Maurer, *Räumliche Umwelt und Identität. Eine sozialökologische Skizze*, in W. Loch (ed.), *Lebensform und Erziehung. Besinnungen zur pädagogischen Anthropologie* (Essen: 1983), p. 27.

defined by position and distance) but "surrounded" by (and embedded in) pre-dimensional lived spaces, for instance "the space of sound, the space of the wind blowing against us and sweeping us away with it, the space of gestures, the space of water for a swimmer or a diver with their eyes closed".[7]

This also implies, switching to non-philosophical disciplines, the distinction between routine spaces (pedestrian zones, stations, etc.), counterculture spaces and openly heterotopic spaces (illusory and with compensatory function); between space as a result of a first spacing (construction or placement of things) and space as an indispensable subsequent synthesis (transformation of goods and people into spaces through perceptual, representative and mnemonic processes);[8] between an abstractly homogeneous and governmentally controlled space (globalization, global cities, web space, etc.) and an axiologically fragmented and hierarchical space (digital gap, ghettos, peripheries, etc.); between neutral zones and the new spaces that the so-called *Erlebnis* society views as "scenarios".[9] As soon as we give up the idea that we exist "in" space, i.e. in a relative reference system, we have to admit that we always experience space "in a certain way", animated by this or that feeling suggested by the space itself. It must be admitted, in other words, that "being in", freed from the objectivistic sphere of metric-geometric three-dimensionality, comes with a spatial dimension of optical-motor nature charged with (more or less intense) emotionality.

The debate on the lived space, at first sight, seems to do nothing but bring to light the tacit millenary opposition between relativistic topology and absolutist topology, that is, between a conception for which space is nothing in itself and springs from the ordering of bodies, and a view for which it exists and is endowed with its own reality, acting as a great "container" of all bodies, regardless of how we act or how we feel it. It may certainly be true that today it is not possible to reduce space as conceived by physical science to an abstractly metric-geometric space, homogeneous and therefore a-qualitative. Yet this is precisely the conception that the mathematical sciences have deposited in = common sense through

---

7 Hermann Schmitz, *Einführung in den Beitrag von Graf Karlfried von Dürckheim aus philosophischer Perspektive*, in Graf Karlfried von Dürckheim, *Untersuchungen zum gelebten Raum*. ed. by J. Hasse (Frankfurt a. M.: 2005), p. 109.

8 M. Löw, *Raumsoziologie*, cit., p. 158 ff.

9 Gerhard Schulze, *Die Erlebnisgesellschaft. Kultursoziologie der Gegenwart* (Frankfurt a. M.-New York: 1992).

their successful applications, so that "the daily representations of space for most people of our civilization are more or less heavily 'colonized' by the physicalist intuition of classical physics in the form of three-dimensional Euclidean space".[10] As sophisticated as the notion of space in today's theoretical physics is, therefore, the phenomenological (and atmospherological) approach should oppose precisely the notion of it that is universally "considered" scientific, which can be summarized in Euclidean isotropy and three-dimensionality. that.

The physics of the past has also provided rather complex interpretations of the notion of space. One example is Newton's absolute space (independent from bodies as opposed to relative space), which was later tamed by common sense because of the obvious unthinkability of infinity. Another example is Leibniz's relativistic space as the "ordering principle of positional relation",[11] such that "strictly speaking one should not say 'this body is in this place', but only that 'it is found, seen by that other body, in this place'".[12] And again, think of Kant's gnoseologistic conception of space not as an object but as the a priori pure form of sensitivity, as a form of possible objects; or, lastly, consider the Einsteinian conception of the relativity of space with respect to the observer's reference system. And yet, despite these enormous variations in the academic field – and despite the disintegration of the traditional unity of space in contemporary art – the idea of space as a container is and has remained the most influential one, which immediately comes to mind in everyday life. With "space", in short,

> we think [...] immediately of the three-dimensional space of mathematics, not [...] just because it was an ancient subject of school learning [...] but also because a large part of our practical action is based on objective spatial references, for example when by measuring and calculating we overcome our environmental world, we build a house, we design the furnishing of a room. The predominance of this objective mathematical space in our conscious behavior and experience does not mean, however, that it is also the foundation of the lived space.[13]

---

10 Dieter Läpple, *Essay über den Raum. Für ein gesellschaftswissenschaftliches Raumkonzept*, in H. Häußermann a. o. (eds.), *Stadt und Raum* (Pfaffenweiler: 1991), p. 164.

11 Alexander Gosztonyi, *Der Raum. Geschichte seiner Probleme in Philosophie und Wissenschaften* (Freiburg/München: 1976), p. 363.

12 Carl-Friedrich von Weizsäcker, *Zum Weltbild der Physik* (Stuttgart: 1990), p. 138.

13 Lenelis Kruse, *Räumliche Umwelt. Die Phänomenologie des räumlichen Verhaltens als Beitrag zu einer psychologischen Umwelttheorie* (Berlin: 1974), p. 33.

As Merleau-Ponty brilliantly reminds us: "besides the physical and geometrical distance which stands between myself and all things, a 'lived' distance binds me to things which count and exist for me, and links them to each other. This distance measures the 'scope' of my life at every moment".[14] This is why space is perceived slightly differently by different generations, ethnic groups, genders and cultures, and this is also why there is a sort of iconic and dizzying polydaemonism of spaces.

> For the spirit clinging to life there are first of all as many spaces and times as the images which it is possible to have a lived experience of in a space-time sense: therefore not only a nightly space next to a daily one, a domestic one next to a celestial one, the space of a wood next to the space of a temple, an East, a South, a West, a North, but possibly also as many house spaces as there are houses, and finally as many house spaces as there are moments of interiorisation of the spatial manifestation through which the house takes shape.[15]

Even without reaching these relativistic excesses, the lived space is precisely what a neo-phenomenological atmospherology should devote attention to.

3. All this also applies to atmospheric spaces as spatialised feelings: they are, in fact, the specific emotional qualities of what I (like Bollnow) call "lived" or "experienced" space. As we will see shortly, the concept of "lived space" had an impressive scientific career in the first half of the Twentieth century and is now back to the fore in the social sciences speaking of a *spatial turn*. "Lived space" is the space we experience in the lifeworld and to which plane geometry turns out to be completely blind. While physical space, made of places and measurable distances, is based on an abstract uniformity (isotropy and Euclidean three-dimensionality), "lived" space claims to have an absoluteness and an irreversibility related to the felt body (above/below, right/left, up/down) and its actions. This was proved, although with all due differences, by the phenomenological-psychopathological field as well as the anthropological-existentialist one (up until at least the 1960s: Heidegger, Binswanger, Minkowski, Straus, Dürckheim, Merleau-Ponty, Bachelard, Bollnow, Schmitz, and many others of course).

---

14 Maurice Merleau-Ponty, *Phenomenology of Perception* (1945) (London: 2005), p. 333.

15 Ludwig Klages, *Der Geist als Widersacher der Seele*, 3 vol. (Leipzig: 1929-32), p. 24.

I will not delve into the (philosophical) history of lived space here.[16] Rather, I will only highlight the turning points that anticipated and prepared Bollnow's theory of lived (or atmospheric) space. The first was Martin Heidegger (1927),[17] for whom the vulgar (quantitative) conception of spatiality was nothing but the neutralisation of a more originary "circumspection" [*Umsicht*], at the centre of which lies the mood or emotive attunement (*Stimmung*). He then transformed "true" dwelling and building, as well as the notion of "place" as a non isotropic spatial determination, into a sort of poetical correspondence to the appeal of Being or, in his terms, to the essential fourfold (earth, sky, divinities, mortals).[18]

Immediately afterwards, one must mention Eugene Minkowski, with his subtle analyses of clear space and dark space as well as his study (1933)[19] of the non-metric but qualitative value of "distance" and its possible pathological deformations. His work was based on the conviction that, far from moving in space, it is the I that creates space with a sort of "a priori spatial dynamism".[20]

An even more significant contribution came perhaps from Erwin Straus' distinction (1935) between a gnostic perception, relative to "*what* is objectually given", and a pathic feeling, relative to "*how* it gives itself ",[21] also exemplified by the contrast both between geography and landscape and between walking and dancing. Nonetheless, it is worth noting that the originary lived space, as a presential-homogeneous-ecstatic-unaware space, can become even pathological (autism) when it loses contact with a historical and localistic determinateness: this is an exceptionality and marginality that must be avoided, by making sure one does not identify atmospheres and a-directionality.

Karlfried von Dürckheim's inquiry into lived space (1932) starting from the "surrounding reality of the felt-body"[22] is certainly less known but perhaps

16 Tonino Griffero, *Atmospheres and Lived Space*, "Studia Phaenomenologica" 14 (2014), pp. 29-51.

17 Martin Heidegger, *Sein und Zeit* (Halle: 1927).

18 "Spaces receive their essence not 'from' the space but from places" (Martin Heidegger, *Building Dwelling Thinking* (1954), in Id., *Basic Writings* (New York: 1977), p. 103.

19 Eugene Minkowski, *Le temps vecu: etudes phénoménologiques et psychopathologiques* (Paris: 1933).

20 Eugene Minkowski, *Vers une cosmologie. Fragments philosophiques* (Paris: 1936), p. 58.

21 Erwin Straus, *Vom Sinn der Sinne* (Berlin-Gottingen-Heidelberg: 1935).

22 Graf Karlfried von Dürckheim, *Untersuchungen zum gelebten Raum*, ed. by J. Hasse (Frankfurt a. M.: 2005), p. 36.

theoretically even more relevant. I will prescind here from his many and slightly specious distinctions, but an anticipation of the theme of atmospheres can surely be found in what he calls "functional space": it exists in the operative variant, based on non-objective but felt distance and closeness; then in the self-related variant where the space exceeds the self like the felt-body (from the skin or dress to the community);[23] but also and mostly in the variant of the essence space, with its physiognomic-qualitative characters.[24] In fact, it is by virtue of the "invite qualities",[25] which for me are *tout court* atmospheric, that one "feels 'solemn' in a church, 'objective' in a laboratory, etc. […] One unwillingly moves differently in a church or in a workplace, in a wood or a street, in a Northern landscape or a Southern one, at home or at someone else's place".[26] And this is certainly not due to projectivistic reasons.

> Every natural space is also felt as the space of a specific life. This is not a transference of vitality from the sphere of the human so that, so to speak, particular natural beings living their life in that space are empathised with. It is rather a life expressing itself starting from nature itself: a life whose time, form and history give sense and meaning to the being-so of the space.[27]

Of course, one can be fond of vast spaces while another person can prefer narrow ones.[28] But this is precisely because "all people overall feel these position qualities, even though some feel good and others do not".[29] Here it is worth making at least a sketched distinction[30] between an essence (in my jargon, an atmosphere) and a subjective mood that does not necessarily correspond to it. Dürckheim provides a sort of compromise solution – unfortunately largely relegated to the infantile and artistic sphere – between the lived sense immanent in the present space and the more

23 "Church also means 'Sunday'. The different spaces of a house have the quality of their hour […] Every space in its overall quality is co-determined by the quality of the hour in which it is present and by the quality of the functions and aspects of life that are realised there" (Ibid, p. 107).

24 In particular, character features (a space can be heroic, harsh, pleasant, etc.), emotional qualities (a room, for instance, can be "serene") and position qualities (the space addresses us in a free or oppressive way, etc.).

25 Graf Karlfried von Dürckheim, *Untersuchungen zum gelebten Raum*, cit., p. 16.

26 Ibid, pp. 34, 49.

27 Ibid, p. 45.

28 Children, for instance, prefer closed spaces (like nests or caves) and absolutely private ones.

29 Graf Karlfried von Dürckheim, *Untersuchungen zum gelebten Raum*, cit., p. 79.

30 See Jürgen Hasse, *Fundsachen der Sinne. Eine phänomenologische Revision alltägliche Erlebens* (Freiburg/München: 2005), p. 142.

or less contingent vital directions of the subject. According to him, the atmospheric is favoured by an afinalistic relation with space,[31] by a "certain passivity and a vast availability",[32] if not even by a personality that is not excessively outlined, as well as by an "ingressive" impression.

> The specific existence of the vital qualities of different spaces becomes evident and tangible mostly when passing from a space to another. It is therefore clear how the overall vital behaviour changes when one leaves the house to go out; when one leaves the street to walk into a field and then penetrates into a wood or, once the last houses are left behind, gets to the countryside; or when a very congested city road turns into a quiet corner.[33]

Dürckheim might be the first European who broke the two-millennia long illusion that the human being is an a-spatial innerness and that space is only a reservoir for external objects.[34] Still, he was certainly less influential than Merleau-Ponty (1945), to whom we owe the divulgation of the (by now consolidated) critique of the physical-geometrical space in the name of perception, which works as a primordial, anonymous and ante-predicative pact with the world. All fundamental spatial determinations therefore are bodily lived: from depth – reinterpreted as "a possibility of a subject involved in the world"[35] with their felt body – to movement, ascribable to a "variation of the subject's hold on his world",[36] to high and low as directions of meaning (both physical and desiring) of the "essential structure of our being".[37] All these dimensions, as "great affective entities"[38] as well as synaesthetic ones, constitute a (mythical or anthropological) lived space whose symbolic pre-theoretical and pre-thetic pregnancy should be reawakened by phenomenologists. Without being petrified by it, they e should recognise that it is the anonymous operative intentionality of primordial perception that legitimises the quasi-objective nature of the emotionally connoted space we have defined as atmospheric.

---

31 "It suffices to utter the word 'finalistic space' and a world – indeed, the world of essence – collapses" (Graf Karlfried von Dürckheim, *Untersuchungen zum gelebten Raum*, cit., p. 82).

32 Ibid, p. 71.

33 Ibid, p. 40.

34 As emphatically stated by Schmitz, *Einführung in den Beitrag von Graf Karlfried von Dürckheim aus philosophischer Perspektive*, cit., p. 111.

35 Maurice Merleau-Ponty, *Phenomenology of Perception*, cit., p. 311.

36 Ibid, p. 312.

37 Ibid, p. 331.

38 Ibid, p. 332.

This brings me to Gaston Bachelard's *The Poetics of Space* (1957), to which we owe a careful phenomenological thematisation of the affective resonances aroused by a *corpus* of (irreducible) poetic images of space. These are pre-reflective, allusive and dreamlike images in which space, taken away from "utilitarian geometrical notions"[39] as well as psychoanalytical and metaphorising deferrals, functions as an archetypal shelter for the *reverie* and as the presupposition for any subsequent personal axiology (and well-being). Indeed, we all coincide with the spaces we lived-imagined:

> Each one of us, then, should speak of his roads, his crossroads, his roadside benches; each one of us should make a surveyor's map of his lost fields and meadows. [...] Thus we cover the universe with drawings we have lived. These drawings need not be exact. They need only to be tonalized on the mode of our inner space.[40]

Bachelard's topophilia is especially condensed into the house, examined in all the aspects capable of atmospheric irradiation. In fact, he speaks of avolumetric spatialities (mainly intimacies) charged with corporeal suggestions, of a specific atmosphere of the act of polishing, of spaces objectively charged with determined impressions and of immanent and transmodal emotional qualities: "for the sense of taste or smell, the problem might be even more interesting than for the sense of vision [...] But a whiff of perfume, or even the slightest odor can create an entire environment in the world of the imagination".[41] This poetic-literary approach is founded upon a psychic-imaginative consonance between subject and object, which is genially preserved by poetic expression.

> The two kinds of space, intimate space and exterior space, keep encouraging each other, as it were, in their growth. To designate space that has been experienced as affective space, which psychologists do very rightly, does not, however, go to the root of space dreams. The poet goes deeper when he uncovers a poetic space that does not enclose us in affectivity. Indeed, whatever the affectivity that colors a given space, whether sad or ponderous, once it is poetically expressed, the sadness is diminished, the ponderousness lightened. [...] When a poet tells me that he "knows a type of sadness that smells of pineapple," I myself feel less sad, I feel gently sad.[42]

---

39 Gaston Bachelard, *The Poetics of Space* (1957) (Boston: 1994), p. 55.
40 Ibid, pp. 11-12.
41 Ibid, p. 174.
42 Ibid, pp. 201-202.

This is an isomorphic and irenic stance that is far from isolated and that also reoccurs in Bollnow's approach.

3. This line of research, which I have radically summed up here, must be complemented by Otto Friedrich Bollnow's "urbanized" analysis (1963)[43] of spatiality as an "existential" space (in a Heideggerian sense) that is totally other than metric space, and of its relationship with moods (*Stimmungen*).

> Space is by no means homogeneous, rather every place in it is laden with special meanings. There is a distinction between preferred and avoided areas. Memories of pleasant or unpleasant kinds are linked with the individual places [...] Just as the sun rises anew for us every morning in the east above the fi xed earth, although we have long known 'better' from the Copernican system, so, despite all our knowledge about the infi nity of the universe, space, as we concretely experience it, whether in a particular case it is narrower or wide, has always remained for us fi nite in its nature. (Bollnow, *infra*, pp. 91 and 326).

In *Human Space* he provides the framework of a (very soft) Heideggerian-*kulturkritisch* polemic towards the increasing homogenization of space, also due to the increasingly widespread road traffic and the indifferentism of the landscape. He also argues for the revaluation of the harmony between naive topology and Aristotelian anisotropy, thus highlighting the "usual" dimensions of the lived space (high/low, forward/backward, left/right, etc.). It is within these dimensions that the life (and the axiology) of the ego takes shape, domesticating them as forms of the objective spirit (Dilthey) or as the objectified spirit (Hartmann). Bollnow circumscribes the existentialistic-Heideggerian "thrown projection" of *Dasein* with the recognition that man, by nature extraneous to spatial infiniteness, is originally in a medium that is not at all hostile but rather decidedly warm and protective like the (archetypal) one of the cradle/case/cave. Sometimes Bollnow's examples of the dyscrasia between physical space and lived space are very effective, such as when he points out that the few centimeters between a point on my wall and one on the wall next to it belonging to a different flat actually mark two totally alien worlds. The book also has the merit of reminding us of theories that today are a little forgotten, like Kurt Lewin's odology. However, it only alludes, quite contradictorily, to "non-mood action space" (*Ibid., infra*, p. 279),

43 Otto Friedrich Bollnow, *Mensch und Raum* (1963) (Stuttgart: 2004).

and provides a somewhat anodyne solution to the central problem of the subjective or objective character of atmospheres.

> Even in the same person, the need for space varies according to his psychological state and his needs at the time [...] Conversely, the character of the space surrounding the individual has an effect on his mood. So we have a reciprocal infl uence: the psychological state of the person determines the character of his surrounding space, and conversely the space then affects his psychological state. [...] Space has its particular mood, both as an interior space and also as a landscape. It can be cheerful, light, gloomy, sober, festive, and this character of mood then transfers itself to the person staying in it. [...] Man himself is governed from within by a certain mood, and is inclined to transfer this to the surrounding space, where the concept of transference should only be used in a temporary sense for the preliminary clarification of this direct sense of belonging together and agreement. One speaks of a mood of the human temperament as well as of the mood of a landscape or a closed interior space, and both are, strictly speaking, only two aspects of the same phenomenon. [...] Mood is itself not something subjective 'in' an individual and not something objective that could be found 'outside' in his surroundings, but it concerns the individual in his still undivided unity with his surroundings. (*Ibid., infra*, pp. 255-257).

This is the curse of any "but-also" stance: it undermines any approach that wants to mediate between very different instances. In fact, Bollnow recognizes, on the one hand, that we are captured by the *Stimmung* of outer space, and, on the other hand, however, that the same space is "tonalized" by our subjective *Stimmung*. As for the typologies of Stimmung, Bollnow does not miss any of them. He distinguishes between a) the objective-embracing space in which the subject and things are present, b) the intentional space formed by distances and directions whose fulcrum is the subject, c) the own-felt space that one acquires thanks to habitual movement. He also differentiates, in relation to what one inhabits or embodies, between a) one's felt body, understood as the original point of space endowed with its own specific bulkiness, b) one's own home archetypically understood as a protective extended body (phylogenetically, as a cave), and, finally, c) the surrounding space, in which one also feels protected by virtue of an I/world resonance prior to any dualism.

Even from the little that has been said here, it is absolutely clear that Bollnow's book is one of the most important sources of the later and more advanced neo-phenomenological inquiry into lived space. To Hermann Schmitz, founder of the so-called New Phenomenology (since 1964), we actually owe not so much the nth reflection on the lived space, but rather an ambitious and systematic amendment of the prevailing spatial conception. For him, there are three levels of experience of space.[44] First of all there is a) the *local space* (*Ortsraum*), founded on relative dimensions (straight line, divisibility into parts, surfaces, reversibility, distance, place, etc.), which can be explained – to avoid infinite regress – only by starting from a corporeal space, such as b) the *directional space* (*Richtungsraum*). This is the pregeometrical dominion of a motility that is not (yet) reduced to local translation (expiration, gestural expressiveness, dance, sport, glance, etc.) and that is rather founded upon the narrowness/vastness dynamic. It is also the starting point of a felt-bodily communication with the surrounding environment, whose pre-local directionality depends on motor suggestions.

> Optical objects exercise not only a function of orientation, but also a function of attraction. That is, [...] they do not only attract the observer's attention, they also induce them to come close [...] The very sight of an open door, a piece of furniture of surprising shape and colour, a glance at a distance, or a source of light is often enough to transport a person into a finalised movement.[45]

Directional space, in turn, is rooted into an even more primal spatiality, devoid both of surfaces and dimensions: this is c) the *space of vastness* (*Weiteraum*), the place of the "primitive presence" – which, for Schmitz,[46] is given by the interwoven series "here-now-being-this-I" – as the extradimensional apriori of our corporeal feeling. This includes the climatic space (the one that, for instance, makes us say that "there is tension in the air") and the sound space; the olfactive space untranslatable into a figure[47] and the space of silence; the space of the swimmer (surrounded by volumes without width, height and depth) and the space of corporeal isles;[48] the space of feeling and the space enlightened in its peculiar atmospheric voluminousness. Other examples include empty space, the distressing space of twilight, the space of

44 See, lastly, Hermann Schmitz, *Situationen und Konstellationen: Wider die Ideologie totaler Vernetzung* (Freiburg/Munchen: 2005), pp. 186–204.

45 Géza Révész, *Die Formenwelt des Tastsinnes*, Bd. I (Den Haag: 1938), p. 91.

46 Hermann Schmitz, *Der unerschöpfliche Gegenstand* (Bonn: 1990), p. 280.

47 Because of its "naive" spatiality, "what smells and tastes cannot be measured, numbered, divided and, for these reasons, it cannot even be communicated in an objective way [...] It is indissolubly tied to the whole of a mood" (Hubertus Tellenbach, *Geschmack und Atmosphäre* (Salzburg: 1968), pp. 28–29.

48 See Tonino Griffero, *Quasi-Things. The Paradigm of Atmospheres* (Albany, New York: 2017), pp. 55-67.

ecstasy, even the (fundamental and yet unnoticed) unarticulated background that accompanies each of our optical-kinetic motions forwards. Finally, other instances of *Weiteraum* are the ability to walk with others without clashing thanks to the somatic control of the glance, the instinctive and undetermined tendency to run away in the case of panic, the open air we breathe in when we leave a sultry space, the thermal-optical field to which we expose ourselves when we doze in the sun.

These, then, (local space, directional space, and the absolute space of vastness), are three different ways of experiencing space. While being, luckily, melted together in adult life (and particularly in the atmosphericness immanent to dwelling), they still remain, at times, relatively distinct. The first localisation of a burning sensation in a hand, for example, to which we get "guided only by the absolute place of the felt-bodily isle now become blatant and by the habitual trajectories of the motor-bodily schema",[49] is evidently the space of vastness. The second one, which is instead possible only by means of subsequent focalisations on our finger, is more relative (and even more so the third).

In the space of feeling (*Gefühlsraum*) there are also three different levels of atmosphericness corresponding to the local space, the directional space and the absolute space of vastness. In fact, the atmospheres corresponding to the space of vastness are a) atmospheres centred on the felt body and devoid of borders like pure moods, leading to full extensions (satisfaction) or empty ones (desperation). The atmospheres corresponding to the directional space are instead b) vector atmospheres: emotions whose objectual terminations lead to (mistakenly) talk of intentional feelings. They can be unilateral, like those that exalt or depress, but also omnilateral, centrifugal, centripetal or undecided like what is rightly defined as pre-sentiment. Finally, the corresponding atmospheres of local space are c) the atmospheres that, in this or that object, find their point of condensation even without being their real anchoring point. The result is that there are as many kinds of atmosphere as there are forms of spatiality, and even the banal local space (surfaces-points-distances), rationalistic and pragmatically functional to human ex-centricity, is far from devoid of an atmospheric charge (although a partly projected one).

But this is not the place to analyse the atmospherological consequences of the humanities' rediscovery of the lived space.[50] It will suffice to recall

49 Hermann Schmitz, *Der unerschöpfliche Gegenstand*, cit., p. 291.

50 This is one of the basic premises of my own atmospherological research: see Tonino Griffero, *Atmospheres. Aesthetics of Emotional Spaces* (London-New

that, as is also admitted in sociology, spaces themselves develop "their own potentiality and can influence feelings. This potentiality of spaces [can] be called "atmosphere".[51] If Bollnow did not yet use the word "atmosphere" in a technical way, he still certainly dealt with the "thing" to which the word refers: feelings poured out into a certain pre-dimensional space. By valorising atmospheres as lived-affective spaces, especially in an age of break of the traditional bond between communities and their places (virtual world and globalisation), one is also aware of engaging with a far-reaching critical countermovement – something that certainly could not happen without a brilliant forerunner like Bollnow's *Human Space*.

York: 2014); Id., *Places, Affordances, Atmospheres. A Pathic Aesthetics* (London-New York: 2019).

51 Martina Löw, *Raumsoziologie*, cit., p. 204.

Editorial note

We have aimed for an edition that opens Bollnow's discussion to the English-language reader, while also respecting the character of the original book. Among the decisions taken we note the following.

Bollnow used an elaborate system of numbering sections and sub-sections, which we have simplified somewhat. In the contents pages at the start of the book we have retained the original edition's full display of section and sub-section headings.

In the footnotes we have given a full description of a book or article at its first occurence in each part, and have used abbreviated author and title descriptions subsequently for the rest of the part. Bollnow was often quite casual in his manner of referring to sources and, where feasible, we have done some tidying.

For the literature from which Bollnow quotes and to which he refers, we have where possible found existing English-language translations and used those English-language versions in giving titles, and have given page references to those editions. Our editorial interventions in the text or in the notes have been put in square brackets.

A recurring issue in the translation of Bollnow's text should be mentioned: how to translate 'Mensch' (already there in the title of the book), 'er', 'sein' and other words that have purely masculine referents in English? We felt that 'he or she' and 'his or hers' would seem too cumbersome over the course of the book. So where possible we have phrased to avoid the problem and elsewhere have used just 'he' and 'his'. This is at least consistent with usage at the time Bollnow wrote.

To Dr Ortrud Bollnow, née Bürger

11 September 1963

Introduction
On the History of the Question

The problem of time in human existence has preoccupied philosophers to such an extraordinary degree over recent decades that one could almost describe it as the fundamental problem of contemporary philosophy. Bergson was probably the first to formulate it convincingly as that of 'durée', concretely experienced as opposed to objectively measurable, and soon afterwards Simmel introduced this question to Germany. Later Heidegger, in the course of his existential ontology, decisively placed the question of the temporality of human existence at the centre of his entire philosophy, thus making it visible for the first time in its full significance. Sartre and Merleau-Ponty in their turn took up these ideas and disseminated them in France. But the same problem, starting from this impulse, has also proved extremely productive in the individual sciences, and has provoked a very extensive discussion, rich in new questions and results, in psychology and psychopathology as much as in the history of literature and the other disciplines of the arts and humanities. Here we will merely refer, among the extensive and complex literature, to the seminal work of Minkowski on 'temps vécu' [lived time].[1]

The problem of the spatial condition of human existence or, to put it more simply, of the concrete space experienced and lived by humans, has in contrast remained very much in the background, which is surprising when one considers the traditional, almost proverbial, link between the questions of time and space. Admittedly, as early as the 1930s, in psychology and psychopathology the question of experienced space was vigorously taken up, evidently under the strong influence of Heidegger, in close connection with the simultaneous research into time. Dürckheim, in his *Untersuchungen zum gelebten Raum* [Investigations into experienced

1 Eugène Minkowski, *Le temps vécu. Etudes phénoménologiques et psychopathologiques*, Paris: 1933, [*Lived time. Phenomenological and psychopathological studies*, translated by Nancy Metzel, Evanston: 1970].

space],[2] was probably the first to develop this question in the German-speaking area. At about the same time Minkowski, in the book on 'temps vécu' already mentioned, also introduced the concepts of 'distance vécue' and 'espace vécu', which he soon afterwards developed further in *Vers une cosmologie.*[3] Out of the psychopathological literature we will mention only the work of Straus[4] and Binswanger,[5] to which we will repeatedly return in the course of our observations. But these very interesting approaches did not impinge on the narrower area of philosophy and seem in fact soon to have been forgotten outside medical circles. Compared to time, which concerns the innermost centre of humanity, space seemed philosophically less rewarding, because it seemed to belong only to the outer environment of mankind.

From a totally different direction, Cassirer encountered a related question in his extensive *Philosophy of symbolic forms.*[6] In his pursuit of the development of human thought from its magical– mystical beginnings up to the formation of the modern scientific consciousness, he also had necessarily to occupy himself with the development of the concepts of space and time. He worked his way through an enormous amount of evidence from the fields of ethnology, history of religion, linguistics and the various individual human sciences, with rewarding results for systematic philosophical questioning. It is particularly interesting for our purposes to see how he explored the initially unfamiliar and incomprehensible structure of mythical space. He did admittedly perceive mythical space as a bygone stage in human development, overtaken by today's scientific concept of space. Conditioned

2 Karlfried Graf Dürckheim, 'Untersuchungen zum gelebten Raum', *Neue Psychologische Studien*, vol. 6, Munich: 1932, p. 383 ff.

3 Eugène Minkowski, *Vers une cosmologie*, Paris: 1936.

4 Erwin Straus, 'Formen des Räumlichen. Ihre Bedeutung für die Motorik und Wahrnehmung' (1930), *Psychologie der menschlichen Welt. Gesammelte Schriften*, Berlin, Göttingen, Heidelberg: 1960, p. 141 ff. ['Forms of spatiality', *Phenomenological psychology. The selected papers of Erwin Straus*, translated by Erling Eng, London: 1966, p. 3 ff.].

5 Ludwig Binswanger, *Über Ideenflucht*, Zurich: 1933; 'Das Raumproblem in der Psychopathologie' (1933), Ausgewählte Vorträge und Aufsätze, vol. 2, Bern: 1955, p. 174 ff.; *Grundformen und Erkenntnis menschlichen Daseins*, Zurich: 1942.

6 Ernst Cassirer, *Philosophie der symbolischen* Formen, vol. 3, Berlin: 1923-9. [The page numbers given by Bollnow do not correspond to the pagination given in Philosophie der symbolischen Formen, *Teil 2: Das mythische Denken. Gesammelte Werke. Hamburger Ausgabe*. vol. 12, Hamburg: 2002, in reference to the original edition and have been adjusted accordingly [*Philosophy of symbolic forms*, translated by Ralph Manheim, vol. 3, New Haven: 1953-7]].

by the direction of his question, he did not see the problem of experienced space as it is still present in the minds of humans today, and therefore did not ask to what extent spatial structures analogous to mythical views of space may have a more general significance, still valid for people living today, or at least how the mythical forms may be made rewarding for the understanding of experienced space. In addition, because of his emigration, Cassirer's work came to be largely forgotten in Germany and therefore did not exercise the influence on later development that was its due.

Since then, in the domain of philosophy, Lassen, himself under the influence of Cassirer, was probably the only one, in the context of his special question, namely a phenomenology of experience, to emphasize the basic importance of spatiality for the structure of human existence by comparison with the priority of temporality represented by Heidegger.[7] His work too, however, seems to have met with little attention.

Only in more recent times has the question of experienced space come more strongly to the fore. On the one hand, in the yearbook *Situation*[8] (of which unfortunately only the first volume was published), the circle of Buytendijk collected, from the point of view of phenomenological psychology, a series of important works on the development of concrete experienced space, to which we will also need to refer in detail. On the other hand, Bachelard, after a series of books, profuse with ideas, on the four elements,[9] had developed a systematic 'poetics of space.'[10] Thus the general acceptance of this question seems to have been achieved from a philosophical perspective too. The problem of the spatial element of human existence takes its place with a weight and question of its own beside that of temporality. In any event it seems idle to speculate in advance about the possible precedence of one question over another. It might be more rewarding to tackle the new problem of experienced space as impartially as possible and see what comes of it. But all previous approaches have only been in the form of individual contributions from home or abroad, originating from various disciplines, and dealing with the problem from

7 Harold Lassen, *Beiträge zu einer Phänomenologie und Psychologie der Anschauung*, Würzburg: 1939.

8 *Situation. Beiträge zur phänomenologischen Psychologie und Psychopathologie*, vol. 1, Utrecht and Antwerp: 1954.

9 Gaston Bachelard, *L'eau et les rêves*, Paris: 1942; *L'air et les songes*, Paris: 1943; *La terre et les rêveries de la volonté*, Paris: 1948; *La terre et les rêveries du repos*, Paris: 1948.

10 Gaston Bachelard, *La poétique de l'espace*, Paris: 1958; Bollnow quotes from: *Poetik des Raumes*, translated by Kurt Leonhard, Munich: 1960 [*The poetics of space*, translated by Maria Jolas, Boston, Mass.: 1969].

their own particular point of view. What has been missing so far is an approach to a coherent systematic interpretation. This is what will be attempted here.

Contrast with mathematical space

For a start we will try to outline a little more precisely the guiding question. Even though it will soon become evident that the problem of experienced space cannot be developed simply as a counterpart to that of experienced time, the first steps can still be taken following the process successfully adopted with the latter. Just as, with reference to time, the abstract mathematical time to be measured with clocks has been differentiated from time specifically experienced by the living human being, so one can also differentiate in the case of space between the abstract space of the mathematician and physicist and specifically experienced human space. If, in everyday life, we speak without further consideration of space, we are usually thinking of mathematical space – space that can be measured in three dimensions, in metres and centimetres – as we have come to know it at school and which provides the basic system of reference when measuring spatial relationships in everyday life: for example, if we are thinking about how to furnish a new apartment with our old, perhaps generously sized furniture. Rarely, on the other hand, do we become aware that this is only a certain aspect of space, and that concrete space, directly experienced in life, by no means coincides with this abstract mathematical space. We live so naturally in this environment that its singularity does not surprise us, and we give it no further thought. Investigating it is for this reason a special philosophical task, which takes for granted a reversal of the way of looking at it that has become almost self-evident to us, and a return to the basic principles of life which are as a rule disregarded.

Just as Bergson explained 'durée', the time actually lived by humans, by opposing it to the more familiar mathematical time, we can also best visualize the singularity of experienced space, at first still difficult to grasp, by contrasting it with the more familiar mathematical space. In doing so, for the sake of simplicity, we will confine ourselves to the well-known three-dimensional Euclidean space, and base it on an orthogonal system of axes.

The decisive quality of mathematical space is its homogeneity. This means:

1. No point is distinguished above any other. The coordinates in this space have no natural origin, and for reasons of practicality one can make

any point as required the origin of a coordinate system by means of a simple shift.

2. Likewise, no direction is distinguished above any other. By means of a simple turn, any direction in space can be made into an axis of a chosen coordinate system.

Space is unstructured in itself, and regular throughout, and in this way extends in all directions into infinity.

However these qualifications do not apply to experienced space.

1. It has a distinct centre, which is in some way, as will be discussed in more detail, given in the location of the experiencing human being in the space.

2. It has a distinct system of axes, which is connected with the human body and its upright posture, opposed to the force of gravity.

In anticipation, we can immediately expand on this with some further qualifications:

3. Areas and locations in it have qualitative differences. Based on their relationships, a structure of experienced space is built up, rich in content, for which there is no analogy in mathematical space.

4. At the same time there are not only flowing transitions from one area to another, but also sharp demarcations. Experienced space manifests pronounced instabilities.

5. The problem of infinity too becomes considerably more complicated. Experienced space is first given as a closed finite space, and only through subsequent experience does it open up to an infinite extent.

6. As a whole, experienced space is not an area of neutral values. It is related to the human being by vital relationships, both supportive and obstructive in nature. Whether supportive or obstructive, it is the field of human conduct of life.

7. Every location in experienced space has its significance for human beings. Thus it is the categories used in the humanities that we must employ in order to describe experienced space.

8. It is not a question of a reality released from a specific reference to humanity, but of space as it is present for humanity, and accordingly of the human relationship to this space; for it is impossible to separate one from the other.

The concept of experienced space

Let us formulate these relationships as concepts. When we refer to experienced space, we mean space as it is manifested in concrete human life. Dürckheim, in the work cited above, instead speaks of a lived space, and Minkowski uses the same term in this context, 'espace vécu.' This term is in some ways more apt than that of experienced space, because the latter can too easily be understood in a subjective sense, as the way in which a space is experienced by humans, which as such is already independent of the manner of its being experienced – in other words where the qualification 'experienced' applies only to the subjective colouring which is imposed on the space. The term 'experienced space' can therefore easily be understood as meaning the same as 'experience of space' in the sense of a merely psychological reality. By contrast, the term 'lived space' is preferable as it expresses no psychological meaning, but refers to space itself and, in so far as humans live in it and with it, to space as medium of human life.

Nevertheless I hesitate to use this factually much less ambiguous term; for 'living' is an intransitive verb. 'Living' means being alive, as opposed to being dead. It can also be modified by adverbial elements. One can live well or badly, but the word cannot be combined with an object in the accusative. One may say, at most, that one lives one's life, as the poet says: 'I live my life in widening circles,'[11] or in the same way one may speak of a 'life unlived.' But one cannot say that man lives *something*, such as space or time, and therefore one cannot describe space or time as 'lived.'[12] Thus, despite all my reservations, I will stay with the term that is linguistically correct, although factually less apt and more easily misunderstood, 'experienced space' [erlebter Raum]; for it seems to me inadmissible to infringe the laws of language, even for the sake of greater clarity. I will at most speak occasionally, where it seems more appropriate for the sake of clarification, at the same time of 'experienced and lived' space.

One might perhaps also have been able to speak of 'Lebensraum' as the space available for the expansion of life, if this word had not entered the German language in another, narrower sense. To avoid confusion, we had better do without this term and instead speak of experienced space. But this experienced space is not, as should be explicitly stressed to avoid misunderstanding, anything psychological, anything merely experienced or pictured or even imagined: it is the actual concrete space in which our life takes place.

---

11 'Ich lebe mein Leben in wachsenden Ringen', Rainer Maria Rilke, *Stundenbuch. Gesammelte Werke*, vol. 2, Leipzig: 1930, p. 175; see also p. 242, 'All life is being lived ... God, do you live it – life?' ['Alles Leben wird gelebt ... Lebst du es, Gott, – das Leben?'].

12 Examples in *Trübners Deutsches Wörterbuch* for the accusative are modern and seem adverse to syntax.

Factually we are here in total agreement with the way that Dürckheim and Minkowski, at the very beginning of this question, framed their concept of experienced space. When Minkowski, for example, in the final chapter of his profound work extends his observations on 'temps vécu' to 'espace vécu', he begins by contrasting the latter with the mathematical concept of space. 'Space,' he writes here, 'cannot be reduced to geometric relations, relations which we establish as if, reduced to the simple role of curious spectators or scientists, we were ourselves outside space. We live and act in space, and our personal lives, as well as the social life of humanity, unfolds in space.'[13]

And Dürckheim, from the start, formulated the problem in such an apt and comprehensive way that his remarks can be placed here, at the beginning of our own observations. 'Lived space', he says, 'is for the self the medium of physical realization, counterform or extension, threatener or preserver, place of passage or resting-place, home or abroad, material, place of fulfilment and possibility of development, resistance and borderline, organ and opponent of this self in its immediate reality of being and life.'[14] In these formulations, it is important to note the typically repeated contrasting terms: 'threatener or preserver', 'organ and opponent', etc. Space is, as has already been profoundly perceived here, given to humanity in a double manner, as supportive and as obstructive, in fact even more profoundly, as something that belongs to humanity like a limb, and then again as something which faces us from the outside as hostile or at least as foreign.

In this double definition, as 'possibility of development' and as 'resistance', space is for Dürckheim not a neutral, unchanging medium, but full of meanings in the references to life that have opposing effects, and these meanings again change according to the various locations and areas of space. These meanings too are not to be attributed to merely subjective feelings, but they are genuine characters of lived space itself. Thus Dürckheim stresses: 'The concrete space of the developed human being is to be taken seriously in the entire fullness of the significances experienced by him, for in the singularity of its qualities, structures and orderings it is the form of expression, test and realization of the subject living in it, experiencing it and reacting to it.'[15]

How strongly this space is linked as a correlative to the human being living in it again emerges from the fact that it is not only different for

13 Minkowski, *Le temps vécu*, p. 367 [p. 400].
14 Dürckheim, 'Untersuchungen', p. 389.
15 Dürckheim, 'Untersuchungen', p. 389.

different individuals, but also changes for the individual according to his specific state of mind and mood. Every change 'in' the human being entails a change to his lived space. Dürckheim stresses: 'Concrete space is different according to the being whose space it is, and according to the life that takes place in it. It changes with the person who conducts himself in it, changes with the topicality of certain attitudes and orientations which – more or less immediately – dominate the whole self.'[16]

Here we must also differentiate against the term which Bachelard has recently used to sum up his significant contribution to the philosophy of concrete experienced space, namely that of a 'poetics of space'; for this term may be too cautious and therefore finally inappropriate to be applied to what he has so brilliantly expounded in individual analyses about the house and the universe, about lofts and cellars, chests and cupboards, about the whole experienced human world of space. This is certainly understandable in view of Bachelard's philosophical background. It originates from the philosophy of the natural sciences and a concept of realization oriented on this. Seen from this point of view, experiences in experienced space seem to him to contain no objective realization. He therefore interprets them as something merely subjective, that is, as the work of the poetic power of imagination.

On the other hand, however, he sees within the frame of his expanding metaphysical world view which he himself, in connection with Novalis, once described as 'magical idealism'[17], in this power of imagination an achievement that goes well beyond what is normally understood by this name. For him it has, as a human creation that finds its expression in language, as 'imagination parlée', only to dream along with the 'dream of things', the 'imagination matérielle' or 'imagination de la matière' which itself produces reality.[18] As a result, creative writing acquires for him a particular dignity: it is 'not a game, but a power of nature. It illuminates the dream of things.'[19] Therefore he sees philosophy as dependent on the achievement of poets which precedes it: 'How much the philosophers would learn, if they would consent to read the poets!'[20] Accordingly, in his own method, which, in reference to Minkowski, he describes as phenomenology, the interpretation of poetic images takes up a broad space; for 'poets and painters', to use the phrase he borrows from Van den Berg,

16 Dürckheim, 'Untersuchungen', p. 390.
17 Bachelard, *La terre et les rêveries de la volonté*, p. 5.
18 Bachelard, *La terre et les rêveries de la volonté*, p. 1 ff.
19 Bachelard, *La terre et les rêveries du repos*, p. 324.
20 Bachelard, *Poetik des Raumes*, p. 239 [p. 208].

'are born phenomenologists.'[21] In this deeply formulated sense of poetic power of imagination we will, even without examining this concept in detail, easily be able to include the results of his analyses of poetic space in our investigations of concrete experienced space.

The spatiality of human life

Even though we have refused to regard experienced space, in the sense of mere experience of space, as something merely psychological, it is on the other hand not an object removed from the subject. As we have stressed from the start, it is a question of the relationship between the human being and his space, and thus also of the structure of human existence itself, insofar as this is determined by his relationship with space. It is in this sense that we speak of the spatiality of human existence. This term does not imply that life – or human existence [Dasein] – is itself something spatially extended, but that it is what it is only with reference to a space, that it needs space in order to develop within it.

It is in this sense that Heidegger in *Being and time* very clearly worked out the question of the spatiality of human existence, even if he could not develop it more detail in the general context of that work. Just as, according to him, one must distinguish between temporality as a structural form of human existence and time as an objective process, so we must also distinguish between space – whether it is experienced or mathematical space is irrelevant to this question – and spatiality. Spatiality is a definition of the essence of human existence. This is the meaning of Heidegger's statement: 'The subject (Dasein), if well understood ontologically, is spatial.'[22] That it is spatial does not therefore mean that the human being occupies a certain space with his body, in the same way as any other mass, and also occasionally – like the proverbial camel at the eye of a needle – is prevented from slipping through openings that are too narrow. It means that the human being is always and necessarily conditioned in his life by his behaviour in relation to a surrounding space.

This is also what Minkowski has in mind when he stresses: 'Life spreads out into space without having a geometric extension in the proper sense

21 Bachelard, *Poetik des Raumes*, p. 22 [XXVIII].

22 Martin Heidegger, *Sein und Zeit*, Halle a. d. Saale: 1927, p. 111 [*Being and time* (1962), translated by John Macquarrie and Edward Robinson, Oxford: 1967, p. 80].

of the word. We have need of expansion, of perspective, in order to live. Space is as indispensable as time to the development of life.'[23]

At the same time we are still expressing ourselves carelessly if we say that life takes place 'in space.' Human beings are not present in space as an object, let us say, is present in a box, and they are not related to space as though in the first place there could be anything like a subject without space. Rather, life consists originally in this relationship with space and can therefore not be separated from it even in thought. It is basically the same problematic of 'being-in' that Heidegger develops with reference to 'Being-in-the-world', when he stresses: 'Being-in, on the other hand, is a state of Dasein's Being; it is an *existentiale*. So one cannot think of it as the Being-present-at-hand of some corporeal Thing (such as a human body) "in" an entity which is present-at-hand … Being-in is thus the formal existential expression for the Being of Dasein, which has Being-in-the-world as its existential structure.'[24]

The question of space is thus a question as to the transcendental nature of humanity. This on the other hand does not mean that space is simply there, independent of the human being. There is space only insofar as man is a spatial being, that is, a being that forms space and, as it were, spreads out space around itself. And this again is the well-understood meaning of the Kantian thesis of the 'transcendental ideality' of space. Nevertheless, space is more than a mere form of human experience. Here the Kantian approach must be extended by the inclusion of full life with its multiplicity of vital relations. Space then becomes the general form of human living behaviour. Meanwhile mathematical space results from experienced space, when one disregards the various concrete vital relations and reduces life to a mere subject of understanding.

As this space-forming and space-spreading being, man is however necessarily not only the origin, but also the lasting centre of his space. This again should however not be understood in a coarsened manner, as though man carried his space around with him as the snail does its shell. Rather, it makes total sense when one, without thinking too hard about it, says that man moves 'in' his space, where, therefore, space is something fixed in relation to man, within which human movements take place. And so we can probably also understand the other Kantian thesis, that space has 'empirical reality.' How these two definitions can be reconciled even with an extended method of observation still remains an open question, which

23 Minkowski, *Le temps vécu*, p. 367 [p. 400].
24 Heidegger, *Sein und Zeit*, p. 54 [p. 79].

we must see here from the very start as a guiding perspective, but for the time being put aside; for it cannot be dealt with before concrete analysis, or independently of it.

The spatiality of human life and the space experienced by the human being thus correspond to each other in a strict correlative. Every statement about the one at the same time contains a corresponding statement about the other. At the same time the path of investigation necessarily starts from the exploration of experienced space, and then draws conclusions on the structure of human spatiality. For the analysis of experienced space produces a wealth of definitions of content and a multiplicity of questions, such as would not have sufficiently come into view with a direct approach to the structure of spatiality. For this reason we will deliberately put aside the question of human spatiality and will attempt for a start, as impartially as possible, to approach the analysis of space experienced and lived by the human being.

The present investigation aims to make evident, in an initial, preparatory manner, the importance and the productiveness of the question of experienced space. In order to take a view of the multiplicity of the questions that thrust themselves forward, one must first look around on all sides in order to gather together from a philosophical point of view what is made available for this purpose as a contribution by the individual sciences, and see to what extent it can be assembled into a uniform picture. The collection of this complex material must therefore be accorded a wide space, and inevitably digressions in various directions will sometimes threaten to break through the uniform path of representation. Only in the great number of the perspectives that come together here can the productiveness of the guiding question be preserved.

Completeness, of course, cannot be achieved here. It must suffice to bring together suitable examples according to the various directions. In particular, two groups of questions have been deliberately eliminated, because their problematic, leading to entirely new connections, would have broken through the circle of these first, elementary reflections. These are, first, the question of conscious construction of space in the visual arts, and second, the transition from directly experienced to mathematical-physical space.[25]

---

25 A discussion of the detailed description of this development given by Cassirer in the third volume of *Philosophy of symbolic forms* would be outside the scope of the present work. For the development of the mathematical-physical concept of space, see the excellent account by M. Jammer, *Concepts of space* (Cambridge, Mass.: 1954).

I
THE ELEMENTARY STRUCTURE OF SPACE

1. The Aristotelian Concept of Space

In order to free ourselves from inhibitions about the view of space conditioned by modern science, which is today almost taken for granted, it is advisable first to glance at other views of space which are not yet influenced in this way. In doing so, however, one immediately encounters the difficulty that although these are everywhere basic to unreflecting thought, they are seldom consciously and explicitly expressed as such. In the fourth book of his *Physics*, for the first time in the history of Western thought, Aristotle examines in detail the problem of space, summarizing the Greek view of space and at the same time dealing in depth with the various opinions of it. Here we find the familiar parallelism of space and time or, to use his own terms, 'topos' (τόπος) and 'chronos' (χρόνος), typical of all later developments. It will not be our task here to examine in detail Aristotle's highly differentiated presentation. I will only single out a few points which illustrate the unfamiliar, not to say surprising, aspects of his observations.

Natural place

This includes, first of all, the teaching that space in itself has a natural structure and that each of the four elements that were distinguished at that time (fire, air, water and earth) has its own particular place where it belongs and to which it repeatedly aspires. Thus, Aristotle remarks: 'For unless prevented from doing so, each of them moves to its own place, which may be either above or below where it was. Above and below and the other four directions are the parts or forms of place.'[1] This, for a start, is quite different from the way we are accustomed to think of space. Here space is by no means perceived as homogeneous, but rather parts and kinds (μέρη

1 Aristotle, *Physik*, translated by P. Gohlke, Paderborn: 1956, 208 b [*Physics*, translated by Robin Waterfield, Oxford: 1996].

and εἴδη) are distinguished in it, which are later referred to as directions (διαστάσεις): up and down, in front and behind, right and left. This is, as we might say today, the system of reference given by the human body, which structures space, and to which we must later return in some detail. But Aristotle goes further, stating that these definitions are not only valid for human beings, but exist because of nature. 'These directions', as he says, 'are not just relative to us.'

In the sense in which they *are* relative to us, they are not always the same, but depend on our position – that is, on which way we are facing. That is why the same object might well be, at different times, to our right and to our left, above us and below us, in front of us and behind us. But in themselves each of the six directions is distinct and separate. "Above" is not just any random direction, but where fire and anything light moves towards. Likewise "down" is not just any random direction, but where things with weight and earthy things move towards. So their powers as well as their positions make these places different.'[2] Aristotle rightly remarks that these directions, as far as they relate to human beings, also change with the position of the human being. What is right for one person is left for the other, and what was in front of me just now can suddenly be behind me, as soon as I have turned around.

So far, the approach is quite natural, and modern thinking would take from this the demand to free oneself from such subjectively determined definitions. But with Aristotle it is quite different; for him these definitions are from the start not only relative with regard to the human being, but exist because of nature. 'It is not every chance direction which is "up", but where fire and what is light are carried; similarly, too, "down" is not any chance direction but where what has weight and what is made of earth are carried.' There is no further reference to the two other contrasting pairs of concepts, and clearly detachment from the relativity with humans would here have presented even greater difficulties. At least with reference to height and depth there is a natural structure to space, in which every element has its place where it belongs and to which it returns, if not hindered by other forces. Aristotle states in this connection that space not only exists, but that it also possesses 'a certain power', that it 'exerts a certain effect', or however else one might translate 'ότι έχει τινά δυναμιν.'[3] It is therefore a space pervaded by inner powers, which one might almost see as a field of force in the sense of modern physics.

2 Aristotle, *Physik*, 200 b.
3 Aristotle, *Physik*, 208 b.

However, at this point a qualifying statement is necessary. When we said just now that each of the elements aspires towards its natural place, we translated the Greek word 'topos' (τόπος) as 'place', not, as the parallelism with time would suggest and also as it is mostly translated in versions of Aristotle, as 'space.'[4] And this is actually the literal translation, for 'topos' means place, location, position, and then also a reference in an author's text. So the sentence quoted tells us that everything in space has its natural place. 'Space' in turn would be translated into Greek as 'chora' (χωρα), which itself comes from 'choreo' (χωρέω), which means primarily to give room, to make space, then, more generally, to give way, to shrink back, and in particular with reference to vessels: to hold something, to have room to receive something. From this origin, 'chora' is then (and we will return to this later in another connection) space in the sense of gap, scope, distance, etc.

Space as a vessel

One could then at first presume that the awkward translation, traditional in the approach to Aristotelian physics, of 'topos' as space, has produced an apparent problem that did not exist at all in the Greek text. But the difficulty is not to be resolved as easily as that. For in the natural arrangement of 'topoi' it is a case of structure in space and to that extent a very definite and at first very astonishing statement about the construction of space. Beyond this, however, it remains questionable whether what Aristotle meant by 'topos' is really correctly translated as 'place.' If, by doing so, one at first avoids the difficulties resulting from translating it as 'space', the further progress of Aristotle's discussion soon leads to new difficulties, where the translation as 'place' cannot be sustained. For while 'place' is a particular point that I can indicate with my finger, the word 'topos', at least in the way that Aristotle uses it, always implies a certain extent, a spatial volume.

Proceeding from the question of what happens when two bodies change places, when there is now water where just now there was air, Aristotle states that space seems to be 'like a vessel', for a vessel is 'a movable place',[5] while inversely space is 'an immovable vessel.'[6] So the 'topos' has

4 Gohlke therefore emphasizes: 'The translation of τόπος creates difficulties because it can mean both place as well as space' (p. 322). Thus he uses both translations or alternatively "Space and place", where Prantl [who translated Aristotle in 1857] would have spoken of "space".'

5 Aristotle, *Physik*, 209 b.

6 Aristotle, *Physik*, 212 a.

a certain spatial extent, it 'contains its object.'[7] Aristotle defines it more precisely as 'the immediate limit of the container,'[8] like a kind of skin, therefore, which is drawn around it. And this property cannot appropriately be rendered by the word 'place.'

The comparison with a vessel expresses with particular clarity the contrast with our modern views of space: space is not a system of relationships between things, but the boundary, completed from the outside, of the volume taken up by a thing. Space is the hollow space bounded by a surrounding cover, and therefore it is necessarily exactly as large as the thing that takes it up.[9] As a hollow space of this kind, space is necessarily finite. It is possible to speak of space only insofar as something is surrounded by something else. Beyond this, the word loses its meaning. For this reason Aristotle expressly stresses: 'A body is in place, then, if there is a body outside it which contains it, but not if there is none.'[10] This once again clearly expresses the difference between the terms space and place; for places necessarily lie side by side, while spaces (that is, 'topoi' in the Aristotelian sense) can lie within each other, the smaller space within the larger, surrounding space. And so there is a succession of steps toward ever more extensive spaces, and the question arises as to an all-encompassing space.

This idea transfers itself to the universe as a whole. Aristotle stresses: 'And so earth is in water, water is in air, air is in fire, and fire is in the heavens; but there the sequence stops – the heavens are not in anything else.'[11] And because space always assumes a surrounding other, heaven is no longer in space, but space in the widest possible sense is everything that is surrounded by heaven. 'Heaven is not itself space,[12] but it [that is, space] is only its [that is, heaven's] inner boundary, which touches the edge of the movable body, without moving itself.'[13] Space is thus necessarily finite space, that is, the hollow space surrounded by the vault of heaven.[14] The questions of Aristotelian astronomy, in particular that of this unmoved mover, can be disregarded here. The important thing for his concept of

7 Aristotle, *Physik*, 211 a.
8 Aristotle, *Physik*, 211 b and 212 a.
9 Aristotle, *Physik*, 211 a.
10 Aristotle, *Physik*, 212 a.
11 Aristotle, *Physik*, 212 b.
12 Gohlke here translates 'place' [Ort].
13 Aristotle, *Physik*, 212 b.
14 Gohlke correctly says: 'The vault of heaven therefore has an inner, yet no outer boundary' ['Die Himmelskugel hat hiernach also nach innen eine Hülle, nach außen dagegen nicht'], Aristotle, *Physik*, p. 324.

space is that space for him is always a hollow space bounded from outside and filled in itself, in this sense necessarily a finite space, and that a question as to an empty space beyond the filled space has no concrete meaning. There is no empty space.

Here I will break off, because we are not interpreting Aristotle here, but exclusively drawing attention to some points that puzzle us in our familiar ideas about space, and are therefore appropriate for giving us some useful points of view for further investigation. With this in mind, I will summarize: anything like a homogeneous mathematical space extending into infinity is not even contemplated by Aristotle, because the Greeks approached the question from quite another direction. Their primary question is: where does something belong? In other words, they immediately think of the natural structure of space, in which everything has its own place, suitable to it. And it has this place by nature, not one assigned to it by human beings. It is a cosmically ordered and at the same time necessarily finite and manageable space. Space therefore does not extend further than the things that fill it. Certainly Aristotle at first only relates this thought to the four 'elements', but probably he would extend it further to the individual things in space arising from nature, which equally have their natural place. And in this context, finally, one might also include the human ordering of space, which for its part assigns its (human) things to their space, but which should at the same time be immediately integrated into the surrounding cosmic order. This opens up a wealth of new questions.

2. Word Usage and Etymology

Everyday linguistic usage

With a brief glance at Aristotle, we have loosened up to some extent the fixed ideas conditioned by the modern physical concept of space. We are now ready to consider more objectively what is meant by the term 'space' [Raum] as it is naturally understood. In doing this, we will from the start disregard a derived scientific usage where space is spoken of as a human concept, as in Euclidean and non-Euclidean spaces. We will also disregard the jargon widely in use today, in which the concept of space is used in an undefined, figurative sense, very difficult to grasp in detail, as when reference is made to 'industrial', 'political' or even 'creative' space. These terms generally denote something like areas in which the observed phenomena take place. Rather, we will consider the word 'space' in its direct, powerful, natural linguistic sense, which is not yet burdened by such distortions.

In doing so we notice that the German word for space, 'Raum', when accompanied by the definite or indefinite article, occurs only in the sense of a room as a part of the house, as a generic term, therefore, which encompasses living room, bedrooms, kitchen and the other parts of the premises [Räumlichkeiten]. 'Raum', in this sense, is an independent part of the house, separated off by means of dividing walls, which in turn may serve various purposes. Thus one speaks of 'Wohnräume' [living rooms], 'Büroräume' [offices or workrooms], 'Nebenräume' [side rooms], etc. A very typical example is that of the assembly or meeting room. If the meeting takes place in the open air, we speak of the meeting-place or area, but not of 'Raum', which makes it especially clear that 'Raum' here always means a part of a building, that is, something closed off from the outside world, a hollow space. This linguistic usage, by the way, is not found in other languages. In French, for example, the word 'pièce' is used, and the question that interests us is eliminated straight away by linguistic usage. We can therefore disregard this meaning of the word.

Otherwise, however, the word 'Raum' – used without an article – occurs above all as a component of certain fixed phrases, and we will have to rely on these if we want to understand what is meant by the term when it is not yet encumbered by science. In this sense one speaks of 'having room' or 'needing room' to spread out, thus 'creating room' for oneself. We read in the Christmas story, for example, that the baby Jesus had to be laid in a manger, because there was 'no room at the inn.' It is also said that for a happy pair of lovers there is 'room even in the smallest hut',[1] a state of affairs to which we will return in more detail in another connection. In a similar sense we also speak of a 'roomy apartment', 'roomy larders', etc. The expression continually used is 'room' [Raum]: a room available for use, not required for any other purpose, a room in which one can move freely. We may also speak in a figurative sense of allowing 'room' for thoughts and feelings, such as suspicion.

'Raum' [space or room] is therefore in the widest sense the 'elbow-room' for a movement, the space or distance between things, the 'free space' around a person. Narrowness and width are the original definitions of this space. Space is tight, so that one feels hemmed in by it, or there is abundant space, so that one can be lavish with it. The so-called endlessness of space is as little con-sidered here as it is by Aristotle, because there is no point in speaking of space unless it can be filled by a specific necessity of life. Space never extends further than the range of life which is to be fulfilled. One may have a great deal of space, but to have endless space can only mean to have more space than one can ever make use of.

Linguistic references

a. This interpretation is confirmed if we invoke the linguistic references supplied by etymological dictionaries. The Grimms' *Deutsches Wörterbuch* gives as the original meaning of the word 'räumen' [to clear a space]: 'to create a space, that is, a clearing in a wood, for the purpose of cultivation or settlement.'[2] This also is the origin of the word 'Raum.' The various older examples, according to the Grimms, use the word 'Raum' 'as an ancient expression of settlers … which at first referred to the activity of

1 'Raum auch in der kleinsten Hütte', Friedrich Schiller, *Der Parasit. Sämtliche Werke*, edited by Eduard v. d. Hellen, vol. 9, Stuttgart and Berlin: n.d., p. 305.

2 'einen Raum, d.h. eine Lichtung im Walde schaffen, behufs Urbarmachung oder Ansiedlung', Jacob und Wilhelm Grimm, *Deutsches Wörterbuch*, Leipzig: 1854 ff.

land clearance and freeing of a wilderness for settlement ... then to the place of settlement itself.' This reference is highly significant. Space in this original sense is not already in existence per se, but is created only by human activity, by the clearing of the wilderness (which is therefore not a 'space'). In the same way, we learn from the Kluge-Götze dictionary that the word came into being from a common Indo-Germanic adjective in the sense of 'roomy', in its earlier senses something like 'free space, resting-place, seat, bed.'[3] In an already somewhat extended range of meaning, 'Raum' also denotes a hollow space, which receives and houses or harbours the human being, in which he can move freely, and which, as such, is differentiated from anything else that surrounds him which is no longer referred to as 'Raum.' A suggestion of harbouring always seems to accompany it. In a related sense, the term 'Laderaum' is used for the place assigned as storage space on a ship. Here too the idea is one of an available place that is closed in all around.

Seen in this way, space is further that which is between things, even if the idea of the hollow space then retreats. Things allow more or less space. One example speaks of 'two rocky mountains which scarcely allow room for the little river to force its way through.'[4] Space is thus the often narrow space needed to allow movement. Likewise, another example reads: 'There was dancing on the floor; that is, anyone who was able to take possession of two feet of space kept turning around on that spot.'[5] Here too, space is the space necessary for movement, which one must first conquer for oneself. This space may be narrow. 'Around one, beside one, not an inch of space', reads another example. Here the human being is wedged in, unable to move freely. Space is thus always free space for something, in particular for a movement, for free unfolding, and in terms of this natural concept it ends where things prevent further movement.

But space can also be wide. Rilke writes in one very fine passage of a joyful experience: 'It was as though things closed together in order to make room.'[6] Space is therefore in all these cases something specific, determined

---

3 'freier Platz, Lagerstätte, Sitzplatz, Bett', Friedrich Kluge, *Etymologisches Wörterbuch der deutschen Sprache*, Berlin: 1883 ff.

4 'zwei Felsberge, die kaum dem Flüßchen Raum lassen, sich hindurchzudrängen', M. Eyth, quoted in *Trübners Deutsches Wörterbuch*, Berlin: 1939 ff.

5 'Auf der Diele ward getanzt, das heißt, wer zwei Fuß Raum erobert hatte, drehte sich darauf immer rund um', Annette von Droste-Hülshoff, quoted in *Trübners Deutsches Wörterbuch*.

6 'Es war, als ob die Dinge zusammeträten und raum gäben', Rainer Maria Rilke, *Briefe aus den Jahren 1914-1921*, edited by Ruth Sieber-Rilke and Carl Sieber, Leipzig: 1937, p. 94.

by the situation. And if one also describes a situation in a figurative sense as constricting, there also lies behind this term the original suggestion of a lack of space for movement.

One speaks in general of a lack of space, of an advantageous use of space or of a waste of space. But however we interpret it, in all these cases of an uninhibited linguistic usage 'space' by no means signifies the three-dimensionally endless, all-embracing continuum, but rather it refers to a life that unfolds within it. Space exists only in relation to a movement perceived as living. If one also speaks of space in relation to an inanimate being (such as the river mentioned above), this is only possible in so far as it moves and therefore can be thought of as animated. The space required largely depends upon the individual claim. 'You would not believe', says Goethe, 'how much room ['Platz'] one finds when one needs little space ['Raum'].'[7] In a similar sense, a well-known German proverb states that many patient sheep can enter a sheepfold. The less room each one claims for itself, the more individuals can find room in a space. Schiller writes confidently: 'The earth has room for all',[8] where 'Raum' is now meant in a more general sense as 'Lebensraum', that is, as a possibility for the development of human life.

The concept of space has now been extended. It has lost the notion of more or less constricting boundaries. Thus we find the term of the 'raumen See', the wide, open sea.[9] We also find 'Luftraum' [air-space] as the space of an infinitely wide-ranging movement, even though often completed only in thought, for example:

> … when we hear the lark outpour,
> Its warbling song, lost in the blue of heaven[10]

We also like to use the heightening plural, when we speak of 'heavenly spaces.' This idea is also suggested by Hesse when he writes:

---

7 'wieviel Platz man findet, wenn man wenig Raum braucht', Johann Wolfgang von Goethe, *Wilhelm Meisters Lehrjahre. Gedenkausagabe*, edited by Ernst Beutler, vol. 7, Zurich and Stuttgart: 1948-71, p. 308.

8 'Raum für alle hat die Erde', Schiller, 'Der Alpenjäger', *Sämtliche Werke*, edited by Eduard v. d. Hellen, vol. 1, Stuttgart and Berlin: n.d., p. 108.

9 Further references to *Trübners Deutsches Wörterbuch*, which I am consulting repeatedly, are omitted.

10 'Wenn uber uns, im blauen Raum verloren, / Ihr schmetternd Lied die Lerche singt', Goethe, *Faust erster Teil. Gedenkausagabe*, vol. 5, p. 176 [Faust part one, translated by David Luke, Oxford: 1987, p. 35].

> serenely we shall traverse space after space[11]

Here too we feel the sense of elation at being freed from constricting boundaries:

> the world spirit wishes not to fetter and constrict us

Compared with the plural which is here establishing itself, interstellar space, in which even 'space travel' has recently begun to develop, is necessarily always expressed in the singular.

b. This picture is confirmed and enriched when we also consider the related verbal expressions. The word 'räumen', to whose original meaning we have drawn attention above, in its further development means something like giving up a previously occupied space. The vanquished opponent 'räumt' [vacates or moves out of] the battlefield, by withdrawing his troops from it. The outgoing tenant vacates his apartment by taking his furniture out of it to make room for a new occupant. The police clear the premises when a fight has broken out there. The shopkeeper makes room for new stock by holding a 'clearance sale.'

'Räumen' in this sense also means clearing out of the way, and finally becomes equivalent to cleaning. One clears the table, one clears the stove or fireplace by removing remains of ash or soot. To make ourselves clearer, we also call this 'abräumen' or 'wegräumen' [clearing away], or 'ausräumen' [clearing out].

The word 'einräumen' in one sense is also relevant in this connection. It means to make room for someone else by withdrawing from it oneself. Thus, in the context of discussion, it also means giving up a position of one's own, because one recognizes an opponent's objection as valid. 'Einräumen' in the other sense means the process of placing in a space – a room about to be newly occupied, a new cupboard or wardrobe, or one being put to a new use, a drawer of a chest, or the like – the things that are to be stored there in future. One does not simply throw them in, but one creates order in this limited space by giving each object that was previously lying around at random a specific place to which it will in future belong.

In the same way, 'aufräumen' means returning objects negligently and indiscriminately scattered in a room, a workshop, etc., to their place,

11 'Wir sollen heiter Raum um Raum durchschreiten' and 'Der Weltgeist will nicht fesseln uns und engen', Hermann Hesse, *Das Glasperlenspiel. Gesammelte Dichtungen*, vol. 6, Frankfurt a. M.: 1952, p. 556.

and thus, after the constricting disorder, again at last acquiring room to move, or 'to breathe', as we say in a loose colloquial sense. In a figurative sense, one can also describe a mental state as 'aufgeräumt.' Here the word means something like clear-thinking, not constricted by any uncontrolled prejudices, in a similar way to the later word 'aufgeklärt' [enlightened], but in addition, in particular, cheerful or genial. 'She was friendly, obliging and open-minded [aufgeräumt] to all',[12] we read in one example, or, in a well-known poem by Goethe:

> St Peter's thoughts had gone astray [war nicht aufgeräumt] — He had been musing on his way.[13]

Here the new meaning is very well expressed. That St Peter was not 'aufgeräumt' means, as with a room that has not been tidied up, that he was not free to meet the claims placed upon him, because he was full of other thoughts; he was not available, in the sense of Gabriel Marcel.

c. As a guide to later investigations, let us sum up the information we have gained from the language in the following ways:

1. Space [Raum] is that which surrounds us, in which everything has its place or location.
2. Space is the elbow-room that man needs in order to move freely.
3. Space in its earliest linguistic significance is the clearing created in a wood to prepare it for human settlement. It is thus originally a hollow space.
4. Space, further, is non-constricting but fundamentally closed space; it is by no means infinite in nature.
5. Even with so-called free space, we are not speaking of an abstract infinity, but of the possibility of an unhindered advance, like that of the lark in the air, or of the breadth of the spreading plain.
6. Space thus becomes the space for development of human life, which is measured by the subjectively relative definitions of narrowness and width.
7. In taking space and giving space, it is a question of the rival relationship in the human urge for development. In their need for space, people collide with each other and need to share their space.
8. Space as elbow-room also exists between objects. But space is here also the elbow-room for movement, the distance between objects. It is only

12 'Gegen alle war sie freundlich, gefällig und aufgerämt', Gottlieb Wilhelm Rabener, quoted in *Trübners Deutsches Wörterbuch.*

13 Goethe, 'Legende', *Sämtliche Gedichte. Gedenkausagabe*, vol. 2, p. 109.

space in so far as it is empty, that is, it extends only to the surface of things, but does not penetrate them.

9. Space is created by human orderliness, and is lost as a result of human disorderliness.

10. To make space [einräumen] and to clear space [aufräumen] are thus forms of organization of the human sphere of life, in which space is created for a suitable activity.

'Orte' and 'Stellen' in space

Having begun by getting to know space as the surrounding whole, we must now turn to its inner structure, and consider first of all the terms available in the German language to describe it. These include 'Ort', 'Stelle', 'Platz' and similar terms. We must therefore determine not only the relationship with what is designated by these terms with space, but also their relationship with each other. In a very rough approximation, this relationship can be described as one of points in a continuum. The Grimms' dictionary defines it as follows: '"Raum" [space] is primarily the given location for expansion or extension. In contrast to this, "Ort" [place] which comes into being in such a space.' And other interpretations will have to be made of the other expressions. We must therefore look into each of these words individually.

a. The most straightforward relationships are those of the word 'Ort.' Here, linguistic history provides useful clues to the more precise understanding of the word. Its primary meaning is given as 'point', in particular 'spear-point. A well-known passage in which this word is first found is in the 'Hildebrandslied.' Hildebrand and Hadubrand stand facing each other, 'ort widar orte', that is, spear-point to spear-point. This origin is also preserved in some other contexts: the shoemaker uses an 'Ort' among his tools, that is, an awl. Geographically an 'Ort' is a point of land projecting into the water, such as Darsser Ort in the Baltic, etc., or, as in Ruhrort, the point at the estuary of a river's tributary. The mineworker works 'vor Ort' when he quarries into the rock at the furthest end of the tunnel. The word 'Ort' always means point.

These linguistic clues very neatly characterize the general meaning of 'Ort' in a spatial context. 'Ort' always refers to a specific point. One can *point* to it. It designates a fixed point in space, in particular a fixed point on the earth's surface. Above all, however, this concept has narrowed to the sense of an 'Ortschaft' [village or small town], that is, a human settlement. In this sense there is an 'Ortsangabe' [statement of place], a 'Wohnort' [place of residence], a 'Geburtsort' [birthplace], etc. But one also speaks of the position of a fixed star as 'Ort', or of a geometric 'Ort', etc., and in a figurative sense of 'Ort' as the location of a quoted passage.

If we try at this point to define the meaning of the word 'Ort' [point], it does not imply extension, a filled surface or a filled space, as with the word 'Platz' [place]. One cannot say that something 'has point' or 'needs point', in the way that it needs its place. 'Ort' is rather always a specifically located and precisely fixed point. It retains this sense of pointing. It is this specific point in contrast to any other. Therefore one cannot exchange 'points' as one exchanges places and positions, but rather one can only move to a different point. It is through this specific character that the 'Ort' is most sharply distinguished from all (however small) spatial structures. A town, city or village is called 'Ort' in German not because of its spatial extensiveness, but because it is located in this particular place.

b. Closely related to the 'Ort' is the 'Stelle' [position], for this too refers to a certain point in space, but its meaning, corresponding to its different linguistic origin, is different again. 'Stelle' comes from the verb 'stellen' [to place]. The primary meaning of this verb is quite literally to make something stand, and from this it derives its various meanings such as bringing to a location, 'aufstellen' [to set up], 'hinstellen' or 'abstellen' [to put down], and so on. 'Stelle' is the fixed position of a thing. Another term linguistically related to this is the 'Stall' [stable], that is, the place for standing, today used more narrowly to mean cattle shed. This meaning of 'stellen' is connected with the corresponding other linguistic expressions which will become important to us for the understanding of experienced space. The 'Gestell', the frame into which something can be placed, is also closely connected with the act of making a place for something. This includes the 'Bettstelle' [bedstead], the frame for sleeping, the 'Fahrgestell' [chassis of a car], and so on.

'Stelle' is thus in this sense the place where one puts something, and where this is later to be found. It is often equivalent to 'Platz.' It is the right place. In a related sense, one can also say that one brings someone to the 'Stelle' [report for duty]. If something is 'zur Stelle' [to hand], this means it is tangible, available. But from this point, this word too has been generalized. The 'Stelle' is *the* place for something, such as the 'Baustelle' [building site], the 'Haltestelle' [bus or tram stop], the 'Schlafstelle' [sleeping place], and so on. The 'Baustelle' for example is the place where building is carried out. The meaning is often so closely linked with that of 'Ort' that it is difficult to draw a distinction between them. Thus one speaks of an 'Unfallstelle' [scene of the accident], but a 'Tatort' [scene of the crime]. At the same time 'Stelle', in a freer meaning, can refer to something found at a certain place, distinguished from its surroundings. For example, an apple can have a 'faule Stelle', a rotten spot, etc.

Similarly, the word 'Stelle' can also be transferred to the literary world, and here too it is closely linked with the quoted 'Ort.' There is a 'Belegstelle' [quotation], a 'Bibelstelle' [biblical passage], and so on; I cannot find the 'Stelle' [place] in a book where I saw an interesting sentence. Here the word 'Ort' refers to the work and the page number, the 'Stelle' however also means the quoted sentence itself.

From here, the word 'Stelle' can be transferred to other frames of reference, and thus become functionalized. For example, there are numbers with several decimal places [Stellen]. Again, a 'Stelle' may be a job [position, place], for example as a bookkeeper, that an individual is looking for, and in the newspaper there are whole pages of 'Stellenangeboten' [job offers]. There is an 'Arbeitsstelle' [place of work], a 'Lehrstelle' [a vacancy for an apprentice], or someone is without a place [a job] and applies to the 'Stellenvermittlung' [job centre or employment agency]. Nevertheless, a certain differentiation seems to exist here: when someone is looking for an 'Arbeitsplatz' [job], the word 'Platz' in the general sense seems to mean that he will be accommodated or taken care of there. 'Stelle' on the other hand rather refers to a certain task that he will have to undertake there. In the functional sense there is also a 'Stellvertreter', a representative, who in case of need takes the place of the actual holder of the job. Likewise, there are also 'Amtsstellen' [official posts], and instructions may come from the 'höchster Stelle', the highest authority.

c. The closeness of the word 'Platz' to 'Stelle' has already been mentioned. One puts something in the right place or in the right position, without any difference between the two expressions being detectable. Nevertheless, place is not exactly the same as position, and we must try to distinguish between the two concepts. The history of language does not give us many clues here. Place comes from Greek: πμαυεία (όδός), the broad street, the main street of larger cities, gives us the Latin 'platea', which changes meaning from street to courtyard and square [Platz], from which derive the Italian 'piazza', the French (and English) 'place', and so on.

In the course of medieval development the meaning becomes extended, so that 'Platz' now generally means an open space. Thus there is a

'Bauplatz' [building site], a 'Festplatz' [fairground], a 'Sportplatz' [sports field or playing field], a 'Richtplatz' [place of execution], etc. Here a place is universally the open space made ready for something, and unlike similar combinations with '-raum' it means a covered area in the open air. There is a 'Sammelplatz' [assembly point], a 'Lagerplatz' [storage area or campsite], a 'Stapelplatz' [stockyard] and a 'Handelsplatz' [trading centre] for goods, and in a military context a fortified place, of which a 'Platzkommandant' is in command. But in a minor sense, with reference to an individual person, a 'Platz' may also be a place for standing or sitting, for example in a theatre, which has a fixed number of seats, or a railway train. One 'nimmt Platz' [takes one's seat]. And so the 'Platz' becomes in a more general sense the space occupied by a person. In this sense one makes 'Platz' [room] for someone or takes someone's 'Platz' [place].

For all their sparseness, these particulars of linguistic history suffice to give us an indication of the differentiation of concepts. In all the examples, going back to its Greek origin, the word place always implies a certain expansion or extension in space, even a certain dimension of width. This differentiates the word from a point or position and brings it closer to 'space', so that we must now clarify the relationship of these two concepts.

Nevertheless, this approximation is valid only in a very narrow sense. 'Raum' is by far the more comprehensive term. 'Weltraum' [outer space] has no equivalent in 'Platz' [unless one were to say, very inappropriately, that there is 'Platz', room, for very many stars in it]. Only in the context of smaller spaces can the two concepts be compared. 'Platz' is always a place which is limited, created by humans and made ready for human purposes. This is valid in larger contexts of urban development. The market place, for example, is the place kept free of buildings for the conducting of market business. It is always the human shaping of the world that determines that 'points' become places. In the desert, for example, or in the high mountains and in inhospitable regions, there are probably points where one could in theory meet, but not 'places.'

This however is also valid on a smaller scale, where humans allot a place to an object in a space designed by humans, and this place is closely related to the point in the sense mentioned above. Nevertheless the difference is also noticeable here. A place is allotted to a thing, but it can be located at any given point. Again, the position [Stelle] is where one deposits something. It is assumed that there is indeed room [Platz] for it. With room, however, one must take care that the required extent of space is available. In case of need, room must be made, by clearing away something else. There is an interesting difference between 'Bauplatz' [plot of land] and 'Baustelle' [building site]. The plot is the site made available for building. Perhaps it may be acquired for later use. But it becomes a building site only when building actually takes place on it, and it remains one only as long as the work continues.

Here space and place are quite close together in meaning, but it is precisely here that the difference too is perhaps most clearly to be grasped. One makes room so that another person can pass by, that is, one moves aside. One can offer another person one's place, for example one's seat. One can dispute someone's right to their place or alternatively their 'space.' Here the difference is clear: in the battle for someone's space it is a question of drawing the boundaries between the individuals' spaces more tightly or extending them. But a place can only be surrendered or maintained as a whole. I can only create the place for something by taking something else away. The place is a limited quantity at one's disposal, which can be divided in one way or another. This also applies in a figurative sense to the place of work or job. In working life, the older generation makes place for the younger, by leaving its workplace or job to the latter and going into retirement. Here, then, no 'space' is gained, but an available 'place' is newly allocated. It would be a different matter, something less easily quantifiable, if the older generation allowed the younger 'space' for its own development. This is why Schiller says: 'There is space for all on earth', but on another page, 'Make place for the Landvogt! Disperse the crowd!'[14] or: 'Woman, make place, or my horse will stride over you.'[15]

This is also valid in a more general sense: place designates the closely bounded area of space into which something just fits, up to its limit, but not beyond. 'Space' however also means the room for movement, the elbow-room for a movement. Thus a free 'place' is a space not being used, one that is still disposable, that is empty. In this sense, much space can be available, but necessarily there is a finite amount of 'place.' A free 'space' on the other hand opens up an expanse for movement. It can be opened up to an infinite extent. Thus one can differentiate: things too need a place, but 'space' in the true sense is needed only by man. Place is something disposable in the world, 'space' however is part of the transcendental condition of man. In this sense space acquires the basic precedence over all points, positions and places in space.

14 'Platz, Platz dem Landvogt! Treibt sie auseinander!', Schiller, *Wilhelm Tell. Sämtliche Werke*, edited by Eduard v. d. Hellen, vol. 7, Stuttgart and Berlin: n.d., p. 212.

15 'Weib mach' Platz, oder mein Roß reitet über Dich hinweg', Schiller, *Wilhelm Tell. Sämtliche Werke*, vol. 7, p. 255.

d. More for the sake of completeness, let us also mention the 'Fleck' [patch, or spot], which often overlaps with points and positions. When, for example, Goethe writes: 'In Neustadt we found everything in the same spot; the bronze of the king was still galloping in the same position',[16] it is only for stylistic reasons that the word position is substituted for 'patch', where the meaning remains the same. Thus the expressions 'nicht vom Fleck kommen' and 'nicht von der Stelle kommen' mean the same thing [to get nowhere, to make no headway], and 'das Herz auf dem rechten Fleck haben' [to have one's heart in the right place] means the same as having it 'an der rechten Stelle.' Without going into the linguistic history in detail, 'Fleck' and 'Flecken' (as well as 'Flicken') are individual pieces of material, in particular remnants, that can be used for repairs, for patching. 'Besser ein wüster Fleck als ein schönes Loch' [better a messy patch than a beautiful hole], says the proverb. And so there are patches of the most varied kinds, leather patches used by a cobbler on shoes, fabric patches used by a tailor. And as a patch of this kind stands out against its background, so it becomes similar to the spots discussed earlier, for example the 'Schmutzflecken' [spot of dirt or dirty mark], the 'Tintenflecken' [ink stain], 'Fettflecken' [grease mark or spot], and also, in a figurative sense, the 'Schandfleck' [eyesore, blot on the landscape or disgrace].

But in addition, and with greater relevance here, a piece of land is also called a patch. One speaks of a 'lovely spot or patch of land', and also uses the word to refer to an 'Ortschaft' [village or small town]. There is also a 'Marktflecken', a small market town. The fact that both meanings derive from the same Indo-Germanic root in the sense of 'to beat', and thus originally refer to something 'beaten flat', is important for our purposes, since this leads to the meaning of a flat, extended surface. The 'Fleck' always remains twodimensional.

e. Finally, let us also remember the 'Feld' [field] as an extended surface, which is then used in a figurative sense, for example in gravitational field or electromagnetic field, for a well-structured space.

All these definitions of the meanings of words, these reflections on present-day linguistic usage, and digressions into German linguistic history, are not intended to anticipate the practical examination of the problem of

---

16 'In der Neustadt fanden wir alles auf dem alten Fleck, der metallne König galoppierte nach wie vor auf derselben Stelle', Goethe, Brief an Christiane. *Gedenkausgabe*, vol. 19, p. 698.

space. Their only purpose has been to prepare some points of view for this practical analysis in a provisional heuristic sense. It is in this spirit that we will carry them with us as we now turn to the actual analysis, as regards content, of experienced and lived space.

3. The Natural Coordinate System

Vertical axis and horizontal plane: upright man

After these preparatory discussions we will try to visualize in detail the structure of experienced space. We will begin with some very general definitions and try to move on from there to the more specific subdivisions. In doing so we will once again start with the difference indicated earlier between experienced space and mathematical space. In contrast to the homogeneity of mathematical space, as we have said, experienced space is characterized by its lack of homogeneity. We will now pursue that difference in its various aspects. It means, in the first place, that in experienced space there are no axial directions of the same quality, but particular, distinct directions that are inextricably linked with the relationship of the human being with space.

Aristotle distinguished six 'kinds' of space, classed in pairs: above and below, front and back, right and left. These are the directions naturally arising from the position of the human being standing upright in space. Admittedly Aristotle went beyond this and believed that this structure could be found, independently of the human body, in space, where every object had its 'natural' place. Here however the structural system is simplified to the one contrast between above and below, while the other two pairs of opposites – significantly, as we shall see – are abandoned. But we will ignore this extension into the cosmological sphere and will restrict ourselves to the space experienced by the human being in the narrower sense.

And here we immediately observe that the three pairs of opposites are by no means of equal value, but each has its own noninterchangeable character. We perceive front and back in a different way from right and left (we will return to this too). Above all, the concept of above and below stands out, since it is conditioned by the upright posture of the human being. Of this we can indeed say that it arises from nature and not from human arbitrariness; for right and left, front and back, change when the person turns around, but above and below remain the same, even if the person lies down or moves in space in some other way. They are determined by the direction of gravity. It is the direction of standing up and falling down, of rising and falling and thus also of lying on the ground. In this sense the above/below direction is objectively given.

An abundance of transferred meanings are brought into play even with this simple opposition of above and below. To pick out one fairly arbitrary example, in which the direct experience from life of the dimension of height still resonates, I will quote a statement by Kästner. He stresses 'that such a great number of miracles take place on mountains', and continues: 'Every mountain ascent contains a distant echo of this event. This comes from the power that is captured in the word "above", it arises from the energy of the word. Even someone who has long ceased to believe in heaven and hell cannot exchange the status of the words above and below. … Above is above.'[1] This also applies to human social existence. Man tries to be 'on top' in all situations of life. He tries to subjugate others. The individual psychology of Alfred Adler made this opposition into the basis of an interpretation of all human life. But for the time being we will not speak further of these transferred meanings.

The situation is quite different with the contrasting directions of front and back, and right and left. 'Front' is what lies before me in the direction of my face or, more generally, of my body. But I can turn around, and then what was formerly in front of me is now (for example) behind me – or right instead of left – or some other direction in between. But it is now significant that when I turn around, I do not turn my space around with me in the sense of a body-bound system of coordinates, but I turn around *in* space, the space remaining fixed around me, while I turn. This means that my body, with its inbuilt axial system, is not valid as an axial system of space, but however much the space is related to me, it still acquires a peculiar independence, not dependent on my current physical position. I do not move my space, but I move in space.

But however much I may turn in any direction, the vertical axis still remains unaltered, and as a result the horizontal plane is also fixed. What is in front, the single point of direction, is changeable, but the plane as such is unchangeable. We can therefore establish our first, most straightforward structural principle: vertical axis and horizontal plane together form the simplest system of concrete human space.

1 Erhart Kästner, *Ölberge, Weinberge*, Frankfurt a. M.: 1960, p. 95.

Similarly, Kant in his observations 'On the first ground of the distinction of regions in space' started out from the position of the human body standing upright. Here he says: 'Since through the senses we know what is outside us only as far as it stands in relation to ourselves, it is not surprising that we find in the relation of these intersecting planes [that is, of the three planes, standing vertically one upon the other, given by the physical directions above and below, in front and behind, right and left] to our body the first ground from which to derive the concept of regions in space. The plane to which the length of our body stands perpendicular is called, in reference to us, horizontal; it gives rise to the distinction of the regions we indicate by *above* and *below*.[2]

The earth's surface

Of course this pattern is still much too abstract and only to be used as a primary aid to clarify the difference between experienced and mathematical space. We must now look around in both directions, the vertical and the horizontal. To begin with the latter, the horizontal plane is not a simple abstract orientation scheme, but the term designates a tangible reality. It is the ground upon which I stand and which gives my life a solid basis. But this ground divides space into two very unequal halves: one is the physical space beneath me, into which I cannot (in practice) enter, because the solidity of the ground offers resistance to me. The other is the air space above me, into which I (in practice) equally cannot enter, but for the opposite reason: because the lack of resistance in the air continually allows me to fall back to the ground.

So these are two very different hemispheres. And it is to the border between these two areas, the surface of the earth, that man is bound with his life. The meagre extent to which he is able to remove himself from it, by climbing trees or crawling into caves, by building houses and towers, or digging wells and mines, or even from time to time by raising himself above the surface of the earth in an aircraft, all this cannot change the fact that man is fundamentally bound to this two-dimensional space, just as it is shown in the atlas. Even aircraft flights only act as a link between two points of the earth's surface. A life in planetary space, even if space travel

---

2 Immanuel Kant, *Gesammelte Schriften*, edited by Königl. Preussische Akademie der Wissenschaften, vol. 2, Berlin: 1902, p. 378 ff. [*Kant's inaugural dissertation and early writings on space*, translated by John Handyside, Chicago and London: 1929, p. 21 ff.].

gave us the opportunity for this, is something of which we simply can have no precise idea.

That this earth surface is structured by mountains and valleys does not essentially change this situation: for even if it is perhaps folded to some extent by heights and depths, it still remains a formation with the structure of a surface on which human life takes place. For this reason one has in mind only this flat surface area when speaking of the 'Lebensraum' [living space] of a nation. The meagre extent to which man can penetrate heights and depths by means of structural or civil engineering at best forces one to replace the designation of a horizontal plane with that of a horizontal layer, which, without sharply delineated upper or lower borders, always remains comparatively thin. Perhaps we can also express it in other terms: near space is three-dimensional, but distant space extends only in two dimensions. At any rate, the decisive dimension of the outer development of life is always its breadth.

Here a further difference between the upper and the lower hemispheres must be stressed: the downward view is limited by the opacity of the earth – even the ocean is transparent only to a very limited depth – but the transparency of air space enables an uninterrupted upward view. So it is only a semi-space that opens up to my gaze, which is limited downward by the surface of the earth, upward by the vault of the heavens (which looks like a flattened shell), and which is united as a finite space surrounding me by a boundary line where these two surfaces meet, the horizon. The phenomenon of the horizon therefore forms a decisive further difference between concretely experienced space and mathematical space, and we need to deal further with it in this context.

The firmness of the ground and the forms of its loss

But the earth's surface, in its material character, has a specific significance. Even if it cannot be described as a horizontal plane in the mathematical sense, even when it includes mountains and valleys and man can to some extent rise above it, this does not change the fundamental fact that man needs firm ground underfoot in order to be able to move, and that the solidity of the ground provides the basic situation on which all the security of human life relies.

If this solid ground is absent, man must fall, and if it is only partially absent, as when an abyss opens close to him, at a steep cliff in a mountain area, or at the unprotected edge of a high tower, he becomes dizzy, because the basis of his ability to stand is endangered. He thinks he is losing his balance, that he is about to plunge into a bottomless pit; he is gripped by a nameless fear, and he will really fall if he does not promptly succeed in regaining his foothold.

This phenomenon is fundamental to the understanding of the whole of human life, for the spatial pattern, in a figurative sense, applies to the whole situation of mankind. When Kierkegaard describes fear in general as 'the dizziness of freedom',[3] what is meant is that all fear is understood in terms of this specific fear, that is, the fear of falling into bottomless space. Similarly, from a physician's point of view, Plügge describes the sense of crisis in terms of falling into an abyss.[4]

This is also valid in another figurative sense. Even when we say that a child 'schwindelt' [literally 'is dizzy'], that is, is fibbing, when he or she tells fantastic, unrealistic stories, or when, in the business world, a 'Schwindelunternehmen', a swindle or scam, collapses like a house of cards, this is all to be understood as part of the same pattern. 'Castles in the air' is a term used for structures without any real basis that we build up in our daydreams. Philosophy too is constantly in danger of losing the 'firm ground of facts' beneath its feet, and it needs 'the courage for triviality' to linger over the simplest facts, in order to assess their entire significance. Everywhere the concept of spatiality offers the 'foundation' for an understanding of the intellectual world. Even the term just used in a figurative sense, 'foundation' [Grundlage], and indeed, more generally, that of 'ground' itself in its logical meaning, develops from here and must be understood from this point.

It is also interesting in this connection to pursue a specific phenomenon, such as that of extravagance [Verstiegenheit], as developed by Binswanger in a revealing study.[5] For extravagance too, as a typical form of 'frustrated existence', is to be understood in the spatial relationship of height and width, and is connected very closely with the phenomenon of vertigo which has just been discussed. As Binswanger describes it: As an existence that not only conceptualizes distance and strides into distance, but also conceptualizes

3 'Schwindel der Freiheit': Soren Kierkegaard, *Der Begriff der Angst*, translated by Christoph Schrempf, Jena: 1884, p. 57.

4 Herbert Plügge, 'Über Anfälle und Krisen', Psyche, vol. 2, 1948/9, p. 401 ff.; see also *Wohlbefinden und Missbefinden. Beiträge zu einer medizinischen Anthropologie*, Tübingen: 1962.

5 Ludwig Binswanger, *Drei Formen missglückten Daseins. Verstiegenheit, Verschrobenheit, Maniriertheit*, Tübingen: 1956; see also 'Traum und Existenz', *Ausgewählte Vorträge und Aufsätze*, vol. 1, Bern: 1947.

height and climbs into heights, human existence is intrinsically fraught with the possibility of 'Sich-ver-steigen' [in German, either getting lost while climbing, or becoming presumptuous].' Extravagance depends for him 'on a certain disparity between climbing up and stepping into the distance.'[6] When a mountaineer has lost his way [sich verstiegen] on a rock face and cannot get any further without help, he has dared to climb too high without adequate knowledge of the structure of the mountain. This is how Binswanger sees the extravagance of the schizoid psychopath, indeed extravagance as a possibility in human life in general, when man, aspiring to a higher viewpoint, to an ideal way of observation, to 'overcome the "weight of the earth" [Erdenschwere] and lift himself above the pressure and the "fear of the earthly"',[7] has removed himself so far from the reliable foundation of experience that he has now become bogged down in a similarly hopeless situation. Extravagance in Binswanger's formulation thus means the 'unusual prevalence of the height of decision over the width of "experience ".'[8] It is a 'condition of being cramped or held spellbound by a certain problematic point of human existence.'[9] Help thus consists in the lost or wandering person being brought back to earth and being given the possibility of a new beginning by means of broadened experience and the command of the situation that it brings with it.

Here it is not a question of individual characteristics but only of how the intellectual situation of human existence can be comprehended only on the basis of a spatial scheme.

Front and back: man on the move

In establishing the scheme so far of vertical axis and horizontal plane, we have already simplified the situation in a way which can no longer be maintained. When we took as our starting point the fact that man can turn in a circle and in doing so turn towards any point at will, and that in doing so the definitions of front and back, left and right, could be interchanged at will as a result of this turning, we were, without giving it very much consideration, starting from the assumption of a person standing in a leisurely way, looking around in the landscape. In this way the image developed of a uniform horizontal plane, on which no direction is different

6 Binswanger, *Drei Formen*, p. 1.
7 Binswanger, *Drei Formen*, p. 4.
8 Binswanger, *Drei Formen*, p. 6.
9 Binswanger, *Drei Formen*, p. 7.

from any other. In normal human life, that is, as long as man is occupied with some task, it is however quite different, and here a human being is certainly able to distinguish between front and back. If, for example, I am giving a talk in a lecture hall, then the 'front' is where my audience is sitting. I am standing facing them, and it would not occur to me to turn around, unless I wanted to write something on the board. Turning around would be contrary to the purpose of my activity, and my audience would no longer understand what I was saying. And for my audience, on the other hand, 'in front' is where the lectern stands. That is where their attention is directed, and it would not occur to them to turn around, unless perhaps they should be distracted by the sounds of a latecomer to the audience. And thus it is generally valid to say that 'in front' for a human being is the direction in which his or her attention is focused. So one discovers what is in front and what is behind one, not by standing idly around, but only when one is occupied with some task. It is from this activity alone that the surrounding space derives a certain orientation, and this then determines the directions, forward, backward and to one side.

This applies in the most original and vivid form when man approaches a spatially determined target; for here he not only turns his attention from his task, from a fixed position, but he also aims to reach his target himself by his own movement in space. In walking, or driving, and so on, on a certain path in the direction of a target to be reached, the contrast between front and back acquires a quite definite, irreversible meaning, determined by the direction of the path. The movement of walking is trapped in this simple contrast of front and back. 'In front' is the direction in which the human being is walking. He must not lose sight of it, as long as he is on the move. Here he needs to be careful, using foresight in the literal sense, that is, the posture that looks ahead while walking and assesses the path ahead for possible obstacles and opportunities for better progress. 'Back' on the other hand is the road already travelled. It is no longer in one's line of vision and it is as though it no longer exists.

We can, of course, also look back. But to do so we must turn around, and to turn around we must pause in going forward, that is, interrupt our progress. There must always be a particular reason for this, whether the traveller hears steps behind him which make him uneasy, or feels tired and wants to make sure of the distance he has already come, in order to assess how much still lies ahead. The original movement, therefore, must always be interrupted in some way when one looks back at one's path. The look back may then be extended into observation of the whole panorama. It is then, but only then, that the landscape appears before one's eyes in its full extent. But each time, I must first stand still, that is, interrupt the movement of walking or driving.

Movement on one's way acquires at the same time a directly moral character, and from this there immediately arises the figurative meaning. Man strives to go forward or he draws back, and in this drawing back there is at the same time an ethical evaluation, namely the reproach of not having fulfilled a task. It is a failure, an avoidance of challenge, whether out of weakness or cowardice. The striving towards 'progress' is part of the basic purpose of human life, but this is accomplished only in continual struggle with an 'opponent.' The resistance which confronts his striving presents itself as a warlike image. Progress becomes battle.

But man can retrace his steps and return home. This is something quite different from drawing back; for in drawing back he keeps his eye on his objective, or on the opponent who is barring his way. He moves backwards, his feet feeling their way uncertainly, unable to see where he is going, and still ready to make a renewed forward effort at any moment. In drawing back, therefore, his direction remains the same, and it is within this directedness that he is drawing back. But in going back, the human being actually turns around in order to make his way back. What was 'back' for him is now forward, and vice versa. And what, seen as a whole, is a return journey, now also becomes a journey forward, in so far as it is once again a distance to be traversed. Man can return with a clear conscience only when he has reached his goal and then returns home again, or when he has become resigned to giving up his goal as unattainable. The polarity of going and returning is thus different from that of pushing forward and drawing back.

The three forms of looking back, retreating and returning thus represent the three basic forms of natural forward movement in an opposite direction.

The dimension of width, the view to left and right, is here totally eliminated. Movement on one's way takes place only in the one-dimensional contrasting directions of forward and back. The width dimension of the terrain only comes into play if the path forks, that is, at a crossroads, or where the path is lost, with no direction, in a pathless terrain. Here the simple view of forward and back is not sufficient; here man must look around himself in order to find his true path. And it is only here that the full extent in width of the terrain becomes apparent.

These definitions are of great importance not only for the concrete experience of space, but also beyond that, for human life in general; for the journey is not some temporary or occasional resting-place, but describes a basic situation, perhaps *the* basic situation of man in the world, and thus becomes one of the great primal symbols of human life, which pervades its whole interpretation to such an extent that one can hardly draw a line between its 'literal' and 'figurative' meanings. Life is perceived as a lifelong journey, and man as a traveller on this journey, a 'homo viator.' In this journey, or movement, the concepts of front and back at the same time acquire a temporal meaning: in front of us is what lies before us in the future as a stretch of life still to be traversed, while behind us is the stretch of life's journey already completed, the past.

As far as behaviour on life's journey is concerned, it is just as with 'actual' travel in the spatially extended terrain: normally man faces forward, towards the future. But there are also moments of looking back, of reflection, whether the human being is pleased at having reached his destination, or whether he has encountered difficulties and been forced by them to reconsider. However, there is no direct equivalent in the journey of life to returning or drawing back, although progress on this journey is also perceived as a battle, the battle of life.[10]

Man at the crossroads, faced with the choice between the right and the wrong road to take, is also one of the great primal symbols of human life.

If we immerse ourselves in this way in the symbolic meaning of front and back, we immediately notice the great difference between this and the relationship of above and below. In both cases, admittedly, it is a case of a contrast of values, which comes into being not just in the figurative meaning, but which leads to a wholly concrete experience of space, but this contrast has at times quite a different character. Aspiration to heights has a character quite different from pressing forward into the distance, and downfall from a high place is quite different from an exhausted collapse along the road[11].

Right and left sides

A further difference is found in the contrast between right and left. If we start from the movement of striding forwards, then in addition to the

10 To what extent there is in a temporal context also such a thing as a return to an earlier point in time is a question discussed in my essay 'Das Nachholen des Versäumten', in *Maß und Vermessenheit des Menschen: philosophische Aufsätze* (Göttingen: 1962), p. 214 ff.

11 See Ernst Jünger, *Sprache und Körperbau*, Zürich: 1947; Karl Bühler, *Sprachtheorie*, Jena: 1934, especially: 'Das Zeigfeld der Sprache und die Zeigwörter', p. 79 ff. Ludwig Klages, *Die Sprache als Quell der Seelenkunde* Stuttgart: 1959, especially chapter 10, 'Sprachliche Raumsymbolik', p. 160 ff.

contrast of front and back there is also the sideways direction, extension into width, and while the first contrast designates a pronounced difference in values, the second is originally neutral in value. It is the direction of simple coexistence. But the sideways direction can develop in a double sense, either to left or right. This corresponds to the two sides of the symmetrically structured human body, in particular its two hands, which are mirror images of each other (while the mirror-like correspondence has the particular character that the two parts that correspond to each other cannot be brought into congruence with each other).

Neither of these two sides, geometrically speaking, is privileged before the other. They have fundamentally equal rights, and if it is necessary to decide between them (as with driving on the right- or left-hand side of the road), this is only possible by means of an arbitrary convention. One can decide in favour of one direction or the other. And yet human beings are aware of a noticeable difference in value between them. The word 'right' in its original meaning, in terms of sensory perception, means straight in contrast to crooked or bent. It is linguistically related to 'correct' and 'righteous.' The 'right' is the correct. And if we transfer this meaning to the right-hand side, this contains the implication that it is singled out as the preferred, the correct side. The left side on the other hand is devalued, as the lesser, bad side. In juxtaposition, this results in a value judgement. The right side is the side that is accorded greater respect. The guest of honour is allowed to walk on the right; the younger person yields the right side to the older, the gentleman to the lady. The same tendency is found in superstitious practices. The right-hand side is the auspicious one, the left the sinister one. For example, it is considered a bad omen if one gets up using the left foot first.

This order of precedence is not preordained by nature. If we ignore the difficult question of whether the preference for the right hand is not conditioned by a certain asymmetry in the human body, both sides start out as equal in merit, and the decision as to which should have preference could well have gone the other way. And in some cases it has indeed gone the other way. In the Roman art of prophecy, birds flying to the left presaged good fortune, to the right they meant disaster, just as in a German folk superstition of today seeing a 'little sheep on the left' is an auspicious sign. Perhaps we can see these two tendencies together: precisely because the two directions, right and left, are in themselves symmetrically of equal value, they respond to an interpretative valuation placed on one of them by humans, and perhaps this is the basis of the suitability of this difference for a predictive interpretation.

4. The Centre of Space

The question of the zero point of space

I will resist the temptation to pursue prematurely these metaphors, inherent in human nature itself, which in any case we will need to examine later in more detail. In this first chapter, I will attempt, to begin with, to work out the elementary spatial system that lies at the basis of human life. Here we must recall our earlier observation when we discussed the natural zero point of experienced space. If we regard man as the subject of his experience of space, then the obvious thing to do is to start from the concrete human being, how he is situated as a living being in space and how his own body determines the definitions of above and below, front and back, right and left. Thus one could take the zero point of this present perceived space, which is essentially our field of vision, to be the zero point of experienced space in general. This zero point of vision would then, as we know, be between the eyes, in the region of the root of the nose. If I look around to left and right, my visionary rays are in a sense the vectors of a system of polar coordinates, while I, the person seeing, am myself its zero point.

But as obvious as such a starting point may be, from the perspective of pure perceptive psychology, it does not after all correspond to the natural interpretation. Such a zero point may determine my temporary and incidentally changeable position in space, but not the central point of my space itself. Here we must return yet again to the singular double relationship between man and space: on the one hand, space stretches out around the human being, and belongs to his transcendental condition, but on the other hand man does not carry his space around with him as the snail carries its shell. But we do say, when looking at things impartially, that we move 'in' space, and this in the sense that we are in motion while space remains immobile. And yet again space is not independent of the subject, but even if I move 'in' space, it forms a specific system of reference related to the subject. These are relationships that are curiously entangled with each other, and we will for the time being keep as closely as possible to the naïve view of the person as yet unencumbered by philosophy.

Going away and coming back

In natural linguistic usage, we say that I go away and come back, and all my movements in experienced space take place in it as an obvious alternation of going away and coming back. We use these concepts in daily life without having a clear idea of what the terms 'away' and 'back' are related to. In any case, it means that I remove myself from my resting-point, but that this removal is perceived as only temporary, and that I will return to my starting point. We must therefore distinguish between my present location and the place to which I 'belong.' The latter is the constant resting-point in relation to occasional change. But the question is, where this resting-point, always implicitly envisaged, is to be found.

This varies a great deal in specific cases and can for the time being only be stated provisionally. If I stand up from 'my' seat in a café, for example to get a newspaper, I will then return to the seat I previously occupied. This, as long as I have no further thoughts, is the (relative) point of reference. Or again, perhaps I have left my room only to drink a quick cup of coffee, and will then return to my room. Seen from this point of view, the previous point of reference is now, for its part, an eccentrically situated, temporary resting-point, and the room and the house in which it is located are now the central point of my journeys into town. But the room, again, may be only a hotel room, in which I am staying only for a few days, or a student's lodgings which I have rented for a term. For some reason I have been away, and am now returning from the 'foreign' city to my own apartment and my own family. I have 'left the house' and 'returned to the house'; I have, as we say, returned home.

But what is this strange thing, a 'home'? For children, as long as they are not yet independent, it is in general the house of their parents. But even if a person has his own house and his own family, this does not imply an absolute end-point. Perhaps he does not feel at ease in the place where he is currently living, and longs for his former residence, which he gave up thoughtlessly, or was obliged against his will to give up. He is consumed by 'homesickness.' Behind this there somehow lies darkly the home of his childhood. Behind the house, therefore, 'home' is no longer perceived as the actual point of reference, but as the central area of all spatial relationships.

But even here, no absolute zero point has been found. A person's home too can become foreign to him, and he may since then have created a 'new home' for himself. He may also, in a figurative sense, have lost his way and, in his self-alienation, be attempting to return to his original nature. Or he may feel entirely homeless on this earth and long for an 'eternal home.'

However we may take it, everywhere the assessment of 'going away' and 'coming back' is related to a specific point of reference. But the point of reference changes according to the level of observation, and a complicated hierarchy develops, perceived only indistinctly in its order, in which every spatial point of reference is again relativized by a higher one.

Nevertheless, as long as we do not wish quite yet to abandon the realm of spatial relationships, a reference point emerges to which the human being must be rooted in space, if the relationship with space, with spatiality, is to be at all significant to him. This is the point where he acquires a foothold in space as an intellectual being, where he 'stays' and 'dwells' in space. We call it, in a designation for the time being left indeterminate, his dwelling [Wohnung]. Here, in some as yet vague sense, man's dwelling place emerges as a point of reference distinguished from others, to which all other shorter– or longer-term places of residence refer.

Hence the double motion of going away and coming back acquires a much more concrete character, which cannot in any way be comprehended by means of the mathematical scheme of space. Going away is not some arbitrary movement in space, but a human being goes forth in order to perform some errand in the world, to attain some goal, in short, to fulfil some task or other, but when he has fulfilled it (or even if he has failed in his intention), he returns to his dwelling, to his resting point. It is thus at the same time the alternation, of deep significance to man, that expresses itself in this pendulum movement of going away and coming back, from which every phase at the same time has its peculiar, unmistakable emotional colouring.

Order around the centre

Thus the system of spatial relationships is structured from the dwelling outwards. The places to which I go and from which I return are related to this point as their organizational centre. If we change our dwelling place, the world reconstructs itself in a new way from the new dwelling. If the change takes place within the same city, everything is still newly structured within the new residential area. It is not only the definitions of closeness and distance that change, but also the inner structure of the streets through which I usually pass and that have the character of intimacy for me, that are what is well known to me above all else in the city, and what is only vaguely outlined for me as a fading background. It is always something different that is significant to me in this way in the city, and thus the whole city acquires a different character when I change my address within it. It is just the same when moving to another town to live. From the standpoint of the new city, the landscape and the relationships with the other cities reconstruct themselves in a totally new way; what was formerly peripheral moves into the centre, and vice versa.

Anticipating a little, I have mentioned these relationships here, because at the same time they lead in another direction. What has been said here in respect of the individual human being or the individual human family is valid in an increased measure if we regard man as a member of an overarching community life. Thus the question of the centre of the system of coordinates is to be determined not by the individual alone, but only by the community. Here, what had previously been developed only from the individual is repeated on a higher level. Even the houses in a settlement are arranged around a central point. In more clearly observable medieval conditions, it was the market or the church to which all the streets, and thus the position of each individual house, were related.

In the big city of today, the relationships are perhaps less easily recognizable, but still present in a basically equivalent fashion. I have an equivalent feeling that I am moving towards a centre when I, from my apartment situated on the edge of the city, say that I am going 'into town', which in a literal sense I have actually never left. 'Into town' means the direction towards a centre where I want to conduct my business or do my shopping, and to which, to that extent, I am related in my apartment away from the centre. In the same way, the village is related to the town, the towns to the cities, and these in turn to the capital city. Thus there is a chain of references, according to which my subjective experienced space is each time taken up into and held in a greater whole. But what is the central place where I stop in this return journey? And in what sense am I placing the actual centre of the experienced space there? Probably we have an obscure sense of such a supra-individual centre, which does not coincide with the situation of our own house, but where it is actually located remains somehow uncertain. The chain of references has no natural end.

In earlier times, before the original spatial order was relativized by the discovery of America, things were quite different. Each nation considered its country to be the centre of the world, to which everything else was related. 'Just as the heart lies at the centre of the body', goes a saying in old Iran, 'the land of Iran is more precious than all other countries because it is set at the middle of the world.'[1] It corresponds to this natural feeling about life that, for example, the Chinese called their country the country of the centre, the ancient Germanic people regarded Midgard as the centre of the world,[2] and in the ancient Greek world-view the countries were grouped around Hellas and collectively surrounded by the great Oceanus that flowed around them and held them together. On the disc of Earth, under the vault of heaven, each country felt itself to be the natural centre and distinguished above the others.

Following this line of thought, the task naturally arose of fixing more precisely the centre of the world within one's own realm, and thus the Greeks revered this 'navel of the world' in Delphi, the Jews saw it in the rock on which the temple of Jerusalem was built, the Chinese in the palace of the Celestial Emperor in Peking, or wherever else this point was thought to be located.

This point on the horizontal plane of the earth's surface at the same time expanded to become a world axis, which arose vertically from it. However much the form varies in detail, the principle recurs in its various forms as typically the same. It is the axis which links the three realms of space split into vertical divisions: the world of the supernatural, the underworld and the world of the earthly human. Often it is the sacred mountain that denotes the centre of the world and on which the gods reside. Often it is also a specially erected axis, a sacred pole or pillar. Thus, for example, it is said of a tribe in the west of Canada that they believe 'that a copper pole passes through the three cosmic levels (underworld, earth and sky); the point at which it enters the sky is the "door to the world above ".'[3] In our own culture there is a traditional story of the sacred pillar called the Irminsul, which was destroyed by Charlemagne in the Saxon Wars. A similar function was fulfilled in the Etruscan vaulted tombs by a conically tapered pillar, which had no practical function in the self-supporting vault. Here too, the stone vault represents the vault of heaven as 'image and representation of the axis of the world.'[4]

It is also reported of certain nomadic peoples that they carried their sacred pole with them everywhere, and erected it anew at every place

---

1 Mircea Eliade, *Das Heilige und das Profane. Vom Wesen des Religiösen.* Rowohlts Deutsche Enzyklopädie, vol. 31, Hamburg: 1957, p. 24 [*The sacred and the profane*, New York: 1959, p. 40 ff.].

2 Wilhelm Grönbech, *Kultur und Religion der Germanen.* vol. 2, Darmstadt: 1954, p. 183.

3 Eliade, *Das Heilige und das Profane*, p. 21 ff. [p. 35].

4 Otto Wilhelm von Vacano, 'Die Etrusker in der Welt der Antike', *Rowohlts Deutsche Enzyklopädie*, vol. 54, Hamburg: 1957, p. 85.

where they settled. This example is important because it shows that they took their centre with them even on their wanderings on earth, so they did not fall from the centre, even if they changed their location.[5] But we need not even refer to such distant peoples. Among the ancient Germans, too, the raised pillar which supported the roof above the seat of the head of the household had a similar significance. It is reported that on the search for a new home, it was thrown overboard near Iceland, so as to determine a place for their new settlement.[6] Here too we have an axis of the world which could be carried on a journey.

In a mythologically ordered world the question of the centre is unequivocally solved, and all paths in the world thus have their fixed point of reference, their zero point in the system of coordinates. To a great extent this has persisted in our own world. Even today, on the main roads of Italy, which are still those of the ancient Roman Empire, all distances are reckoned from Rome. Every kilometre– stone gives the distance from the city, without the need for more precise information. In this system, therefore, Rome is the centre of the world in which Augustus, in proud self-confidence, marked the exit point of all roads with a golden milestone.[7] However, we cannot linger here among historical viewpoints, but must turn again directly to the world in which we ourselves live.

The finiteness of the world

This is also the place to add a further comment that is important for the total understanding of space. This original, mythological space based on a fixed centre is at the same time a finite space. Beyond the borders of the known inhabited realm, the world simply stops. Eliade stresses the contrast for primeval man between 'their inhabited territory and the unknown and indeterminate space that surrounds it. The former is the world (more precisely, our world), the cosmos; everything outside it is no longer a cosmos but a sort of "other world", a foreign, chaotic space, peopled by ghosts, demons, "foreigners ".'[8] Similarly, Haberland stresses that in folk tradition, 'Beyond these borders lies the "rest of the world", a

5 Eliade, *Das Heilige und das Profane*, p. 20 [p. 32 ff.].

6 Grönbech, *Kultur und Religion der Germanen*, p. 110.

7 H. U. Instinski, 'Inschriften an römischen Strassen', *Das neue Bild der Antike*, edited by Helmut Berve, vol. 2, 1942, p. 352.

8 Eliade, *Das Heilige und das Profane*, p. 18 [p. 29].

region of whose reality one is aware, but which plays no decisive role in one's consciousness.'[9]

It is Brunner who has probably most acutely formulated these relationships in the case of ancient Egypt. He starts from the assumption that 'our world ... is enclosed on all sides by chaos',[10] but comes to the conclusion that in the realm of this chaos one could not actually speak of space, rather that it was 'spaceless.'[11] For 'among the Egyptians we can speak of space only within the created world. The realm before and outside creation is spaceless ... The idea of an infinite space is inconceivable to the Egyptians, since space and borders belong inseparably together.'[12]

Thus we can summarize the result in the words of Weischedel, 'that the early experience of space is characterized by the image in the cave, which is understood as the enclosing and sheltering dwelling place of mankind.'[13] The notion of a hollow space worked out of a non-space, imposed on us by the linguistic history of the word 'room', is thus confirmed by a wide range of traditional folk material (not further to be developed here). The world-view of Greek astronomy, as we have observed it (if only briefly) in Aristotle, is only a crystal-clear development of this original consciousness of space. There is no thought whatsoever here of an infinite space.

9 E. Haberland, 'Naturvölkische Raumvorstellungen', *Studium Generale*, vol. 10, 1957, p. 586.

10 H. Brunner, 'Zum Raumbegriff der Ägypter', *Studium Generale*, vol. 10, 1957, p. 614 ff. See Leo Frobenius, *Kulturgeschichte Afrikas*, Zurich: 1933, p. 188.

11 Brunner, 'Zum Raumbegriff der Ägypter', p. 188.

12 Brunner, 'Zum Raumbegriff der Ägypter', p. 188.

13 Wilhelm Weischedel, *Das Denken zwischen Raum und Zeit*, Berlin: 1960, p. 7.

5. The Points of the Compass

Orientation in space

When a human being leaves his usual location and, for whatever reason, moves into the expanse of the outside world, he must learn to find his way around, that is, to reach his target and from there find his way back home again. This is not difficult, provided that he is in a familiar area, close to his place of residence. He knows the routes in this area, having gradually come to know them, starting from his house, and he knows how to move along them. But when he leaves this familiar realm and enters unknown territory, he must explicitly make sure of his route; he must determine the direction in which he is going. This is no longer the direction towards a definite target, but all those starting from his residence, the points of the compass, north and south, east and west, as they are brought into being by the course of the sun. Man directs his movements according to the position of the sun. With its help he 'orients' himself in his environment.

The verb 'to orient oneself', as we know, is derived from the 'Orient', the land of the rising sun, and thus literally means to determine the direction of sunrise, although even in everyday life, particularly when we speak in a figurative sense of intellectual orientation, we are rarely conscious of the origin of the word. Kant, in his little essay 'What does it mean to orient oneself in thinking?', determines the original spatial meaning of this word as follows: 'To orient oneself, in the proper sense of the word, means to use a given direction – and we divide the horizon into four of these – in order to find others. When I see the sun in the sky and I know it is noon, then I know where to find South, West, North and East.'[1]

But in naming the determination of the four points of the compass, which after all have fundamentally equal rights, we are giving preference to one of them, namely the east, and we must inquire into the causes of this one-sided preference. This leads us back to certain 'ideological'

1 Kant, *Gesammelte Schriften*, vol. 8, p. 134.

assumptions, that is, assumptions based on the history of religion. Christianity, in which this idea is of course alive in the 'orienting', that is, the alignment of churches with the altar to the east, for its part refers to older traditions. The points of the compass are here originally not at all equal, merely formally distinct directions, but have their quite specific significances and characters, just as the traditional number four has a quite specific significance, deeply rooted in mythology. To understand the forms of orientation of the present day, we must cast at least a fleeting glance over this religious-historical background.

In his *Philosophy of symbolic forms*, Cassirer, considering 'mythical space', that is, space as given for a mythical state of consciousness, explicitly referred to the qualitatively different characters of the points of the compass. At the same time he pointed out that from this spatial scheme, it is not only the well-known number four that needs to develop, but to an equal extent the number five, when one includes the central point between the four arms of the cross, or perhaps, even more frequently, the number seven, when the directions of up and down are added to the division of the four horizontal points of the compass. He says, for example, using only one example out of many: 'In the mythical-sociological world view of the Zunis for example … the sevenfold form of the totemic organization, which runs through the whole world, is particularly reflected in the conception of space. Space as a whole is divided into seven zones, north and south, east and west, the upper and the lower world, and finally the centre of the world.'[2]

Some relevant comments on the numbers five and seven in relation to the points of the compass are also found in Frobenius, where the centre is particularly distinguished as a world mountain or celestial pillar. These concepts denote the vertical axis, which represents not only the centre of the horizontal division, but also, in a vertical sense, rises up towards the divine. I mention it here because at the same time it represents the link with the idea of a world axis which was discussed earlier. Frobenius says: 'In the imagination of the Ural-Altaic peoples the heavens are supported by a 'golden pillar', a 'golden pole', an 'iron tree.' The erection of such celestial columns, that is, simple wooden pillars, is very common.[3]

2 Ernst Cassirer, *Philosophie der symbolischen Formen*, vol. 2, Berlin: 1923-9, p. 108 [*Philosophy of symbolic forms*, translated by Ralph Manheim, vol. 2, New Haven: 1953-7, p. 86].

3 Frobenius, *Kulturgeschichte Afrikas*, p. 176.

Mythical geography

The question of the number of directions in the world involves a further thought. Because space is not homogeneous from the outset, each location in it has its own special character, its 'tone' or 'special accent' (Cassirer). For this reason, the points of the compass in particular are qualitatively different, not only in terms of direction but of their nature. Cassirer precisely followed this connection in the so-called primitive world-view and what he reports in greater detail using the example of the Zuni is only a particularly clear case of a typically recurrent interpretation. The sacred number seven divides not only space, but at the same time all existence, and the result is a continuous arrangement, whereby every living being is allocated a particular place in space, and each particular place in space for that reason also has its own particular character or nature. 'Every reality', says Cassirer, 'occupies its unequivocal position, its definitely prescribed place, within this general classification [that is, within the sevenfold totemic organization of space described above].'[4] He shows how the different 'elements' are assigned to the points of the compass: 'To the north belongs the air, to the south fire, to the east earth, to the west water.'[5] It is just the same with human activities. 'And the various human classes', Cassirer continues, 'occupations, and institutions enter into the same basic schema: war and warriors belong to the north, the hunt and the hunter to the west, medicine and agriculture to the south, magic and religion to the east.'[6] Cassirer speaks of a 'mythical geography.'[7] This is for him 'an expression of a very definite and typical outlook', according to which 'all species and varieties of things have their "home" somewhere in space'[8] and as a result they are therefore all included in a great uniform interpretation of the world. This depends on the 'Schematismus' variously emphasized by Cassirer (a word used by him in a Kantian sense), by means of which intellectual connections are 'mediated' by the understanding of spatial connections.

Thus the different points of the compass acquire quite a different significance. Often, originating from the sacred area in the centre, actual gods of direction develop,[9] and the individual areas acquire their special,

4 Cassirer, *Philosophie der symbolischen Formen*, vol. 2, p. 108 [p. 86].
5 Cassirer, *Philosophie der symbolischen Formen*, vol. 2, p. 108 [p. 86].
6 Cassirer, *Philosophie der symbolischen Formen*, vol. 2, p. 108 [p. 86].
7 Cassirer, *Philosophie der symbolischen Formen*, vol. 2, p. 115 [p. 93].
8 Cassirer, *Philosophie der symbolischen Formen*, vol. 2, p. 108 [p. 87].
9 Cassirer, *Philosophie der symbolischen Formen*, vol. 2, p. 121 [p. 98].

divine and demonic, friendly or hostile characters. Among these directions, east and west again emerge as the most important. 'The east as the origin of light', says Cassirer in summarizing these ideas, 'is also the source of life – the west as the place of the setting sun is filled with all the terrors of death. Wherever we find the idea of a realm of the dead, spatially separate and distinguished from the realm of the living, it is situated in the west of the world.'[10] Brunner stressed it similarly in an essay on the spatial concept of the ancient Egyptians: 'In historical times the dead person lies on his left side, his head towards the north, so that he faces the rising sun, the land of birth and life.'[11] The extent to which this affects the orientation and spatial symbolism of the Christian churches is well known, so that only a reminder is necessary here.

This understanding of the different qualities of the points of the compass also has an effect on the art of prophecy, just as, conversely, the Roman technique of prophecy allows a retrospective look at the understanding of space. Cassirer sums up these relationships as follows: 'The whole of heaven breaks down into four parts, determined by the zones of the cosmos ... From this purely logical partitioning developed the entire system of Roman theology. In searching the sky for omens of man's undertakings on earth the augur began by dividing it into definite sectors. The east-west line, established by the course of the sub, was bisected by a vertical from north to south. With this interesection of the two lines the decumanus and the cardo, as they were called in the language of the priests, religious thinking created its first basic schema of coordinates.'[12]

Thus, in 'mythical geography', orientation in space according to the points of the compass is at the same time linked with an interpretation of space in the various individual characters of its realms. Even if this link has today been broken and the metaphysical regions of the world have become a system of qualitatively similar directions which can be broken down at will into further divisions, a remnant of this deeper significance still resonates today in the understanding of the points of the compass. The south is still associated with the idea of summer and warmth, the north with the idea of winter and cold. In the same way, the side of the house most exposed to the weather elements has its own quite special character, and rooms facing north, into which no ray of sunlight penetrates, are emotionally valued

10 Cassirer, *Philosophie der symbolischen Formen*, vol. 2, p. 122 [p. 98].

11 Brunner, 'Zum Raumbegriff der Ägypter', p. 617.

12 Cassirer, *Philosophie der symbolischen Formen*, vol. 2, p. 124 [p. 100]. See H. Nissen, *Das Templum. Antiquarische Untersuchungen*, Berlin: 1869; Werner Müller, *Die heilige Stadt*, Stuttgart: 1961.

less highly. The evening and the morning sun, too, are so different and the concepts of west and east reflect this. That the points of the compass even today have not quite become concepts purely to be defined in mathematical terms may become evident to us from the more lively and colourful image of the original mythical idea of space.

Other schemes of direction

But that orientation in space is not necessarily linked to the course of the sun, that rather, in certain circumstances, quite different possibilities may form in a geographical scheme of directions, in which these too may again merge with a corresponding mythical background – this is shown by certain interesting examples from the realm of ethnology, given by Jensen. With certain Indian tribes it is the direction given by the course of essential rivers which represents the decisive spatial axis and, despite the bends of the river, is fixed as a permanent direction. 'The Yurok for example', reports Jensen, 'have the two main directions "down-river" and "up-river". Right and left of these directions are called "to the other shore" and "away from the river", where the person in question is thought of as being on one side of the river. These directions, totally dependent on the situation of the moment, dominate the thinking of the Yurok to the extent that for them, for example, a door is situated not on the west, but on the "down-river" side of the house', and so on.[13] At the same time, these two directions have their religious significance. Up-river is the direction from which life comes, down-river is the direction of the realm of the dead. Haberland, in a text derived from Jensen, remarks that these ideas are so strongly rooted in the thinking of the nations in question 'that they are taken along on journeys and transferred into an environment which does not in any way fit into this scheme',[14] that they can therefore be completely separated from geographical assumptions.

Conditions on the Maluku island of Seram, which Jensen describes from his own experience, are particularly striking. The mountain people in the interior of the island, the Alfuros, entirely lack our concept of a fixed direction of the compass. Their basic direction, to which all other directions

13 A. E. Jensen, 'Wettkampf-Parteien. Zweiklassen-Systeme und geographische Orientierung', *Studium Generale*, vol. 1, 1947, p. 38 ff. See Erik Homburger Erikson, *Kindheit und Gesellschaft*, Zurich and Stuttgart: 1957, p. 108 ff.; Haberland, 'Naturvölkische Raumvorstellungen', p. 583 ff.

14 Haberland, 'Naturvölkische Raumvorstellungen', p. 585.

are related, is 'towards the sea' (it is important for the understanding of this information that the island is traversed by a high range of mountains and the settlements of the people in question lie at a middle height with an open view of the sea). This direction 'towards the sea' is considered 'something constant and the same in all places',[15] which of course must give rise to flagrant contradictions of the 'actual' relationships, as we see them. Thus they find nothing strange about the fact that the sun rises in different places in different directions, and refer to their experience that after all the direction of sunrise in the same place changes in the course of the year. The uninhabited primeval forest area of the mountain range, lying behind the view of the sea, is regarded as the limit of their space, where their 'world' ends. Thus Jensen reports of the inhabitants of a spot in the northern half of the island: 'The fact that beyond those mountains there lies, once again, the sea, is denied most vigorously by the inhabitants. ... Seen from [this place] all the settlements of the southern half lie spread out to left and right along the same coast, where one has an open view of the sea [from this place]. The individual directions "towards the sea", according to their view, thus run in approximate parallel from all points of their settlement area.'[16]

The coastline surrounding the island thus appears as a straight line running left and right into infinity, and the circular area of the settlement is accordingly deformed into a strip. Haberland summarizes very aptly: 'The Seramese are not capable of imagining their island as a complex whole, but believe it to be an endless coast, to which the rivers flow down from the ridge of the mountains behind which, for them, another world begins.'[17] 'At any rate', Jensen stresses, 'the mountain people of Seram regard their homeland not as an island, but as a continent, which stretches out behind their settlement into the limitless distance.'[18] Here the realm of spirits and fabulous beings begins. This scheme of orientation, reduced to the crudest simplification, means that the position of a place can be determined by its distance from a corresponding spot on the coast. In the area in which the people in question move, this scheme is totally adequate. A lack of consistency with 'reality' would appear only if they ventured beyond their accustomed area. Then, admittedly, they would experience the need for re-orientation such as was experienced by the European peoples when they ventured beyond their original area, for example on the discovery of America.

15 Jensen, 'Wettkampf-Parteien', p. 44.
16 Jensen, 'Wettkampf-Parteien', p. 44.
17 Haberland, 'Naturvölkische Raumvorstellungen', p. 585.
18 Jensen, 'Wettkampf-Parteien', p. 15.

Preferred places

But the individual character of directions and places in space is important in another respect for the understanding of experienced space. Even if the mythological world picture in general has disappeared, if the individual characters of space have lost their supra-individual and as it were objective, mythically based validity, these places and directions still retain a quite specific character of their own in the life of the individual human being. It is only that the latter is not generally speaking related to the geographical points of the compass. For the human being living today, space is by no means homogeneous, rather every place in it is laden with special meanings. There is a distinction between preferred and avoided areas. Memories of pleasant or unpleasant kinds are linked with the individual places. And even if some of them are distinguished by such a heightened significance that they provoke an almost religious thrill in us, most are perceived only obscurely in emotional terms, and only rarely rise to clear consciousness, so that they usually escape our notice. For this reason a reference to the more noticeable manifestations of the mythical idea of space seems rewarding, because it draws our attention to the analogous, but concealed, conditions in the experienced space of the human being no longer bound to mythology, and thus directly contributes to our theme.

We recognize the formation of such a division of space in terms of significance most clearly when, leaving our familiar environment, we suddenly find ourselves transplanted into a new landscape which is still unfamiliar to us. In *The magic mountain*, Thomas Mann has aptly described how our sense of time becomes transformed and renewed when on a holiday journey in an unknown situation. We notice something similar in our sense of space. In the new location, we discover a space devoid of meaning – at least still so for us. Only by staying in this location will we fill it with significance and emotional meaning. For clarification I will add a description of a perceptive listener which seems to me to reproduce the situation very aptly: 'When people go on holiday, a space undoubtedly opens up for them which is at first fairly homogeneous and of uniform value. But very soon this space breaks up into familiar paths and places, preferred or avoided, and most often there then emerges a particularly favoured spot, a quiet corner which thus becomes the pivot of the whole experience of the holiday space. This may be the sandcastle or the campsite, a spot by the seashore, a "camp" in the undergrowth, such as groups of young people tend to create during the summer holidays. When one then observes that such a favourite place has already been occupied by others, one cannot help regarding the other as an intruder.'

This experience was once formulated in classic terms by Goethe, when looking back in later life he described the view of the Alsatian landscape, as it appeared to him when he first ascended the Strasbourg cathedral tower. He writes: 'Such a fresh view of a new land, in which we are to spend some time, still has such an individual quality, as pleasant as it is ominous, that the whole lies before us like a blank slate. As yet, no sorrows or joys of ours are inscribed upon it; this cheerful, colourful, lively surface is still mute for us; the eye lingers on objects only in so far as they are significant in their own right, and as yet we have neither an inclination nor a passion to pick out particularly this location or that; yet a sense of what is to come is already disturbing the young heart, and an unsatisfied need quietly calls for whatever is to come or may come, that which in any case, whether for good or evil, will imperceptibly take on the character of the region which we now inhabit.'[19]

Directions *of travel and regions of life*

What applies to individual places also applies in a greater measure to the regions and directions in space that all have a significance in our lives, and here too what we have come to know about the points of the compass of the mythological world picture also applies to the smaller scheme of directions of our everyday life. Here I am thinking first of all of the situation of the person who leaves his house in the morning. As soon as he walks into the street, he must take a particular direction, and thus he steps out into the world of decisions. When a human being walks out of the door of his house, Simmel remarks, 'life flows forth out of the door from the limitation of the isolated separate existence into the limitlessness of all possible directions.'[20] And in fact it is the directions of travel, as opposed to the quiet equilibrium of domestic life, that force one to make decisions. They make the outside world appear as the realm of necessary decisions.

In today's living conditions, with a house situated in a street it is usually the case that when leaving the house, one must turn either left or right in the direction of the street. The choice of one or the other then determines the further purpose of the outing. One direction is 'into town' (or, in the

19 Goethe, *Dichtung und Wahrheit. Gedenkausagabe*, vol. 10, p. 393.

20 Georg Simmel, 'Brücke und Tür' (1909), *Brücke und Tür. Essays*, edited by Michael Landmann, Stuttgart: 1957, p. 4 ['Bridge and door', translated by Mark Ritter, 1994; now *Simmel on culture*, edited by David Frisby and Mike Featherstone, London: 1997, p. 173].

country, 'into the village'), to one's usual place of work or other destinations for conducting everyday business. This is the route that one takes, as it were, by default. But the other side leads away from this accustomed path, into the open, for an excursion or other activity. In any case the first step out of the house involves a decision between two quite different worlds. Once the first step has been taken in one or other direction, then – as long as one does not decide in favour of an explicit return and a new beginning – no transition is possible from one realm to the other. So every direction has a significant character of its own. With the direction one takes, one enters into a quite specific sphere of life, and the life rhythm of work and relaxation, everyday habit and new beginning, is already delineated in the spatial scheme of the route on which one is setting out.

In his novel series *A la recherche du temps perdu* [In search of lost time], Proust superbly develops the whole structure of his hero's life by means of the polarity of two such spatial directions. From the house of his grandfather in Combray there were two possible routes for taking a walk: one passing by M. Swann's house towards Méséglise, the other towards Guermantes. But both, in the terms of the narrative, were not only spatial directions, which led towards very different landscapes, but because of the personal circle associated with them they were also, in the intellectual sense, two quite different worlds, within which the further development of the story took place. The importance of this unequalled source of the significance for life of spatial connections makes it appropriate to give this text here in some detail:

> For there were, in the environs of Combray, two 'ways' which we used to take for our walks, and so diametrically opposed that we would actually leave the house by a different door, according to the way we had chosen: the way towards Méséglise-la-Vineuse, which we called also 'Swann's way,' because, to get there, one had to pass along the boundary of M. Swann's estate, and the 'Guermantes way.' Of Méséglise-la-Vineuse, to tell the truth, I never knew anything more than the way there, and the strange people who would come over on Sundays to take the air in Combray, ... whom we would assume to be 'people who must have come over from Méséglise.' As for Guermantes, I was to know it well enough one day, but that day had still to come; and, during the whole of my boyhood, if Méséglise was to me something as inaccessible as the horizon, which remained hidden from sight, however far one went, ... Guermantes, on the other hand, meant no more than the

> ultimate goal, ideal rather than real, of the 'Guermantes way,' a sort of abstract geographical term like the North Pole or the Equator. And so to 'take the Guermantes way' in order to get to Méséglise, or vice versa, would have seemed to me as nonsensical a proceeding as to turn to the east in order to reach the west. Since my father used always to speak of the 'Méséglise way' as comprising the finest view of a plain that he knew anywhere, and of the 'Guermantes way' as typical of river scenery, I had invested each of them, by conceiving them in this way as two distinct entities, with that cohesion, that unity which belongs only to the figments of the mind; ... while, immediately beside them, ... the purely material roads, at definite points on which they were set down as the ideal view over a plain and the ideal scenery of a river, were not worth the trouble of looking at them ... But, above all, I set between them, far more distinctly than the mere distance in miles and yards and inches which separated one from the other, the distance that there was between the two parts of my brain in which I used to think of them, one of those distances of the mind which time serves only to lengthen, which separate things irremediably from one another, keeping them for ever upon different planes.[21]

Unfortunately it is impossible to include here the whole of this wonderful description of these two spatial-intellectual worlds, and the reader is strongly recommended to refer to it in the novel itself. But one more passage will be quoted here, which sums up, from the point of view of old age, the enduring significance of the worlds opened up by the two directions, with their individual emotional connotations for the rest of life:

> But it is pre-eminently as the deepest layer of my mental soil, as firm sites on which I still may build, that I regard the Méséglise and Guermantes 'ways.' ... The 'Méséglise way' with its lilacs, its hawthorns, ... the 'Guermantes way' with its river ... have constituted for me for all time the picture of the land in which I fain would pass my life.[22]

---

21 Marcel Proust, *Auf der Suche nach der verlorenen Zeit*, vol. 1, *In Swanns Welt*, Frankfurt a. M. and Zurich: 1953, p. 200 ff. [*In search of lost time*, translated by C. K. Scott-Moncrieff (1922-39); now in the public domain, http://etext.library.adelaide.edu.au/p/proust/marcel/)]

22 Proust, *Auf der Suche*, p. 273 ff.

Not only has the landscape of youth determined the picture by which every other landscape will later be measured, but the two directions in space have at the same time become the safe lifelong foundation for the structure of intellectual worlds.

6. Horizon and Perspective

The double aspect of the horizon

In our introduction, we described finiteness as a further feature that distinguishes concrete human space from abstract mathematical space. But at the same time we hesitated over this first enumeration, because the finiteness of space cannot be asserted with the same conviction as its other features, but first requires explanation. A space is called finite when it has a border or limit, where it comes to an end. In the case of a mountain cave, this border is supplied quite obviously by the surrounding rock. Experienced space is not as a whole enclosed by such material walls. But, if one looks at it to begin with in the light of day, it has a border of another kind in the horizon, which in fact, according to its original Greek sense, means that which bounds or limits.[1] It limits the human field of vision. But this limit has something enigmatic and incomprehensible about it, so that we must first ask in what sense the horizon is a border of experienced space and thus makes the latter a finite space. Van Peursen has dealt with this question in a thoughtful essay in *Situation*, on which we can to a great extent rely.[2]

So what is a horizon? A simple geographical definition would perhaps determine it to be the line where the vault of heaven seems to rest upon the surface of the earth. Within the landscape, it limits our natural field of vision on all sides, as long as it is not obscured by some object or other. The horizon opens up when a human being emerges from a narrow mountain valley onto a plain. We speak of a free or open horizon. Moreover, the horizon may become narrower and wider. It widens at the top of mountains, where, if the gaze roams over the expanding surfaces before it, it may expand to an overpowering degree. But the curious thing is that man never

---

1 Cornelis Anthonie van Peursen, 'L'horizon', *Situation*, vol. 1, 1954, p. 204 ff.

2 In how far a sense of finiteness is preserved even when no horizon is visible, as in night space, will be discussed on p. 224 ff.

climbs higher than his horizon. The horizon is not left behind, but climbs with the climber; it always remains at the height of the human being. One experiences this in a very impressive way when one climbs a mountain on the sea coast, and sees how tree after tree, hill upon hill is overtaken by the horizon, and in fact sinks below the horizon. The horizon, incidentally, always defines the horizontal; at the moment when a point on the nearby mountain slope is reached, I know that I am on the same level as that point.

The same is true of horizontal movement. However tempting a distant prospect appears, man can never reach the horizon. The further we wander, the further the horizon recedes. One cannot even say that one is approaching the horizon. The things that stood on the horizon, the towers of a far-off city, or the crest of a mountain range, may come nearer as one approaches them, and the masts of a ship at sea may rise above the horizon. The horizon always remains the same. As I move, it moves with me. This is particularly noticeable where individual forms retreat and the horizon is delineated with particular obtrusiveness. A traveller in the steppes reports that there is something frightening about being imprisoned for ever by the same, eternally accompanying horizon. 'Precisely because of too much riding and too much freedom, and of the unchanging horizon, in spite of our desperate gallopings, the pampa assumed the aspect of a prison for me, a prison that was bigger than the others.'[3] If one defines man as a being that can cross all boundaries, the horizon is the one boundary he cannot cross. It is an absolute limit.

On the other hand, however, the horizon is not only a limit, and the example of the frightening experience of being imprisoned was an abnormal, borderline case. In general, the horizon does not restrict people, rather the opposite: it extends in front of them a wide field of vision and movement reaching forward freely into space. It is a boundary, but not a restricting boundary. Even as it recedes, it positively entices one into the distance. Van Peursen has very clearly worked out this double character of the horizon: at the same time it broadens out spatial development for humans and immediately restricts it again. 'The horizon', he says, 'defines the limit which humans cannot reach, but also the area in which man extends himself through his vision, through his wishes.'[4] He stresses the 'double aspect of the horizon': 'to be both inaccessible boundary and space for pushing forward.'[5]

---

3 Jules Supervielle, quoted by Bachelard, *Poetik des Raumes*, p. 252 [p. 221].

4 Van Peursen, 'L'horizon', p. 208.

5 Van Peursen, 'L'horizon', p. 208.

But what then 'is' the horizon? Geographers call it the 'imaginary line' where the vault of the heavens meets the earth. But then again, there are various kinds of imaginary line. The horizon is different from the Equator, which of course is also not a visible line on the surface of the earth. But nevertheless the Equator has its defined situation on earth. One can reach it and cross it and possibly even mark it on the earth's surface (in Mainz, for example, the 50th parallel has been marked by a metal strip inlaid into the pavement). But one cannot reach the horizon, because it has no fixed place at all in space. While bordering space, it is not itself in space. But this is only to repeat the question: what then 'is' the horizon?

Van Peursen has developed this question very convincingly in his essay. The horizon is not something that could simply be found independent of mankind. It is not a thing in the world. It is 'unreal.' But for that reason it is again not something that only exists in the human mind, something merely imagined, but it necessarily belongs to the world. All things that are encountered by humans in space must be encountered by them in the context of a horizon. A world without a horizon is impossible. Van Peursen says: 'Without a horizon the world would not be poorer, but it would not remain the same. A world without a horizon cannot be imagined.'[6] It is the horizon that brings visible objects together into unity. On the other hand, the horizon also belongs equally inseparably to man. Man only lives within a horizon and can never escape the bond with this horizon. 'Man cannot negate the horizon. Defeating the horizon would mean abolishing mankind. The horizon is linked in some way with humankind.'[7]

So the horizon belongs to a realm which cannot be assigned entirely to mankind or to the world, but includes both in their original unity. We may best define it by means of the Kantian concept by stating that it belongs to the transcendental condition of the human being-in-the-world. For this reason the horizon is not anything within space, but belongs inseparably to the spatiality of human existence. The human being always extends his space from the centre in which he stands, in the frame of a limiting and unity-forming horizon, and the fact that man never reaches his horizon, but his horizon travels along with him, shows only that the horizon belongs inseparably to the human being (here one can really say 'like the shell to the snail'), and thus the human being always remains the centre of the space enclosed by his horizon. 'The horizon places man in the centre of

6 Van Peursen, 'L'horizon', p. 207.
7 Van Peursen, 'L'horizon', p. 207.

reality.'[8] The placing of man in the centre of his space and the horizon that encloses it are thus necessarily dependent on each other.

Here one could perhaps ask whether the vault of heaven, in its appearance as an 'azure bell' or as a surface covered with clouds, is to be perceived as a natural continuation of the horizon; for it is only in the heavens that the enclosing circle extends to become an enclosing covering, and the horizon achieves its full spatial extent.

Van Peursen here adds another very interesting thought, which leads to further consequences: it is at the same time the horizon that allows man to be at home in the world, to dwell in it. For 'man could not live in an endless world, and an endless field of vision would make him anxious', he would feel forsaken. It is the horizon that gathers the space around man into a finite and manageable environment. 'The horizon shows this element of protection.'[9] 'The horizon', says Van Peursen, 'covers him and gives him a home.'[10] It makes the world into a sort of sheltering house, even if it is a house of a particular kind, which man cannot leave and seek out again, but one with which he is bound up. On the horizon we see revealed something that we will encounter again in a different context, the original sheltering character of space. Space is not a strange medium for man. He feels at home in it; indeed he feels himself to be at one with his space.

Perspective

Perspective too is bound up indissolubly with the horizon. Perspective – as the word has come to be used primarily of architecture, from the problems of figurative representation – is the aspect that an object offers to me from a particular point of view. Every object appears to us in a particular perspective. This means in the first place that I can only ever see the object from one side, never from all sides at once, and that therefore, if I look at it from one side, other sides remain hidden. Every view is necessarily one-sided. This however also means that the object only ever offers itself in certain 'perspective reductions', that parallel lines seem to converge on each other in infinity, and so on. If I walk around a building, the perspectives are constantly changing. I may perhaps choose the most favourable of these for the purpose of depiction. But however much the

8 Van Peursen, 'L'horizon', p. 217.
9 Van Peursen, 'L'horizon', p. 233.
10 Van Peursen, 'L'horizon', p. 234.

perspectives change, I am always bound to *a* perspective. I cannot escape perspectivity as a whole. I can never see an object independently of a particular point of view, never see it as it is 'in itself.'

Perspective however also means that objects change in size according to their distance from the observer. Objects at a distance appear smaller. This includes the so-called 'air perspective', which makes distant objects appear lighter and more bluish. And finally we must also take into account that objects at the front conceal those behind them, removing them from our gaze. Thus, as a result of perspective, objects are ordered according to their closeness or distance, with reference to man as the centre of his space. Thus perspective is on the one hand the expression of the 'subjectivity' of his space, meaning that man in his space is bound to a particular point of view, that he can only ever see it 'from inside', but on the other hand it also enables him to recognize this dependence of his on his point of view.

Thus, horizon and perspective belong indissolubly together. Perspective orders things within the horizon, but the horizon, in which all parallel lines converge, gives perspective a firm foothold. (This of course is only true of horizontally running parallels, but this once again shows the difference between experienced and mathematical space: in the former, apart from vertical parallels, which according to the rule of art always remain vertical, there are only horizontal parallels.) Horizon and perspective therefore bring man into the 'finiteness' of his existence in space, but at the same time it is they that allow him to function in space. Not only do they place man in a certain situation in space, but they also make it possible for him to recognize this situation and thus attain a firm foothold and a clear view in his space.

Perspective and horizon in the figurative sense

But the concepts of horizon and perspective are also used in a figurative sense, indeed the literal and figurative meaning overlap each other to such an extent that it is often difficult to distinguish between them. One says of one's relationship with the world of the intellect that it sometimes appears in a particular perspective. Intellectual connections are also seen from a certain point of view, a particular world view, are of a subjectively limited nature, and so on. And here too it is at the same time accepted that there are other perspectives, conflicting, but basically with equal rights. And here too it is true to say that man cannot escape being bound to a particular, one-sided perspective. It is perspectivism, as emphatically propounded, for example, by Nietzsche, which however must not be equated with a sceptical relativism, but is a necessary characteristic of all human understanding as being finite.

Perspective however does not only mean one-sidedness in the sense of an imperfection attaching (unfortunately) to human cognition, but it also has its positive side. Just as there is a favourable point of view for the depiction of a building, so there are also rewarding, enlightening perspectives for the illumination of intellectual connections. Things are lit up in a new and deeper context if one observes them from a suitable perspective.

Similarly, there is also a horizon in an intellectual sense. One speaks of the intellectual horizon of a person or an age, meaning, in an analogous way, the environment of what humans can envisage in the intellectual sense and what belongs in their world. The intellectual horizon too can be narrower or wider. A saying ascribed to the German mathematician David Hilbert is that the intellectual horizon in some people has a zero radius, and that was what they would call their point of view. This expresses the concept that the narrow-mindedness with which a human being holds fast to his preconceived opinions is often linked with the limitation of his horizon. On the other hand, the horizon extends with manifold contact with strange forms of human life, through reading, multiple acquaintanceship and, in the literal sense, travel. The extended horizon makes man capable of judgement, particularly when faced with unexpected new tasks. The breadth of the horizon is thus a sign of the superior spirit. But however much the intellectual horizon of a human being may expand, basically the same is true as of a purely spatial horizon: no human can escape from attachment to a field of vision drawn around a particular point of view and therefore always restricted. In the intellectual sphere too, the horizon belongs to the essence of human life.

But it is also true in the intellectual sphere that the horizon is by no means a deplorable limitation, but is necessary for life itself, because it gathers it into the unity of a defined 'Gestalt.' Without a horizon, it would dissolve. This too has been clearly presented by Van Peursen: 'All cultural works have limitations that give them a place. A system of thought exists thanks to these limitations. It aims at decisions, gives starting-points, allows one to make definitions, to clarify … All this can only happen in areas circumscribed by horizons. The horizon prevents one from getting lost, and gives one the means to determine one's situation and to work out the path of one's intellect.'[11] Thus the unregulated extension of an intellectual horizon,

11 Van Peursen, 'L'horizon', p. 212.

in particular through knowledge acquired externally and not relating to one's own centre, can endanger the natural security of life. This was what Nietzsche had in mind in his day, with respect to the superior strength of historical knowledge, when he stressed that 'everything living can become healthy, strong and fruitful only within a horizon.'

II
THE WIDE WORLD

1. Expanse, Distance and the Foreign

A new question

While observing the behaviour of humans in space, we noticed above all the one basic dynamic of 'there and back again. Man does not move arbitrarily in space, rather all his movements are ultimately based on an opposition between going and returning. But so far we have only remarked in passing on this starting-point, in order to determine from it a natural centre within space. We must now return to this concept.

The designation of the spatial centre as a zero point already is insufficient. We must ask what it is that gives the zero point this outstanding significance, so that the return to it appears to be the deepest fulfilment of man's being. And in this way we will find that the mere unexpanded middle point is replaced by a spatially expanded individual area with quite specific characteristics of its own. This area, to which we 'return home' and where we feel 'at home', this area of 'homeland' and 'house', needs to be more precisely understood. But equally, we must ask ourselves what it is that drives man out of this centre, when the meaning of his life is supposed to consist in his return, and how different a space he enters in this way.

Thus the double movement of going away and returning at the same time mirrors a division of space itself into two areas, of which a narrower inner area is concentrically enclosed by a wider outer one, namely the narrower area of house and home and the wider outer area, from which man advances forward and from which he once again returns. This division into two areas emerges as the most important in the structure of total experienced space. It is these two areas that we will examine more precisely in what follows. The order in which this examination takes place, whether we start from one area or the other, is basically unimportant, and however one begins, it will never be done without a certain measure of force, because the two areas can only artificially be separated from each other. I will try to take the path from the outer to the inner area, that is, I will begin from the situation where man has removed himself from the centre of his space, and will try from that point to return to the nature of the centre and the process of returning home.

Pushing forward into the infinite distance of space

Before we can get down to opening up this outer area of space according to its different directions, a brief historical view is required. For this wider area can be given in very different ways. Today we very readily think straight away of the infinite distance of outer space. But this is not the necessary or original concept, and what a historical view shows us in terms of earlier possibilities, again throws light on certain hidden features of our own consciousness of space. Once again we recall the interpretation of the German language, which developed the concept of space from the idea of the clearing, and we recall even further back the ancient idea that space was limited by the heaven of fixed stars as the outermost of the circling spheres. We can summarize this as the cavity theory of space. Here, space is everywhere fundamentally limited and easily comprehended. Here too there is certainly a distance, that is, plenty of room available for movement, but to speak of an infinite expanse is not as yet sensible or meaningful.

This background must be borne in mind if one wishes to grasp what a cataclysmic alteration of the sense of space has taken place in early modern times: in the experience of a new expanse, which has come about through the opening up of infinite space.[1] We must place at the beginning the event already much singled out as significant: Petrarch's ascent of Mont Ventoux in 1336; for the view from the top of the mountain is the situation in which humans most directly experience the sense of expanse. But a long stage of development had to be passed before human beings climbed mountains at all, merely for the sake of the view of far-off places, and in that respect Petrarch's ascent is rightly described as a turning point on the way to the modern sense of space.

But it is surprising at first how little expression is given in Petrarch's account to this new sense of space, in fact how little he writes about what he sees from up there. From contemplating space, he immediately goes over to contemplating time, to looking back over his own life in critical self-examination. And after returning once more for a moment to the wide view

1 Jacob Burckhardt, *Die Kultur der Renaissance in Italien* in *Gesammelte Werke*, vol. 3, Darmstadt: 1955, p. 190 ff. [*The civilization of the renaissance in Italy*, translated by S. G. H. Middelmore, London: 1929].

from the mountain peak, he turns his attention straight from the greatness of the mountains to the greatness of the soul: 'Beside its greatness, nothing is great.'[2] This is an astonishing outcome. Burckhardt too remarks: 'We indeed await in vain a description of the view, but not because the poet is insensitive to it, but on the contrary, because the impression has too powerful an effect upon him.'[3] But I believe that this connection can be more precisely defined: it is neither that he is indifferent to the view of the landscape, nor that the too powerful effect upon him leaves him speechless, but rather that the mood of the soul induced by the spatial expanse is directly converted into a new expanse of the soul itself. So the direction of his thoughts towards the immeasurable expanse of the soul stands in an indissoluble relationship with the expanse of the spatial view. It is the same expanse of the view that is now directed towards temporal distance, and it is the same emotional feeling of the immeasurability of space that is also manifest in the immeasurability of the inner world, as the immeasurability of the soul. The emotion of the inner soul is made possible only by the uplifting experience of spatial expanse. And one senses from the account, even from the return to the plain, how profound is the emotion experienced at the top of the mountain.

This same alteration of the sense of space, however, is what is now expressed in the advance into the expanses of the ocean. What happened a century and a half later, on the discovery of America, and in fact on the enlargement of the known world in the age of discovery, is only the heightened development of what began with Petrarch's mountain climb. Today we must first of all visualize what this meant for the sense of space in the new age; for it was not just that new, hitherto unknown lands were added to those already familiar, but it was a radical transformation of our entire sense of space. It was the opening up of entirely new worlds. It was the expanses of the oceans that lured explorers to unstoppable advances into the open horizons, whereas earlier they had kept anxiously to the coastlines. It was thanks to this intoxicating sense of expanse that Charlemagne later boasted that the sun did not go down on his empire.

These discoveries were as inspiring as they were dizzying; for the discovery of distance necessarily went along with a relativization in spatial orientation in general. No longer could one, with the same naïve certainty, believe the place of residence of one's own people to be the centre of the

2 Petrarca, *Dichtungen, Briefe, Schriften*, edited by Hans Wilhelm Eppelsheimer, 1956, p. 87.

3 Burckhardt, *Die Kultur der Renaissance in Italien*, p. 202.

world. As soon as the surface of the earth had rounded itself into a sphere, there was no longer a distinctive centre. No country was distinguished above any other. So the intoxication of distance could only in passing conceal the fact that with the new discoveries, the secure foothold of a centre had been lost, and man's place on earth had been relativized beyond recall. This was when, to use Sedlmayr's phrase, in a quite directly spatial sense the 'loss of the centre' began.[4]

Certainly it was some time before the final conclusions were drawn from Columbus's discovery. The foreign continents, as colonies of Europe, were for a long time considered in relation to Europe as their actual centre, and it is only in our own days that we are experiencing the disappearance of European precedence and the dissolution of the European point of view in a real world history.

But even more profound are the changes that took place in a corresponding fashion in the area of astronomy, in the space of the heavens, and are associated with the discovery by Copernicus. As we have already mentioned in passing, the ancient sense of the world, that of the Ptolemaic system, remained that of a closed space, finally that of a great cavity, even if in its most perfect form, that of a sphere. The outermost of the spheres, that of the firmament of fixed stars, was at the same time the border of the entire world. Copernicus's discovery, however, did not simply mean a change in the system of coordinates: that the central point was moved from the earth to the sun, but at the same time it exploded the earlier idea of the firmament of fixed stars. Behind it, new expanses, new worlds opened up, wider even than those discovered by Columbus.

Giordano Bruno seized upon these new possibilities with inspiring zest. As he wrote in one poem that he placed at the head of his 'Dialogue on the infinite universe and worlds' (the title itself is significant):

> Confidently I may unfurl my wings,
> I fear no crystal vault,
> [by which he means Ptolemy's firmament of fixed stars]
> when I divide the blue fragrance of the ether
> and hasten upwards to worlds of stars,
> leaving this earthly sphere behind.[5]

4 Hans Sedlmayr, *Verlust der Mitte. Die bildende Kunst des 19. und 20. Jahrhunderts*, Salzburg and Vienna: 1948.

5 'Die Schwingen darf ich selbstgewiß entfalten, / nicht fürcht' ich ein Gewölbe aus Kristall, / wenn ich der Äther blauen Duft zerteile / und nun empor zu Sternenwelten eile, / tief und lassend diesen Erdenball', Giordano Bruno, *Zwiegespräch vom unendlichen All und den Welten*, Jena: 1904.

A much depicted woodcut from this period shows a man pushing with his head through this crystal sphere and looking into the open universe of new worlds.[6] In its own medium it illustrates exactly the same overpowering feeling that must have overcome people of that time in the face of the new vistas that opened up for them, and that was taken up by Bruno in his pantheistic exuberance. He too speaks enthusiastically of 'those splendid stars and shining bodies that are as many inhabited worlds, mighty living creatures and sublime deities, which appear to be innumerable worlds, and indeed are so, not very different from the one in which we live.'[7] The striving for infinity at this period made people dizzy with the perspectives opened up by astronomical thought. They positively revelled in the celestial spaces. For this reason, we can speak of the achievements of Columbus and Copernicus as a positive revolution in the consciousness of space. The concept of the closed nature of a finite space surrounding and sheltering mankind collapses, and opens up into the hitherto unknown expanse of infinity.

But as with discoveries on earth, the new experience of the infinity of outer space at the same time has another, much more dangerous aspect. Its expanse at the same time means emptiness. And when the impetus of the first enthusiasm dies down, returning sobriety allows us to observe a sense of being lost, the ultimate loneliness of man in this space. Only a few decades later, Pascal says in his 'Pensées': 'The eternal silence of these infinite spaces terrifies me.'[8] Here we have not only the other side of Bruno's pantheistic enthusiasm, but at the same time the point at which the consequences of this revolution extend into our own time, and we realize that a reference to these connections is not only an interesting excursus into the history of ideas, to which we could have abandoned ourselves with undimmed pleasure, but it also leads us directly into the burning questions of the present day.

The Baroque interior

By invoking the names of Giordano Bruno and Pascal in explaining the conflicting effect of these developments on man's sense of being, taking

6 Reproduced for example in Günther Müller, *Deutsche Dichtung von der Rennaissance bis zum Ausgang des Barock*, Darmstadt: 1957, p. 175; and in Joseph Vogt, *Wege zum historischen Verstehen*, Stuttgart: 1961.

7 Giordano Bruno, *Von der Ursache, dem Prinzip und dem Einen*, Leipzig: 1947, p. 67.

8 Blaise Pascal, *Über die Religion*, Berlin: 1940, p. 115 [*Pensées*, no. 206].

place over centuries, we have already placed it in the general intellectual context of the Baroque. Indeed, here this intoxication with infinity reaches its final heights. How deeply this transformation in consciousness of space has taken hold of man can be recognized by the fact that it was able even to dissolve the apparently most immovable finite space, the inner space surrounded by solid walls, into infinity. Thus we find in Baroque interiors a clear example of this impulse towards infinity. Although in other respects we have excluded aesthetic questions from our observations, a brief glance at art history may now clarify these connections from another point of view.

Baroque space may, somewhat paradoxically, be described most aptly as an unlimited interior. In other words, the clearly limiting wall which generally determines the nature of inner space, is here consciously veiled in our spatial perception and made to disappear. The means used for this by Baroque architects are well known. The limits of parts of space that were clearly delineated in the Renaissance are veiled by overlapping sculptural decoration, the bordering wall becomes invisible to the observer, because he feels confused by a tangle of projecting and retreating parts, by one view and another, so that he finally no longer knows, and no longer asks, whether anything solid is still to be found behind all these views.

In the bewildering sequence of intersections and viewpoints, solid space breaks up into perspectives leading into the infinite. This is aided by conscious play with illusions, for example in the extravagant use of reflective mirrors. Inaccessible spaces often only serve to produce the optical illusion of an infinite distance.

As the final height of these possibilities let us merely remember the unreal distance from which emerges the silver-gleaming St George of the high altar in the monastery of Weltenburg on the Danube – or from which he rides out, as if caught in the moment when an incorporeal phenomenon becomes corporeal, when, as Pinder says, 'everything becomes a mystical dream, when a silver St George rides out of a bright distance into the twilit altar space.'[9] Dehio describes it in similar fashion: 'It is no longer twilight that reigns in the narrow presbytery, but complete darkness. The back of the area is totally occupied by the high altar. Built up like a triumphal arch. In its centre there is no painting, but an empty opening, and through this we look through into a space of uncertain form and size, a world of light of wavering shapes, seeming infinitely distant. Perhaps the illusory effect would not be as strong without the addition of another artistic medium. For

9 Wilhelm Pinder, *Deutscher Barock*, Leipzig and Königstein im Taunus: 1940, p. 23.

in the centre of the opening stand three overlifesize statues: the knight St George on horseback, seen from the front, on his left the rearing dragon, on his right the fleeing princess. These figures are still in the dark region; but reflected light enters from the back and glides over the golden armour and the silver horse, so that the impression of three-dimensionality is not affected, and at the same time provides communication between the dark at the front and the brightness behind.'[10]

I have quoted this apt account by an art historian verbatim, in order to make this effect of space more vivid (better than any illustration could do it): the inner space dissolves into infinity, without in the process ceasing to be inner space. In fact the extraordinary thing is that this turbulent endlessness of space, this boundlessness, this transition from finite space to non-spatial infinity, this interpenetration of finite and infinite can be experienced only in an interior. For the exterior space becomes clear and visible just where its full breadth opens up, at the endless horizon of the sea. Thus we can also comprehend that the Baroque striving towards infinity is fulfilled precisely in the interior while the outer structure is often, comparatively imperceptibly, left behind.

Narrowness and expanse

We will now try to comprehend this space, extending into infinity, in its inner structure, and in doing so we will pass gradually from the most general definitions to more specific subdivisions. In highly general terms, the German language has three concepts to express the expansion of space in contrast to the inhabited vicinity: expanse [Weite], the foreign [Fremde] and distance [Ferne]. For each of these, the relevant relationship is expressed in a different way. I will try by means of a comparative analysis of these three concepts to work out the spatial reality as comprehensively as possible.

I will begin with the concept of expanse. Perhaps what is meant by this becomes clearest from its opposite. The opposite of expanse is narrowness [Enge]. An article of clothing or a shoe may be tight or loose [eng or weit]. It is too loose if it is not filled adequately by the wearer's body and hangs slackly around it. It can become too tight if the wearer's body has increased in size. A living space can also be too wide. On the other hand one may

10 Georg Dehio, *Handbuch der deutschen Kunstdenkmäler*, vol. 3, Berlin: 1925, p. 575.

feel 'beengt', cramped, by the prospect of a new building too close to one's home. And again, the view widens out when one emerges from a narrow valley onto a plain. There are narrow streets and alleys, there are also narrows in the sea, passages where the land is too close on either side, but again there are wide or spacious places and landscapes. We speak of the endless expanse of the sea.

Not only space, but also the human heart may be tight or open. In a state of fear (the word angst, like 'Enge', literally means narrowness), the heart clenches tightly, and in a state of happy fulfilment it expands once again. From this notion there arises at the same time a wealth of figurative meanings of narrowness and expanse. There are 'engherzige' [narrow-minded] interpretations of existing legislation, and on the other hand, a 'weitherzig' [wide-hearted, that is liberal] attitude of mind. A person may have a clear [weit] conscience, if he is not inhibited by excessive pangs of conscience. There is the regrettable narrowness of an intellectual horizon, but also the oppressive narrowness of poor living conditions.

Narrowness, to summarize these examples, always refers to the prevention of free movement by something that restricts it on all sides. An article of clothing is 'eng', tight, in this sense, if it clings closely to the body, and a house is too narrow if it does not allow the people living in it sufficient space to roam freely. 'Wide' on the other hand describes liberation from this restriction. A door, in this sense, may be opened wide if it allows one to pass freely through it. A person may also open his or her mouth or flare his nostrils wide, if unable to comprehend something strange or surprising.

In general, therefore, man perceives restricting space as a pressure which torments him; he seeks to break through it and to press forward into the liberating distance. Distance thus always means the openness of a field of movement, in which the human urge to expansion, its conquering push into space, is no longer impeded in any way. Hence the references to the wide landscape or in general the wide world. Roads, as the means for overcoming space, lead into the distance. The distance, as a possible space for development, here always refers to human activity, to man as the centre of an expansive, centrifugal urge. 'Wir traben in die Weite' [we ride into the distance], says the song of the German youth movement. Here 'the distance' contains no notion of an actual destination in the sense of a movement towards something, but designates the open field of a forward movement, out of an oppressive confinement. 'The distance' is thus entirely undirected. This also applies in the figurative sense, when the chest expands; it extends itself and becomes open to all the riches of the world.

Of course it is a different matter if one applies the concept of expanse – if only as an adjective – to distant places, and speaks of a long journey. It is still a long way to a certain place – this means that I must travel for a long time until I get there. The concept is often combined with that of breadth [Breite]. 'Far and wide' is a common expression; for example, we say that in a wasteland there is no tree to be seen far and wide. Now breadth generally refers to a transverse direction in relation to length. So there are broad [breite] streets, in which traffic can move, but wide [weite] squares. Above all we should observe this spatial meaning in verbs such as 'to broaden', which refer to an extension of a surface.

The foreign

With the concepts of distance [Ferne] and the foreign [Fremde], on the other hand, we enter quite different realms. Even though both these German words linguistically mean almost the same thing, they have by now diverged into quite different directions. The opposite of the foreign, that which is unknown or strange, is that which is known and familiar, in general one's 'own.' Thus the familiar and the strange are placed in opposition to each other. There are strange people, strange customs and practices, strange lands, etc. 'Foreign' is always the 'other', whatever contradicts our own nature, whatever disturbs us and shocks us out of our own sense of security. Strangers, for a child, are people he does not know, and it is typical of the original relationship that for a long time a child thinks of strangers as bad people. What is familiar is good and what is unknown is bad. The unknown may then become merely odd. A foreign language appears to a naïve person to be comical gibberish and makes him laugh. But the meaning can fade even further: a house is built with one's own money or borrowed money [fremdes Geld]; an inheritance falls into strange hands, and so on.

What remains central is always the spatial relationship. In the earliest linguistic usage, strangers are foreigners, those who do not live where we live. Modern tourism [Fremdenverkehr] seeks to entice these people towards us. But it is a very late development when someone travels to a foreign country merely for the pleasure of change. The word 'Elend', which originally meant exile, where someone must go when driven out of his homeland, also means misery or wretchedness. A child 'fremdelt', is afraid of strangers, when in an unfamiliar world, and what comes out of such a world is 'foreign', strange. As opposed to the free and open expanse, in which man strives towards something outside himself, the foreign is something unpleasant, a menacing area. Rilke, in particular, has expressed in a deeply moving fashion the feeling of being taken over by an overpowering strangeness. He writes of the view from the window of a hotel room:

> It all seemed to warn me off,
> the strange city, whose unconfiding landscape
> gloomed as though I didn't exist. The nearest
> things didn't mind if I misunderstood them.
> The street would thrust itself up to the lamp,
> and I'd see it was strange.

And further he writes:

> and strangeness, in narrowing circles,
> hungrily prowled round my casual flares of perception.[11]

This is how it is in general. One is thrown out of a familiar world into a strange environment. The feeling of intimacy, taken for granted, with the people and things that surround us has been lost. It has moved from the world of the understandable into a world of the inexplicable, in which one feels uncertain and excluded from the lives of others:

> The others they rejoice and let the stranger stand alone[12]

for in foreign parts, one is oneself a foreigner to others. Then one is gripped by irresistibly powerful homesickness. We know of strange, sudden irrational acts, for example by children who try to leave a foreign place in order to return home. Indeed, man can feel altogether a stranger on this earth.

---

11 'Noch war mir die neue Stadt wie verwehrt, und die unüberredete Landschaft finsterte hin, als wäre ich nicht. Nicht gaben die nächsten Dinge sich Müh, mir verständlich zu sein. An der Laterne drängte die Gasse herauf: ich sah, daß sie fremd war' and 'Hungernde Fremdheit umzog das zufällige Flackern meiner Gefühle', Rainer Maria Rilke, *Gedichte* 1906-1926, Wiesbaden: 1953, p. 44 [*Poems* 1906 to 1926, translated by J. B. Leishman, London: 1957, p. 170].

12 'Es jubeln und lassen die andern den Fremden alleine stehn', Joseph Freiherr von Eichendorff, *Heimweh. Neue Gesamtausgabe der Werke und Schriften*, edited by G. Baumann and S. Grosse, Stuttgart: 1957, vol. 1, p. 44.

But this foreign does not have to be some spatially distant realm. It reveals itself in its power to overcome us through the fact that it invades us even in our most sheltered areas. Even in one's own house, strange people and powers may intrude, and even our own lives may become strange to us. Hesse movingly describes, repeatedly (for example, in *Demian*), how for the child the dark power of strangeness as the demonic, deeply shocking to us, penetrates the familiar realm of security. The child is gripped by fear and becomes lonely.

But on the other hand, we may go to foreign parts of our own accord, for example if forced to do so by our work, or if we want to learn something new in foreign lands (as the travelling journeymen used to do). We despise those who have not gone out into the world or learnt to look beyond the steeple of one's own parish church. But there is always a sensible reason for people to travel abroad, never an uncertainly sensed need. We want to expand our knowledge, to learn what we cannot learn at home, or to bring home, as a merchant or a thief, the products of foreign lands. The foreign is always a temporary residence, from which we return when we have achieved our purpose.

Thus we reach a productive confrontation between what we know from home and what we have learnt abroad. Human culture (in the widest sense of the term) grows in the new acceptance and acquisition of what is strange or foreign. But there can also be an excess, a state of domination by foreign influence, in which the strangeness we have adopted suffocates one's own life.

This is why it is important to find the right balance between one's own power of assimilation and the degree of foreignness to be acquired. Nietzsche recognized this very clearly in the second of his *Thoughts out of season*. 'A living thing', he writes, 'can only be healthy, strong and productive within a certain horizon: if it be incapable of drawing one round itself … it will come to an untimely end. Cheerfulness, a good conscience, belief in the future, the joyful deed, all depend … on there being a line that divides the visible and clear from the vague and shadowy.'[13] Nietzsche then applies this in particular to his relationship with his own past, and it serves to escape from an excess of historical knowledge, but it is also, and even primarily, true of the human relationship with other human life forms and here precisely described the demand for a border between what is one's

13 Friedrich Nietzsche, *Vom Nutzen und Nachteil der Historie für das Leben. Groß- und Kleinoktavausgabe*, vol. 2, p. 287 [*Thoughts out of season*, translated by Adrian Collins, in *The complete works of Friedrich Nietzsche*, vol. 5, Edinburgh and London: 1909].

own and what is foreign. Nietzsche adopts the geographical concept of the horizon in a figurative sense in order to describe this demarcation from an excess of foreignness.

Distance

The concept of distance [Ferne] leads us into yet another area. At first it seems to describe in a neutral sense a merely spatial relationship. The opposite of distance is nearness, while the concept of distance has an emotionally neutral meaning. But we must take care to neutralize the concept too much in the sense of a mere gap or difference, and must try to grasp it in its full significance for life. Unlike expanse, in which man can actively advance, unlike the foreign, into which he is exiled, distance has a certain enticing quality, which attracts the passive individual and for which he yearns. There is a longing for distance which is portrayed in the sweetest tones by the Romantic poets. The blue mountains faintly seen on the horizon symbolically embody this distance. We speak of the unattainable distance, and in German the obvious rhyme for 'Ferne' is 'Sterne', stars, as in Tieck:

> You little golden stars,
> you remain always distant from me.[14]
> [Ihr kleinen, goldnen Sterne
> ihr bleibt mir ewig ferne.]

While the foreign is entirely attainable to humans in real terms, and we may be within the foreign even against our will, we can never be in the distance. Like the horizon, it retreats when one approaches it. The distance is by its own nature unattainable. There remains only an unfulfilled longing for the mysteriously enticing distance. And despite its unattainability, we long for the distance which draws us irresistibly towards it. It must therefore be a deep inward condition of life characteristic of man in his very nature that expresses itself in this attraction to the distance.

So what is it that we seek in the distance? With the Romantic poets, perhaps most clearly with Novalis, it is striking how much the longing for the distance is linked with 'the mysterious inward journey', how the return home is the final aim of longing. Homesickness and longing for distance

14 Ludwig Tieck, *Gedichte*, Dresden: 1821, vol. 1, p. 115 ff. [Ihr kleinen, goldnen Sterne / ihr bleibt mir ewig ferne.].

are so close to each other that one must ask oneself if the two things are not basically the same. It is part of the inmost nature of mankind that we seek so far beyond ourselves in the distance.

From this point we may perhaps understand the origin of longing. For how can we seek so far beyond ourselves in the distance what is after all our very own nature? Only when we have lost ourselves in the hustle and bustle of everyday life, when we are no longer 'at home' in our homes, when home has become the foreign to us, in this unsatisfying state of self-alienation the direct path to the renewal of our own nature seems to be denied to us, and then, in the fading distance, the image of our lost home appears to us. Longing for the distance is, in fact, a yearning for our lost origins, when life was still genuine.

Thus, for an animal (if we use its schematically constructed image in order to contrast it more sharply with human nature) there can be no longing for the distance; for an animal is sheltered in its environment, it is deeply rooted in its home and takes it with it, even if it covers great distances on earth. It is only because mankind, according to its nature, is subject to homelessness that we can seek our lost home in the distance. Only for humans, therefore, can there be true distance.

Hans Kunz, in his profound book on the anthropological meaning of imagination, has convincingly worked out a definition of the nature of distance.[15] Only with a certain violence can we extract from the multi-layered connection developed there the train of thought that is of direct importance to us. For him, distance arises from the loss of nearness, from the loss of an original home, in particular from the loss, inevitable in human life, of the sheltering nearness of the mother experienced at the beginning of life. The loss of nearness is transformed into the melancholy allure of the distance, and in the latter he seeks to recapture the former. The distance is therefore not a spatial realm which can somehow be objectively established, but is rooted as a spatial definition in human nature itself. 'Thus, distance', as Kunz formulates it, 'dwells in the inmost centre of existing humanity.'[16]

In everyday life, distance is concealed. So it is not experienced in the same way at all times, but for us to hear its call, we first need a particular awakening event, designated by Kunz an 'invasion of distance' [Ferneeinbruch]. It can be best elucidated in his own words: 'The call of the tawny owl in early February from the old parks of the city; the quail's

15 Hans Kunz, *Die anthropologische Bedeutung der Phantasie*, Basel: 1946.
16 Kunz, *Die anthropologische Bedeutung*, p. 297.

song in the middle of the night or at high noon, when summer broods over the ripening cornfields; a song dying away in the street at night: such … events … can clothe themselves in a shimmer of distance that exercises an unspeakable magic on us.'[17] For Kunz it is always the fading, the drifting, the 'nearness slipping away' of that which affects us so strangely and yet is ungraspable, that allows distance to come into being from the foreign. And always, at the same time, a faint breath of death wafts towards us: 'When through receding nearness the possibility of passing away comes to us as the most common image of death, the invasion of distance takes place.'[18]

Only a being that, like man, is torn through the deep shocks of nothingness and the knowledge of death out of the natural security of the familiar connections of life, out of the original home of his childhood, and feels delivered up to homelessness, is capable of hearing the voice of the distance. When man, shaken to his innermost depths, gives himself up to the call, no sooner possessed than immediately disappearing again, then longing arises within him in the form of a need to follow this call, and the fantasy that springs from this longing, and directed by it, creates a new image of his lost home. For the work of longing is for Kunz ultimately 'the formation of home',[19] and specifically of the irrevocably lost real home of one's childhood as a new ideal home realized only in dreams. Its effect is to that extent a 'cosmogonic event, by means of which man attempts to secure the other, unreal, "supernatural" home',[20] where one must only take note that this 'supernatural' home is not to be thought of as a hereafter separated from the existing human being: 'It remains inseparably rooted in him as something pervasive that prevails throughout his inmost being.'[21]

More cannot be said at this point without allowing ourselves to be torn by Kunz's train of thought, leading us into new depths, out of our own context, in which we pursue the specific phenomenon of spatiality. At any rate, a close link is seen to exist between the distance experienced in space and the innermost nature of man himself. Once again we will leave this thought open to a certain extent, because in any case we must return to it immediately from a different point of view, for a discussion of wandering.

17 Kunz, *Die anthropologische Bedeutung*, p. 288 ff.
18 Kunz, *Die anthropologische Bedeutung*, p. 297.
19 Kunz, *Die anthropologische Bedeutung*, p. 294.
20 Kunz, *Die anthropologische Bedeutung*, p. 308 ff.
21 Kunz, *Die anthropologische Bedeutung*, p. 309.

2. The Path and the Road

The opening up of space

We will now try to examine more closely the advance into the expanse of space. When someone leaves his house, he cannot move as he wishes in the terrain, but is bound to certain predetermined possibilities. The terrain as such offers an impediment to forward movement in space, and one has to see how to advance most advantageously within it. In our conditions of life it is very rarely that one must find one's own way in an untouched landscape. This is the case in high mountain regions or in the primeval forest, where one can proceed only very slowly without a cleared path and under extreme difficulties. But otherwise one will find certain already predetermined paths, and will move on those paths and not in an open landscape, because in this way one can reach one's destination much more easily, or for the most part cannot otherwise reach it at all, quite apart from the fact that in modern cultivated areas we are already dependent on these paths by existing ownership conditions, and cannot deviate from them even if we wished, without coming into conflict with the legal rights of the owner of the land.

The public roads, to use the word first of all in a very general sense, thus emerge as the means with whose help man advances through the terrain. These roads for their part may be of very different kinds, as a narrow footpath, as a driveway which moves through the fields along beaten vehicle tracks, as a regular country road or highway, or a modern motorway. Bridges and footbridges also come into this category, because they enable one to cross over certain impediments, the rivers and streams. Other possibilities for overcoming distances are railway lines, where we see perhaps more clearly the connection with certain predetermined routes. For the time being we can perhaps disregard waterways – rivers, canals and oceans – and also modern aircraft routes. Everywhere there are certain paths on earth that attract traffic on the earth's surface and are channelled in certain ways.

The path thus acquires a special function for the opening up of exterior space. 'The path opens up space', says Linschoten in his excellent work 'Die Straße und die unendliche Ferne' [The road and the endless distance],[1] of which unfortunately only the first half has so far been published. At the same time he refers to the work by Dardel, *L'homme et la terre*, whose corresponding formulation is as follows: 'The real or possible movement which is implied by the path results in an "opening up" of spaced.'[2]

The origin of paths

Wherever human beings move in the terrain, certain paths form out of habit, and these beaten paths prove to be much more convenient means of connection than the pathless spaces in between. Such beaten paths do not exist only in the human world. Animals know them too. These are the well-known game paths, and zoologists report that in primeval landscapes it is often the same paths that generations of animals have successively moved over the centuries. Humans too, if they want to move in the primeval forest, will soon come to depend upon the beaten paths of hippopotamus and elephant.

In the human world, too, we observe how new paths form where, for example on a building site, new traffic requirements have developed. When building begins in a new place, only a few days will have passed before quite specific paths develop where grass has been flattened, and the workers soon limit themselves to these newly instituted paths and avoid the grassy areas between them. It is a sort of arterial system in which the daily necessary errands are undertaken and from which one can read the structural arrangement of the working functions. In its most original form it is perhaps to be recognized in the many short cuts to be found in a forest.

Such paths are not laid out intentionally. They form as a result of being used. Where one individual walks on one occasion, perhaps no path will yet be formed. But when the individual moves in a still pathless terrain, he is usually coming from a frequently repeated starting-point, his house or his village, and again he is going towards a typically repeated destination, another village or his place of work. And where one individual, more or less unconsciously, has gone the most convenient way, others will follow,

1 Johannes Linschoten, 'Die Straße und die unendliche Ferne', *Situation*, vol. 1, 1954, p. 235 ff. and p. 258.

2 Éric Dardel, *L'homme et la terre*, Paris: 1952, p. 41, cited in Linschoten, 'Die Straße', p. 258.

perhaps correcting the clumsy mistakes that the first may have made, and thus create the most favourable path. Soon, preferred lines of connection will appear, which by becoming beaten paths will soon gain the advantage over the pathless terrain.

Road-building

The path, once created, soon attracts traffic and guides it into a predetermined channel. But with increasing traffic, the demands made on the path also increase. Soon it is not adequate as a naturally formed route for walking (or driving), but demands artificial expansion. The path becomes a road, the forms of expansion varying according to the state of technology. In this process, the road increasingly frees itself from its original close link to the terrain; it arbitrarily intrudes on the landscape and subjugates it to the human designing impulse. In this way too, man emerges as ruler of nature. Just as he is the original builder of houses, he is also a builder of roads. And in this lies the essential difference between humans and animals: animals too, as we have seen, have their paths, but it is man who strategically builds roads.

The great teachers of road-building were the Romans. Roman roads have throughout the centuries, even north of the Alps, been the basis of the road system. But it is precisely with the Romans that we recognize a feature inseparably linked with the systematic building of roads: country paths may form of their own accord, but building big paved roads is such a huge task that it can be undertaken only by an overarching state organization. And this is how we understand the connection between the Roman road system and the Roman empire. It is a powerful system of government that brings forth these roads. They are initially military roads, with the purpose of taking troops as quickly as possible from one point to another in the subjugated territories. Linschoten summarizes: 'Europe … learnt to walk – and march – in the militant, administrative and progressive Rome. The roads served for the consolidation, preservation and expansion of the empire; radiating out from Rome, they brought order and structure, and ensured a speedy, safe and economical administration. They formed the fabric of the realm that everywhere lay in the power of the legions; they were the channels of the Roman power system.'[3]

---

3 Linschoten, 'Die Straße', p. 241. See also Joseph Vogt, 'Raumauffassung und Raumordnung in der römischen Politik' in *Das neue Bild der Antike*, edited by

We recognize from this example the inner connection between systematic road-building and a strong political central power. In the same way, under Napoleon III in Paris there were created the large-scale breakthroughs that ruthlessly cut through the narrow twisting street networks that had grown over the centuries.[4] Even today it is one of the delights of the city to follow the juxtaposition of the two networks. Turn a corner, and you find yourself in a different century. But in Germany too, it was only the dictatorial system of National Socialism that was able to push ahead so forcefully the building of the autobahns. Behind these instructive special cases of political dictatorship we recognize the two principles behind all wide-ranging road-building: government and planning. Not only peoples, but the landscape too is subjugated in the road network and designed according to rational viewpoints.

The road network

The road is, to begin with, the connection between one place and another. But it only fulfils its function when it is linked with other roads in a network that allows one to travel from any location in the region in question to any other location. And to this extent the roads really open up space. This road system may be structured in different ways. In countries governed by a strong central power, the roads radiate out from a dominant central point, as is the case today not only with the French country road system, but also with the French railway network. The cross-country routes between the great roads are only sparsely built up, and often the fastest connection between two places on the periphery is the detour through the centre. This radial system emerges even more clearly within the major cities in the relationship of the main roads leading out of the cities to the weakly developed cross-city routes. Here too the most convenient route often leads through the centre. In other countries, such as Germany, a dominant centre such as this is missing; rather, an actual network is developed out of multiply connected streets. These streets open up their area in a similar way to the arterial system of a plant leaf: a network of major roads, from which smaller ones branch off, with even smaller ones branching off from these, until finally even the smallest location, even an isolated house, is reached,

---

Helmut Berve, vol. 2, 1942, p. 109.

4 Fritz Stahl, *Paris. Eine Stadt als Kunstwerk*, Berlin: 1928, chapter 5, p. 160 ff. See also Wilhelm Waetzoldt, *Paris. Die Neugestaltung des Stadtbildes duch Baron Haussmann*, Leipzig: 1943.

even if sometimes, above all in mountainous areas, there is only one vein linking this place to the road system.

We must now consider this road network. It links the built-up areas of the country, the larger towns by means of large thoroughfares, the smaller villages by means of country roads, and so on, according to the importance of the areas. So this is the most straightforward image: first we have the built-up areas and then we build the roads to connect them. But this statement is soon reversed, and this then shows the importance of roads. If we ask the historians why today's cities were built in these particular locations, we learn in many cases that it was because of the favourable traffic situation. So it was first the road links and in particular their intersections that determined the development of cities. Many of the old traffic routes are older than today's cities. But we also learn this in more recent history from the alteration of space through the building of the railways. First the railway lines connected the large cities, but soon intersections were created as a result, which did not coincide with the existing major cities, and here new built-up areas retrospectively developed, which came into being only because of the traffic network, or at least gained in importance because of it. The railway lines that were built in the nineteenth century also make it clear how space acquires from them a totally new inner connection, which is today once again losing its significance as a result of increased motor traffic.

In this context it remains interesting that here too the road network continues to develop its independence. While at first it was the cities that were connected by roads, with the development of modern traffic the existing cities with their often narrow thoroughfares became obstacles, and the roads became independent, as first the smaller places were avoided by means of bypasses and thus to a great extent excluded from through traffic, and later the big cities too were bypassed by ring roads. Thus, finally, the main roads become an independent network, which bypasses cities and which one first needs to abandon if one wishes to reach a particular place.

The alteration of space

a. The homogenization of space

Thus the road network becomes increasingly autonomous and creates its own space, different from that which structured the natural centre of the house. Two features above all emerge here for the general consideration of space. One is the homogenization of space by the road. Linschoten draws attention to this when he stresses: 'Roads not only reconstruct and organize space, they create a new, uncultivated space. But in doing so, they homogenize the world.'[5] This is evident when I leave my own house and take to the road (or perhaps, more obviously, when I drive a vehicle on the road or use the railway): I become part of a network of roads and paths that relates not to my house, but to its own centre. I enter a different, super-individual space where it is left open for the moment whether it has its own central point in a specific traffic centre – which of course is no longer my own centre – or whether in fact it altogether lacks a central point. As soon as I leave my own house and entrust myself to the road, I enter a space which is relatively neutral in relation to my own centre (I say relatively, because there are still certain transitional forms in the narrower environment of the house), in which I find myself in each case at a specific place, without being at home in any such place. Space acquires objectivity by becoming a common system of relationships. The relationships of nearness and distance that are attached to things, permeated with emotional values of the most various kinds, fade into the distance that changes according to where one finds oneself at a particular time.

When we said that 'the road opens up space', it is a space other than the private space that we find in our houses. It is from the outset a supra-individual and neutral space, the space of 'traffic.' The road network forms the arterial system through which 'traffic' pulsates. The individual who entrusts himself to the road is carried along by this traffic. He becomes absorbed by it. At home he was perhaps an individual, but on the road he becomes anonymous.

But the landscape too changes in the structure of the roads. It loses its own character, the individuality of the particular place. The country road does not ask whether it leads through woods or fields. And this is also why Linschoten speaks of 'uncultivated' space. 'The road', he says, 'is not only indifferent with regard to the landscape, but it also makes the landscape itself indifferent, by breaking through the deep intimacy of the countryside, externalizes it and shifts the centre of gravity into the infinite.'[6]

What counts on the road is not the particular nature of the terrain through which it leads, but only its greater or lesser suitability for traffic, the 'road conditions', the gradient and so on. And the more complete the road becomes, only the distances to be measured in miles remain important.

5 Linschoten, 'Die Straße', p. 259.
6 Linschoten, 'Die Straße', p. 259.

Even today the milestones of the Roman roads in part still stand, or are preserved in the names of places (such as Quinten or Ventimiglia). On today's roads, too, information about distance in kilometres is precisely indicated everywhere.

The driver can be certain at any point how many kilometres he has already covered and how many still lie ahead of him. In particular the system of road signs at today's great road intersections intelligibly expresses this network of distances. This however means a basic impoverishment of space; for the road objectivizes individual space by making the original space, which is qualitatively different in its various areas, accessible to quantitative treatment. Space has become subject to mathematics. Thus road-building (with the measuring technology required for it) is at least one of the decisive processes which lead to the formation of a mathematical concept of space.

b. Eccentric space

A second feature is linked with this. The road has no end; for beyond every city to which a road leads, a new road leads to a new destination. While Roman roads reached their limits at the borders of the Roman empire, the modern road system in the sense of the traffic that crosses national borders is by its nature unlimited;

> For every road leads to the end of the world.[7]

Linschoten makes the connection with what we were saying earlier about the pull of the distance: 'The road is the sign of an endless distance. It sets the static landscape in motion, a motion towards the horizon. Nothing in the landscape manifests the attraction of the distance in perspective so much as the converging parallels of road and railway, which appear to the eye by no means to come to an end at the horizon, but invisibly to cross it.'[8]

In contrast to the centred space of our living area, the space of the road, to use Linschoten's term, is an 'eccentric space.' It has no central points,

---

7 'denn jede Straße führt ans End' der Welt', Friedrich Schiller, *Wilhelm Tell. Sämtliche Werke*, edited by Eduard v. d. Hellen, vol. 7, Stuttgart and Berlin: n.d., p. 248.

8 Linschoten, 'Die Straße', p. 260. This naturally only applies to the straight modern road. The simple country lane does not yet present this character. It winds and disappears from sight before it reaches the horizon. A natural vanishing point never becomes visible.

but draws man irresistibly into the endless distance. The road sweeps us along with it. The road, to quote Linschoten again, is 'the expression of an eccentric spatiality, that is, of a world in which man is never quite on his own again.'[9]

Here Linschoten enters on his final analysis: in its attraction to endlessness leading beyond every attainable goal, the road is the expression of the transcendence of man himself. In this spirit, he summarizes his observations: 'Just as they [the road and the railway] pass through the landscape, so they portray man in his nature – as one who passes through. It is from human existence that the road derives its significance. Its "nature", that is, the principle that governs its origin and its development, is nothing other than human nature itself. Its manifestation is the human intention transformed into landscape, the incorporation of its transcendent objectives.'[10]

Thus Linschoten. What he discusses here is certainly a deeply felt realization. The road as an image of human life is, as we have already seen, one of the ancient symbols of humanity, which in the Tao (or Way) of the Chinese becomes a word of metaphysical power. And yet we hesitate to take this realization for the whole and complete truth. The symbol of the journey of life has a completely different character from the symbol of life that we encounter in the modern country road. It shows us man as the wanderer, who – unfortunately – cannot find a permanent resting place; but it conveys nothing of the dizzying attraction of the distance which distinguishes the modern road and its users. Here we already recognize the need to dwell in the sheltering area of the house, which we will examine in more detail in the section that follows. How these two definitions of man, as a wanderer and a dweller, a centred and an eccentric being, fit together, is the deeper question which will lead us further.

Man on the road

In the road, therefore, a one-dimensional structure has been carved out of the two-dimensional surface of the earth, that is the line of the road to be measured in kilometres. From the point of view of experienced space we question the behaviour of the person who moves on such a road. What is the inner state of mind of that person, which is appropriate to the traffic on the road, which is in a certain sense induced by the road? And what,

9 Linschoten, 'Die Straße', p. 259.
10 Linschoten, 'Die Straße', p. 260.

conversely, is the space that opens up to man on the road? What is the experienced space of the road-user? The close connection between space and the person moving in space, which we must later pursue in a separate context, is shown here to an exceptional degree.

a. The forward urge

Specifically there are, in accordance with the varying size of the road, various forms of movement on it: walking – including marching, to which Straus and Lipps[11] have referred in connection with the characteristic experience of space that we find in it; riding, and above all driving various kinds of vehicles, from the horse and carriage to the motor-car. Here too we will ignore the special cases of railway tracks and waterways.

On all these roads it is decisive that there is only one meaningful direction of movement, which is forwards. The driver can move sideways only to a small extent, just as far as necessary to make way for an oncoming vehicle or to allow another to overtake. If he wished to move further sideways, he would have to move out and abandon his vehicle. And to go backwards would be simply to turn back. This would contradict the purpose of the road. There remains only the forward direction, and it is this direction for which the road is designed. There is only one meaningful action on it: to go forward and ever further forward, until our destination is finally reached. To stop earlier would contradict the purpose of the journey. It can only be regarded as a respite, that is, as a temporary interruption to restore one's own strength or for a necessary repair of the vehicle. The road is a technologically created means for reaching one's destination, and one travels in order to arrive there – unless forced by a new reason to undertake a new journey. The road is used for traffic, that is the change from one place to another. On the road, man becomes a 'road-user', who has to follow the rules of traffic. And the traffic needs to move, that is, to circulate like the blood in one's veins.

The road is not a place to linger on, 'for there is no home here', but it drives the user onwards. There is only one meaningful action on it: to attain one's destination by the shortest route and in the shortest time. On the

11 Erwin Straus, 'Formen des Räumlichen. Ihre Bedeutung für die Motorik und Wahrnehmung' (1930), *Psychologie der menschlichen Welt. Gesammelte Schriften*, Berlin, Göttingen, Heidelberg: 1960, p. 160 ['Forms of spatiality', *Phenomenological psychology. The selected papers of Erwin Straus*, translated by Erling Eng, London: 1966, p. 120]. See also Hans Lipps, *Die Wirklichkeit des Menschen*, Frankfurt a. M.: 1954, p. 171.

road, man is always intent on reaching the anticipated goal. This results in the actual power that the road exerts on the person moving on it: it drives him constantly forward. This tendency to haste and hurry is necessarily in the nature of the road itself, and puts the individual under its spell: no hesitation or standing still! Ever forwards, and as fast as possible! No one can resist this temptation. The railway traveller becomes distressed when his train is delayed, even when he knows that he is not missing anything and an unpleasant stay will only be shortened.

In the essay that has already been quoted several times, Linschoten has given a description of behaviour on the road, which is admittedly initially based on the concept of illness, but which, beyond this, characterizes its nature in a compelling manner: 'One walks on the road, and namely one walks forward; one is always in a hurry, in a rush, one person may fall behind others, one may overtake another, and a race of movement into the future takes place.' And here the symbolic meaning of the road immediately emerges. 'The road is the future. This offers a bewildering wealth of conflicting details, everything flows, one is on one's way in hurry and haste, one arrives too late or has to wait, one must adjust one's tempo to others and be able to do so.' And further, the self-alienation of man, his subjugation to the current of the road, is stressed even more explicitly: 'Man in this existence is no longer himself; he is carried along by the general movement and is continually attracted by the always unattainable goal, the point of intersection of parallel lines. "The road draws us".'[12]

What is true in general of man on the road is particularly true of motorists: 'The road draws us.' 'The motorway … demands great speed, wildness, exhilaration, it gives one a new sense of the world', writes Hausmann.[13] The movement, the speed becomes an end in itself. Human nature is transformed in this maelstrom of the motorway, and there is no one who can resist this temptation.

b. The loss of the dimension of width

But for someone who is moving on the road, the entire space is transformed at once, and we experience here particularly forcefully the general correlation between state of mind and experienced space. This transformation takes

12 Roland Kuhn, 'Daseinsanalyse eines Falles von Schizophrenie', *Monatsschrift für Psychiatrie und Neurologie*, vol. 112, 1946, p. 240, cited in Linschoten, 'Die Straße', p. 238.

13 Manfred Hausmann, *Einer muß wachen*, Frankfurt a. M.: 1950, p. 44, cited in Linschoten, 'Die Straße', p. 248.

place gradually, according to the speed of forward movement achieved. This begins with the pedestrian. As soon as the road rises above the terrain as a channel smoothed by a surface of its own, and is separated from the landscape by a ditch to be crossed only with some effort, the landscape recedes. Among the ramblers of the German youth movement, as far as they kept to the country roads, there existed the regrettable type known as the 'kilometre guzzler', who became blind to the landscape through which he was wandering, who was only concerned with the distance he had covered, about which he could boast. But the process which emerges only weakly here is heightened as soon as a vehicle is used, and takes ever more blatant forms with the greater speed of the modern motor-car. For this reason it will suffice to base our discussion on this extreme example.

For someone driving on a country road there is only one dimension, namely the road and the distances to be measured in kilometres. This dimension alone has authentic reality. All one's attention is concentrated on the narrow band of road, for that alone is essential, the area of threats, of dangers, but also of the possibility of moving ahead more speedily by overtaking. In this dimension the thrill of speed gives space a heightened, overwrought reality. The driver is trapped in it, heart and soul. It directs him into the endless expanse that entices him to reach out into space. This is the motorist's decisive experience of space, by no means to be condemned out of hand. The width of his space is measured only by the few metres to the edge of the road. Here too it still has direct reality; for it is the area where all depends on whether there is enough 'space' to bypass an obstacle, to avoid an oncoming vehicle, and so on. It is an area where narrowness and width are of essential importance to life.

But what lies beyond, on the other side of the road's edge, is no longer space in the true sense. It has lost its meaningful reality and sinks into a peculiar quality of imagery. It is an unattainable area, not very different from the moon in the sky or the unscalable mountains. The motorist no longer moves in the landscape, like the wanderer, but rather the landscape moves past him. It becomes a mere panorama. And this de-realization of the landscape background takes place more intensely according to the increasing speed of the vehicle, until finally it disappears entirely.

I remember having once read a short story in a newspaper in which this process was exaggerated to the point of grotesqueness. With this thrill of speed, it is no longer a matter of the place one wants to reach, but the movement implies more than any concrete final point. It implies something more than itself, something infinite. Thus nothing is changed in principle when it arrives back at the starting point. And thus, in this story a utopian picture was painted: the ideal motorway – this is three great loops, which all return to the starting point, differentiated only by the speed for which they are designed. People drive on these loops and enjoy the charm of continual forward motion. At the beginning, so it is reported, the landscape was projected in the form of a film in the human field of vision, so that the drivers were given the illusion of driving through beautiful landscapes. But soon this was given up. The drivers had placed no value on it, because it would only have hindered the main thing, which was simply driving as such. And so, since then, they had only dashed with the necessary speed through the loops, experiencing the thrill of driving, without, in the end, actually moving away from the starting point. Is this only a grotesque distortion? No, it is only the apt expression of the transformation which humans necessarily undergo on the motorway.

Of course, it need not come to this extreme. One can also enjoy the landscape while driving slowly. There are even preferred roads offering good views. But here too, one does not move in the landscape as a living reality. It is only the road that possesses actual reality. The landscape remains in the realm of the inaccessible, and this virtual inaccessibility – the fact that I cannot easily leave my vehicle without hindering the traffic – conditions the consciousness of reality. Even where I am thoroughly enjoying the landscape, it remains merely a view. In this sense we have spoken of a panorama. Only when I get out and leave the vehicle do I re-enter full space, where the view is again transformed into living reality.

c. The fleeting nature of human contact

Together with the alteration of space we also find a corresponding alteration in human connections. One can almost speak meaningfully of a sociology of the country road itself, which then takes on extremely heightened forms in the sociology of the motorist. Schiller writes, certainly under the much more leisurely conditions of his day:

> For here there is no home – everyone presses
> past the other rapidly and as a stranger
> and asks not about his pain …
> They all go on their way
> about their business …[14]

14 'Denn hier ist keine Heimat – jeder treibt / sich an dem andern rasch und fremd vorüber / und fraget nach seinem Schmerz ... / Sie alle ziehen ihres Weges fort / an ihr Geschäft ...', Schiller, *Wilhelm Tell. Sämtliche Werke*, vol. 7, p. 248.

The road demands a quite individual form of human contact. On the one hand there is a natural comradeship among road users, even among motorists (in spite of widespread loutish behaviour). Mutual consideration is taken for granted. One is even – up to a point – ready to help, typically in the case of professional drivers (I gratefully remember the camaraderie I experienced as a driver during World War II). And yet all this friendliness and consideration retains a certain anonymity. One 'asks not about his pain.' No permanent relationship develops, but we break off from each other as quickly as we have come together, and no longer recognize each other if we happen to meet again; in fact it is seen almost as tactless if we refer to an earlier encounter and try to make demands of each other on that basis. It is a light, smooth, but also fleeting contact, without a developing common ground.[15] This is meant in no way in a disapproving manner, but just as the house has its special forms of common interest with the world of the family, the same is true of the country road, whose common ground must be recognized in its individual nature.

15 David J. van Lennep, 'Psychologie van het chaufferen', *Person und Welt. Festschrift für F. J. J. Buytendijk*, Utrecht: 1953, p. 165 ff., cited in Linschoten, 'Die Straße', p. 242.

3. The Wanderer's Path

Wandering

From the great motorway and its possibilities for forward movement, we will now turn, without entering more closely into the various intermediate forms of the country road and the driveway, to the opposite extreme, the narrow hiking path and the form of movement allocated to it. Among the various forms of walking on foot, such as going for a walk, promenading, strolling, sauntering, roaming, and so on, the one we shall be particularly concerned with here, wandering or rambling, stands out. To begin with an approximate definition as an aid to orientation, the term 'wandering' is used to refer to a leisurely, lengthy and coherent movement on foot from one place to another, not driven by urgency or undertaken for some external purpose.

Man has not at all times wandered in the modern sense. The wandering journeyman of a past age, or the wandering scholars, did not wander in this sense. They travelled abroad to study there, certainly also for the joy of adventure, to experience the world. And they went on foot because it was the simplest way, and their means would not allow any other form of transport. Wandering in today's sense, wandering for its own sake, is a result of the critique of modern civilization. The Romantics first discovered it, and it was in the 'Wandervogel' movement of the early twentieth century that wandering developed practically into a way of life.

Paths too are not initially designed specifically for wandering. Even the most modest footpath, like any path, is directed at a destination to which it leads. It serves as a connection. This is why the wanderer initially makes use of the paths that already exist, which lead from one place to another. Not all of these are suitable for his purpose; for their primary purpose is to serve traffic between locations, and the wanderer uses them, as it were, only on sufferance. This may have presented few difficulties in earlier times when traffic was only sparse and slow-moving, and there was always room for a wanderer, even though complaints about the 'dusty country roads' go back a long way.

But this changed as modern motorized traffic became more sophisticated, vehicles became faster and were driven more recklessly, and the roads were increasingly adapted to their needs. The modern motor road is unsuitable for wandering. The motorways in fact are closed to pedestrians, but even on other country roads wandering is becoming ever more difficult. The wanderer would not only risk his own life or at the very least be so obstructed by the vehicles driving by that he would prefer to reduce to a minimum the distance to be covered at the edge of the road (carefully keeping to the safer side of the road), but he would also, for his part, be a hindrance to traffic. He simply does not belong there.

For this reason, the wanderer avoids the great traffic routes. He has a different relationship with the path and the landscape, and with space in general. The wanderer uses the quieter, less frequented paths, he prefers the footpaths, which at the same time lead him further into the interior of the landscape. In this connection, special hiking paths have been created, for example in the Black Forest, by the great ramblers' associations, which not only free the wanderer from the nuisance of the driving road, but also lead him into areas which would be difficult to find on the larger roads, and to highlights of natural beauty which lie away from the purpose-built lines of communication. (One might also think of the special walking paths laid out by health resorts, although these, in accordance with their particular purpose, do not allow actual wandering.) But in spite of all specially created paths, in most cases the wanderer continues to be dependent on existing paths, even though he uses them in his particular way.

This is why we ask: what is the particular nature of wandering which distinguishes it from other forms of travelling? What is the corresponding particular nature of the wanderer's path? And in what way does space open up in wandering? The first question has already been anticipated: the wanderer does not wander in order to reach a particular destination by the fastest route, but he wanders for the sake of wandering. Wandering is a purpose in itself. This does not mean that he does not set himself a goal, to climb a mountain, to see a good view of the landscape and reach a hotel in the evening, but these goals may serve only to give his wandering some content. It may also happen that someone who has set off to reach some particular destination, moved by the magic of the countryside on the way, may adopt the attitude of the wanderer. But then he has forgotten his goal and has experienced a change in his state of mind.

The lack of a goal relates to the second question: the wanderer is in no hurry. He comes to a halt wherever he is pleased by a view or some other sight, always ready for silent contemplation. Indeed he will even come to a halt without any external occasion, merely because he is deep in thought. The wanderer is always prone to reverie.

The path

This corresponds to the form of his path, the actual hiking path. We can imagine its nature most easily by distinguishing it from the country road, particularly the modern motorway. The country road is artificially created. It is specially designed for its purposes, by being carved out of the rest of the countryside. The unevennesses of the terrain are eliminated, and obstacles are cleared out of the way.

The ground is paved and today also asphalted. One can march on it, and this means pushing forward into the world without taking notice of the condition of the ground beneath our feet. The lack of obstacles in the even surface is always taken for granted, as with the pavements of cities. The road is a thoroughly synthetically produced thing. For this reason it is rightly described in Heidegger's pointed phrase as 'equipment for walking' [Zeug zum Gehen][1] and even 'equipment for driving.' As a product of technology, it is sharply distinguished from nature. The road surface separates the foot from the ground. The edge of the road is sharply delineated: what lies beyond it is another world for the road user, a mere sight separated from him as though by a glass wall, and with increasing driving speed it fades more and more into a mere panorama.

The hiking path is the opposite of all this. It is not intent on reaching its goal by the most immediate route. It winds through the countryside, avoids obstacles and clings to forms of terrain where the road-builder would have violated it by a decisive intervention. Here the ground is not artificially prepared. At most, a few stones may be laid over a marshy spot, so that it can be crossed with dry feet, or a footbridge may be built over a stream. Therefore, the wanderer must adapt himself to the ground. He can no longer stride over it in a measured pace, keeping time as when marching. Linschoten puts this very aptly: 'The sand, the rocky path, the natural ground receive him, if only because they force him to change his pace at every moment, to let his foot cling to the ground. The wanderer adapts himself flexibly, he submits to the countryside; anyone who twists his ankle while

1 Martin Heidegger, *Sein und Zeit*, Halle a. d. Saale: 1927, p. 107 [*Being and time* (1962), translated by John Macquarrie and Edward Robinson, Oxford: 1967, p. 141].

walking has not properly understood the countryside. Short or long steps are taken according to the composition of the ground and in living unity with it. Wandering flows irregularly like a stream over the uneven river bed.'[2] This is why the wanderer is no longer separate from the countryside, it is no longer an image that passes away beside him, but he actually wanders through the countryside, becomes a part of it, is completely taken up by it.

Aimlessness and timelessness

From this, the characteristics of wandering are already becoming clear. One is freedom of purpose. Man wants to wander. He wants to escape from his normal everyday world. He seeks out the area where he wants to wander, but not the goal which he wants to reach (or he does so only as a secondary matter). The release from purpose is the dominant characteristic of wandering. The wanderer wants to wander, to be on the road, but he does not want to reach a particular place. I remember the beginning of Eichendorff's *Life of a good-for-nothing*, where the hero sets off in the fresh morning air: 'I felt a real secret pleasure when I saw all my old friends and comrades to right and left, just as they had done yesterday and the day before and forever, setting off to work, digging and ploughing, while I was strolling out into the free world … I felt as though it were an eternal Sunday.'[3] It is the release from the troubles and cares of the everyday, the contrast between the regulated, purposeful work of the everyday and carefree, untroubled wandering. And when the two ladies in the carriage ask him where he is going so early in the morning, 'I felt ashamed that I did not know this myself, and said boldly, "To Vienna"', whereupon they promptly take him with them to Vienna in their carriage.

This purposelessness of wandering, then, is combined with aimlessness. He wanders without thinking of a destination, just as he says:

> Him to whom God wishes to show true favour,
> He sends into the wide world …[4]

It is only the unexpected question addressed to him by another that makes him aware of this aimlessness, and he gives the first answer that

---

2 Linschoten, 'Die Straße', p. 254.

3 Eichendorff, *Heimweh*, vol. 2, p. 349 ff.

4 'Wem Gott will rechte Gunst erweisen / den schickt er in die weite Welt', Eichendorff, *Heimweh*, vol. 1, p. 10.

occurs to him, only in order not to look foolish. Stenzel, in his book on the anthropological function of wandering,[5] which we will consider in more detail, quotes a relevant passage from Manfred Hausmann, who from this viewpoint distinguishes purposeful travel from mere wandering: 'The wishful dream of all travellers is the arrival. Being on the road is unimportant, indeed superfluous, indeed positively wretched. The wanderer on the other hand knows nothing of arrival or of a destination. Whether he strolls through Norway's windless valleys or through the cities' allotment gardens … He knows neither why nor whither. Wandering is subjective, aimless and uncertain. For the wanderer, it is not the arrival that is important, but the wandering, being on one's way, the road.'[6]

Wandering, seen from the viewpoint of a reasonable person, is not a sensible activity. As a counter-example, seen from the reasonable, enlightened lifestyle, here is testimony from Abraham a Sancta Clara's *Huy! und Pfuy! der Welt*, that beautiful picture-book of lessons for all the situations of life:

> The pleasant mountain path often tempts wandering folk,
> Since it leads them away and not towards home.

And this is followed by the proudly emphatic sentence:

> The country road does not deceive.[7]

This sentence is highly characteristic of the concept of 'common sense': 'the country road does not deceive.' We can safely entrust ourselves to it, for it will certainly lead us to our destination. But we must not be drawn onto side-roads, for they may prove deceptive and lead us astray.[8]

---

5 Arnold Stenzel, 'Die anthropologische Funktion des Wanderns und ihre pädagogische Bedeutung', *Erziehung und Leben*, edited by O. F. Bollnow, Heidelberg: 1960, p. 96 ff.

6 Manfred Hausmann, *Einer muß wachen*, p. 42, cited in Stenzel, 'Die anthropologische Funktion', p. 102.

7 'Der anmutolle Steig reizt of die Wandersleute, / der sie noch nebenaus und nicht nach Heimat führt' and 'Die Landstraß trüget nicht', Abraham a Santa Clara, *Huy! undPfuy! der Welt*, Nürnberg: 1707, p. 43. See also Herbert von Einem, 'Ein Vorläufer Caspar David Friedrichs', *Zeitschrift des Deutschen Vereins für Kunstwissenschaft*, vol. 7, 1940, p. 156 ff.

8 This is also related to what one could term the logic [Vernunft] of the road.
It knows best how to arrive at a given goal. Even if the road seems to take a considerable detour, it will have its reasons. Many of those who attempt a more direct route via an apparent shortcut soon regret their decision; they meet with

Of course it is quite different if we place no value at all on reaching a certain destination in the shortest possible time. Then detours need not be irritating, for they only lead us deeper into the countryside. So we cannot speak meaningfully of losing one's way, as long as the wanderer finds his way to some accommodation in the evening. One can only lose one's way if one diverges from a certain path. But anyone who has no particular destination cannot take the wrong path.

But if the wanderer is capable of entrusting himself with patience to the twists and turns of the uncertain course of a footpath, then he himself must be in a corresponding state of mind, a state of lack of purposefulness and readiness to stay calmly in the moment. Here lies at the same time the second characteristic of wandering that we have emphasized: the altered relationship with time. 'The country road is not acquainted with hurry and goes just in the way that suits it', says Linschoten,[9] and those who entrust themselves to it must not be in a hurry either. Rather, they must have time, time to immerse themselves in beauty, to gaze at the flowers and ferns, to contemplate the crawling beetles and darting lizards, the fluttering butterflies and whirring dragonflies, to breathe in appreciatively the summery scent of thyme or of the resin of the pine forests, to observe the woodpecker's distant knocking or to count the cuckoo's calls, to be lulled to sleep by the babbling of the stream or the rustling of the treetops, and so on. I need not conjure up the images that everyone probably brings to such days of wandering from the delightful memory of similar experiences. Once again, let us remember the 'good-for-nothing' for whom it was an 'eternal Sunday.' Perhaps it would be too much to say that time had actually stood still, but it has lost its restless, forward-drawing character. The clock no longer warns us of challenges that lie ahead. It is only the course of the day, the movement of the sun and stars, that reminds us of the presence of time. But, in contrast to the hurry of the country road, it is a different, restful and calming rhythm that takes hold of us here.

The joy of departure

This brings us back from the description of phenomena to the question: why do we wander in the first place? What is it that so irresistibly tempts us to wander? And why is it that it is precisely modern man who feels this

---

unexpected obstacles, have to carry on arduously or even turn back. The country lane knows better, and one should better entrust oneself to it.

9 Linschoten, 'Die Straße', p. 255.

urge to wander? In our description, the features of aimlessness, freedom from purpose, timelessness unavoidably recurred. From this point we are in the best position to understand the function of wandering, specifically in the life of modern civilized man. Wandering is the way in which man tries to break out from the over-increased purposefulness of his existence. Wandering, we can confidently state, is an escape in itself: because man seeks to break out from the hurry of civilized existence, he begins to wander. And in this respect it is no accident that it was precisely in the metropolis of Berlin that the 'Wandervogel' youth movement came into being at the turn of the twentieth century.

Wandering is release from narrowness, breaking through into the open air. This is why the wanderer sings in the consciousness of his superior lightness of movement:

> Let those who will, stay at home with their cares!

He has left behind him the world of cares, the world of the exhausting professional daily routine. He despises the petit-bourgeois. Similarly, the 'good-for-nothing' felt superior to his comrades, departing for their accustomed work. To wander is to shake off one's fetters. As Eichendorff writes, in an excess of overflowing euphoria:

> What a journey this will be
> Through forest and greenery.
> What a glorious life! ...
> The world lies open to me.[10]

This last phrase very aptly describes the feeling of space in an expanse opening anew every morning. 'The world lies open to me.' It is up to man, in the consciousness of his overflowing energy, to push forward into these expanses.

Returning to one's origins

But wandering is more than this morning feeling of freedom, and in the description of the meandering path the freedom from purpose of wandering

10 'Das soll ein Reisen werden / durch Wald und grünen Plan. / Das heißt ein herrlich Leben! ... / Die Welt ist aufgetan', Eichendorff, quoted in Stenzel, 'Die anthropologische Funktion', p. 108.

has already become evident in a deeper sense. It is not actually the joy of departure in search of the endless distance. The wanderer is no longer in such a great hurry for the distance, as soon as he has become captivated by the landscape. Linschoten, whose profound interpretation we are now approaching, refers to Rilke's 'chemins qui ne mènent nulle part' [paths that lead nowhere], to his

> chemin qui tourne et joue
> le long de la vigne penchée,[11]
> [path that turns and twists
> along the winding vine]

and continues with his own description: 'The forest track, the path, are indigenous, they do not prolong themselves, but circulate around their core. They enclose the landscape, just as, conversely, the landscape encloses them … The country path is an organic part of the countryside and is enclosed in the immanence of a whole, which does not flee from itself, does not pass by itself, because it sets no goals and therefore cannot depart from itself. The countryside blooms, without ever crossing its own borders.'[12] The nature of the road, moving further and ever further into the endless distance, its 'transcendence' leading beyond any concrete goal, no longer touches the wanderer. Its paths are 'indigenous', they 'do not prolong themselves, but circulate around their core.' Another passage says: 'Wandering is circling around the centre of gravity of the intimacy that becomes evident through the countryside.'[13] And again, 'that the country path realizes itself in the intimacy of the countryside.' He speaks of the 'domesticity of the countryside.'[14]

In continually new turns of phrase, Linschoten tries to describe the actual joy of wandering, and again and again the word 'intimacy' [Innigkeit] crops up. What this enigmatic word means is not explained further. Certainly it is closely connected to what Kunz called the 'urgency of the distance',[15] just as we feel very close to Kunz's processes of thought. Intimacy at any rate means something like a heartfelt familiarity. 'Innig', derived from 'inne', primarily means, in the literal sense, something like inward. But it is not

---

11 Rainer Maria Rilke, *Gedichte in französischer Sprache*, Wiesbaden: 1949, p. 65 and p. 59.

12 'Lucky is the man who sits by the fire in his house and is at peace', Rilke, *Gedichte in französischer Sprache*, p. 252 ff.

13 Rilke, *Gedichte in französischer Sprache*, p. 255.

14 Rilke, *Gedichte in französischer Sprache*, p. 253.

15 Kunz, *Die anthropologische Bedeutung*, p. 293.

simply the relationship with nature that is called intimate, but intimacy is ascribed to the countryside itself. So it stands for the sense of belonging in which the countryside rests in itself. And yet Linschoten continues: 'Intimacy, the familiar home towards which one strives, does not lie in the realm of wandering feet.'[16] This means that the goal of wandering is not to be found at all in space. But this certainly does not imply that the goal is totally unattainable, only to be striven for in an eternally unfulfilled longing. The goal rather lies in man himself, in the state of satisfaction of his soul. This is where the joy of wandering lies.

From this thought springs the profound statement: 'In real wandering there is something like a return to the ancient inward happiness that can appear only in the cloud of memory, but then again as the harbinger of a future fulfilment. The countryside, centred on its own secret middle point, is manifested only to him who in his wandering returns to the "basis of all things".'[17] And Linschoten continues elsewhere: 'If wandering is a return to the calm and quiet of nature, and in the deepest sense an entry into the immanence of the countryside, then the footpath is a way back, a way of returning to one's familiar home.'[18] Here we notice a definition that resonates multiply in various turns of phrase: the 'return to the ancient inward happiness', the return to the 'basis of all things', the 'way back' that leads to the 'familiar home.' It is the ancient Romantic fundamental problem, deriving from Novalis, that breaks through again: the way back, the way to the origin, to the origins of human life. But what is there imagined as an unattainable goal of longing, here becomes fulfilled; man has returned. Thus it is here possible to speak of a 'familiar home.'

But on the other hand, this form of return is not to be understood in spatial terms. It is a return in man himself, a return to the origins of existence and to the 'basis of all things.' If memories of childhood too are unavoidable here, it is beyond that also the return to a deeper layer of nature, where man still lives 'before' the mastery of the world by technology and the separation of subject and object that took place as a result, 'before' rational fusion, 'before' the world of profession and technology – in a word: before self-alienation, before ossification and hardening. It is a rejuvenation of his whole nature that man experiences in wandering.

16 Kunz, *Die anthropologische Bedeutung*, p. 255.
17 Kunz, *Die anthropologische Bedeutung*, p. 256.
18 Kunz, *Die anthropologische Bedeutung*, p. 257.

The function of wandering

Hence comes the enormous significance of wandering for human life. Just as Antaeus in Greek legend continually gains new strength from contact with Mother Earth, man rejuvenates himself in wandering. And because man in general is a being that can fulfil his nature only in continually repeated rejuvenation,[19] wandering acquires an enormous 'anthropological' importance. While man in his timeless and purposeless wandering totally retreats from the constant forward-pushing hustle and bustle of his everyday life, he gains contact again with a deeper basis of life, resting in timelessness.[20]

Stenzel developed this concept very finely in the work already cited. As man returns from the differentiated and specialized, and therefore largely externalized, existence of his professional life into this still undifferentiated but (still) living basis, he not only becomes rejuvenated himself, but also gains a new, more intimate relationship with the world, and the things that have become petrified by technology become manifest again in a life of their own. This is the meaning of Linschoten's 'intimacy.' Stenzel summarizes what is usually much too externally expressed as 'pleasure in nature': 'It is a question of experiencing nature, as it takes place in wandering, no longer about the scientific connection with nature, but about a much more original relationship of a more aesthetic character.' And he immediately qualifies this: 'Admittedly the description "aesthetic" only applies to the external aspect of this relationship. Rather we can say that in this connection it is a question of a direct relationship with being and reality. Thus new light falls again on the achievement of the "return to origins". If man conducts his life with an awareness of its foundations and origins, everything that formerly appeared to be dead and externalized existence acquires new and now genuine life, it becomes "externalized" by being seen continually in relation to the inmost, original underground of life, out of which it has grown.'[21]

Here, where we are only concerned with the problem of space, we will not go further into the question of the relationship with nature that opens

19 On Fröbel's 'renewal of life' see O. F. Bollnow, *Von Arndt bis Fröbel. Die Pädagogik der deutschen Romantik*, Stuttgart: 1942, p. 222 ff. See also Heinrich Lenzen, *Verjüngung als pädagogisches Problem, nach Herders Lebenswerk*, Mainz: 1953.

20 See O. F. Bollnow, *Neue Geborgenheit. Das Problem einer Überwindung des Existentialismus*, Stuttgart: 1958.

21 Stenzel, 'Die anthropologische Funktion', p. 116 ff.

up in wandering. But it is important in this connection to note how a certain behaviour in space and towards space, that is, wandering on a quiet path, affects man's whole state of mind, so that here again we encounter the close connection between the inner nature and spatial state – a new indication of how space-related human nature is from the start.

But here an amplification is needed so that the reference to the high significance of wandering is not misunderstood. The return to origins which is so joyfully experienced here must not mean that man should continue in this original state, and that all future development should be seen only as a fall from his original nature. When we speak here of the high anthropological significance of wandering, this does not mean that man should now spend his life wandering aimlessly around in the world, or that the vagabond is the ideal of human life. This would be to misjudge fundamentally the sphere of work and profession or trade, and the resulting modern mechanized and industrialized world from which man can or should no longer emerge at all. This would be to miss entirely the actual seriousness of life. Man would lose his grip on himself. This is where the youth movement went wrong in many ways, when it considered wandering as a permanent way of life. But since wandering from the beginning came into being as a counter-movement against a rigidified lifestyle, so it later remains related to this in its nature. This means, to express it rather succinctly: wandering is a holiday occupation, that is, of its nature a temporary release from the serious life of work. In this return to one's origin, which is what wandering is according to its deepest nature, man should regenerate himself, rejuvenate himself, but to the same extent he should then return, rejuvenated, to the seriousness of life, in order to fulfil his tasks there. What is important is to see the polarity between the two possibilities and within this polarity the often misunderstood right to leisure, which is in fact not merely relaxation and recovery, but a fulfilment of man's nature in its deepest sense. With a meaningful understanding of leisure, wandering now acquires its great significance in the whole context of human life.

III
THE SECURITY OF THE HOUSE

1. The Meaning of the House

The house as centre of the world

Starting from the basic dynamics of human life in going away and returning, we first turned (in one-sided but unavoidable abstraction) to one area of space that was structured as a result – the world out there in all its expanse, with its basic directions and areas, with its paths and roads – and tried to clarify certain basic characteristics of its structure. But man cannot live in this world alone. He would lose his foothold if he had no firm point of reference to which all his paths were directed, from which they derive and to which they return. This brings the problem of the centre of experienced space back into the foreground, when after our first introductory thoughts we had for the time being almost lost sight of it. Man needs such a centre, in which he is rooted in space and to which all his relationships in space refer.

But the situation here is the same as with the question of areas of the world: the mythical view according to which the centre of the world, in an 'objective' sense, is moved into the place of residence of one's own people, where it was symbolized in a direct and vivid way by some sacred focal point, could be maintained only as long as knowledge of the surface of the earth remained comparatively limited. It could not hold its own once the new continents had been discovered and the shape of the earth had been shown to be spherical. Now no country can any longer be privileged over the rest, and all points of the earth's surface (if we ignore the poles, as being outside experienced space in practical terms) are fundamentally equal. But even if such a spatial centre, assumed to be objectively in existence, has been lost, human life continues to be based on such a centre. This is the place where humans 'dwell', where they are 'at home' and to which they can always 'return home.' And as with the question of areas of the world in general, so it is here with the centre: mythological viewpoints show us on an enlarged scale what is also contained in a smaller and therefore less easily recognized form in the structure of our own experienced space. This too is today still based on a centre and built up from a centre, even when this centre now more strongly relates to the individual. It is the house in which he lives. His house becomes the concrete centre of his world.

Hermann Broch puts it very aptly in the inscription for a house that he wrote once, which sets one thinking:

> In the centre of all distance
> stands this house,
> that is why I love it.[1]

The stated reason for its being loved, that is for its human value, is that it stands in the centre of all distance. This means, first of all, in the sense discussed here, that the house stands in the middle of the world. It defines the area of the near and dear, which is encircled by the distance. The house itself is contrasted with the distance, as that which most belongs to us, and that is why it should be loved. But the phrase ‘centre of all distance’ at the same time has a profound double meaning: it can mean, at the same time, where the distance is densest, most ‘distant’, in the actual heart of the distance. Our own house, apparently the nearest and most familiar thing to us, is in reality the most distant, and because, in dwelling in the house, one is oneself already in the distance, it is vulnerable and needs to be loved.

Admittedly man today, if he regards his house as the centre of the world, is at a distinct disadvantage with regard to the mythological world image. For mythological man, the centre of the world was objectively rooted with reference to the fixed centre of space as a whole. Dwelling was therefore no problem to him. But since this objective centre has been lost, the anchoring in an objective system is also lost. Man is then in danger of being uprooted. He becomes homeless on earth, because he no longer has special ties to any place in particular. He becomes an eternal fugitive in a world that impinges menacingly upon him. This is in fact the danger that threatens man today. But from this, conversely, his task is also created. If it is important for man once again to find a centre for his space, if, as is still to be shown, the fulfilment of his nature is linked to the existence of such a centre, then he will no longer find this centre as something taken for granted, but must create it himself, consciously base himself in it, and defend it against all external attacks. The creation of this centre thus becomes a decisive role for mankind. And he will fulfil this task in the making of and dwelling in his house. But the mere outward ownership of one’s dwelling-place is

1 ‘In der Mitte aller Ferne / steht dies Haus, / drum hab es gerne’, Hermann Broch, *Gedichte*, Zurich: 1953, p. 68.

not enough. Rather it is one's inner relationship with it that enables it to fulfil its achievement of providing security. This is what Heidegger means when he says that man needs to learn how to dwell.[2] The problem of the house and of dwelling now takes up the central position in our discussion of experienced space.

Dwelling

The way in which man lives in his house is called dwelling. And so we must first examine this concept if we want to determine man's relationship with his house. Dwelling is a basic state of human life whose full significance is only slowly being recognized. Man dwells in his house. In a more general sense, he also dwells in a town. But dwelling is more than merely existing or being located; for both these states are in only an external relationship with space. The existentialist, if we regard him as an extreme example of human existence, does not know 'dwelling.' 'Thrown' into the world, as the typical phrase has it, he finds himself in some basically arbitrary location, which he did not choose and which remains foreign in its nature to him. He knows the world only as the pressure of a restrictive situation. So he remains an eternal stranger on earth, not bound to any particular place, always on his way, but never reaching his goal.

But to dwell means to be at home in a particular place, to be rooted in it and belong to it. This is why it is so important to note how in the development of the present-day intellectual movement – particularly in its examination of existentialism – the concept of dwelling has recently pushed its way into the foreground; how it is taken up by various authors and has passed, perhaps unnoticed even by themselves, into their linguistic usage, and in this way often acquires a further significance which is no longer confined to dwelling in a house. For this very reason, this concept however seems particularly well suited for the definition of a profound general change in the sense of space which results from the examination of existentialism. Man is learning once again to dwell in his world.

Saint-Exupéry, in his *Citadelle*, the 'city in the desert', was probably the first to stress the significance of dwelling. 'I have discovered a great truth', he writes, which is 'to know that all men dwell, and that the meaning of

2 Martin Heidegger, 'Bauen, Wohnen, Denken', *Vorträge und Aufsätze*, Pfullingen: 1954, p. 145 ff., p. 162 ['Building, dwelling, thinking', *Poetry, language, thought*, translated by Albert Hofstadter, New York: 1971, p. 161].

things changes according to the meaning of their home.'[3] So dwelling is here no longer a random activity like any other, but an aspect of human nature which is decisive with regard to man's relationship with the world in general. The fictional hero of his observations says proudly: 'For, above all else, I am he who *dwells*';[4] for only in dwelling can we, as is shown here, attain the fulfilment of our true nature.

Here Saint-Exupéry's thought coincides with that of Heidegger, who, in his Darmstadt lecture on 'Building, dwelling, thinking', coming from quite a different direction, created the formula: 'To be a human being means to be on the earth as a mortal. It means to dwell.'[5] So human nature as a whole is here determined by dwelling.

Since then Bachelard, in his *Poetics of space*, has dedicated a penetrating investigation, which we have yet to examine in detail, to the 'primeval function of dwelling', as he sees it incorporated in the house.

But above all we should here name Merleau-Ponty, who uses the word dwelling [habiter] almost as a code word, in which his relationship with the world as a whole is reflected. And in fact he uses it not only to characterize man's relationship with his house, but at the same time he uses the understanding he has won from it to characterize man's relationship with the world as a whole. He mentions, for example, that we dwell in the world and the things in it, but in a more general sense we also dwell in space and time and existence in general. We must therefore ask: what is this new relationship with the world, for whose characterization we are forced to use the concept of dwelling?

To understand the meaning of the word 'dwell' it is helpful to look once again at linguistic history. The German equivalent, 'wohnen', developed from the general basic meaning of 'be at ease or content' to the definition in spatial terms as 'stay, linger, be in [a place]', and even then the present basic sense of a continuing residence was still rare; rather, the word at first signified only the action of staying in a particular place in a general sense. Thus the living room [Wohnzimmer] is the space usually occupied by the family during the day. At the same time the word may become important in the Christian context, when we read: 'The Word was made flesh and dwelt among us.'[6] Here too, dwelling refers to an intimate, close relationship.

3 Antoine de Saint-Exupéry, *Citadelle*, Paris: 1948; *Die Stadt in der Wüste*, Bad Salzig and Düsseldorf: 1951, p. 36 [*The wisdom of the sands*, translated by Stuart Gilbert, London: 1952, p. 15 (original translation modified)].

4 Saint-Exupéry, *Die Stadt in der Wüste*, p. 36 [p. 15].

5 Heidegger, 'Bauen, Wohnen, Denken', p. 147 [p. 147].

6 John, 1: 4.

This meaning is also contained in the compound word 'innewohnen', to be inherent in something. The word 'Wohnung', dwelling-place, is also used initially in an abstract sense. It describes the residence taken up by man in a particular place, and is only subsequently transferred to the specific spatial complex in which he dwells. In this sense the word 'Wohnung' is normally used today to mean a flat or apartment, a self-contained part of a house inhabited by a family. In a larger house there may be several apartments.

Dwelling is thus closely related to 'Aufenthalt' – a place where one stays, or 'stance.' In this case too it is rewarding to look briefly at the history of the word. The prefix 'ent' [re-], which may mean something like 'against', explains the term 'sich enthalten' in the sense of 'to offer re-sistance', and this is then further clarified as 'sich aufenthalten', 'to stay upright, to resist unwaveringly.' This term is initially used of a single combatant who cannot be made to fall, then to a body of fighters and finally to a fortress which resists its enemies. Thus Dürer, for example, writes: '...to build a stout fortress, from which in time of need one may resist [sich aufenthalten] and defend oneself from enemies.'[7] The place we stay in is thus initially the place from which one can assert oneself against an enemy, and only subsequently, in a weaker sense, a place where one stays for a longer period of time. This too is a useful clue, for it makes one realize that it is not simply given to man to stay in one place; residence must first be asserted against the claims of an enemy. This is a meaning which is today largely applied to the word 'dwell.'

So this means that in order for man to dwell in a fixed place on earth, it is not enough to settle fleetingly in some arbitrary place, but rather a special effort is demanded. Man must ground himself at this point, he must to some extent dig his claws into it, in order to assert himself against the onslaught of the world which may dislodge him again from this place. This is the factor that came to be expressed in the linguistic history of the word 'Aufenthalt.' Saint-Exupéry, in the work mentioned above, developed this idea in a penetrating manner. 'I am a builder of cities,' he writes, 'I have halted the caravan on its way. It was only a seed in the rushing of the wind ... But I resist the wind and bury the seed in the earth, so that the cedars may grow upwards for the glory of God.'[8] The decisive factor is here clearly enunciated: only in being rooted in a particular place can man attain the stability that allows him to assert himself against the onslaught of the 'desert', that is, of time, which destroys everything.

---

7 Quoted in *Trübners Deutsches Wörterbuch.*

8 Saint-Exupéry, *Die Stadt in der Wüste*, p. 32 [p. 12].

So to dwell means to have a fixed place in space, to belong to this place and be rooted in it. But for man to stay in this place, for him to be at ease there, the dwelling-place must not be thought of as a mere point, in the sense in which we have been speaking of a natural central point of experienced space, to which all his paths are related. In order to dwell there at one's leisure, this place demands a certain expansion. Man must be able to move there in a specific area. Dwelling demands a specific dwelling-space. I refer to a dwelling in this sense without making any statement about the type of dwelling other than that it is the spatial area in which one dwells.

Space and security

But for man to be able to dwell in his dwelling-place, so that he can find stability, security and peace in the face of the world's onslaught, he needs to secure this area by suitable means. Saint-Exupéry for example writes that firm defences are necessary, without which one cannot live. And indeed, in the German language, as Heidegger has pointed out, the 'Frieden' [peace] in which one lives is related to the 'Umfriedung' [enclosure] of the dwelling area. So in order to dwell in peace, we need protective walls and a sheltering roof. Thus the mere dwelling becomes a house in the real sense. But there are connections with the house that we will leave aside for the time being: the fortified city and every secured area of space in general, and not only walls and roofs but also fences and hedges. For the sake of simplicity we will for now restrict ourselves to the house.

It is the house, therefore, that provides man with security, and the problem of dwelling intensifies into that of the house. The history of the world in this case gives little aid to understanding it. The house is initially a general means of shelter, a hide-out, and then narrows into the house in which men dwell. Proverbially it is often combined with another word in an alliterative term, 'house and hearth.'

> A house is good security,
> A refuge in both joy and sorrow,[9]

says Fischart. Here man can move freely and without constraint, here he can be at peace with himself.

---

9 'Ein Haus ist ein gut Sicherheit, / ein Zuflucht beid zu Freud und Leid', Johann Fischart quoted in Grimm, *Deutsches Wörterbuch.*

With the walls that mark the boundaries of the house, with the borders of the dwelling place in general, an element of instability is created in experienced space, to which attention has been drawn in our introductory remarks. Space is now divided into two sharply distinguished areas. By means of the walls of the house, a special private space is cut out of the large common space, and thus an inner space is separated from an outer space. Man, who according to Simmel is generally distinguished by the ability to set limits and at the same time to overstep these limits, places these limits most visibly and directly in the walls of his house. This double concept of inner and outer space is fundamental to the further structuring of the whole experienced space, indeed for human life as a whole.

The two spaces have totally different characters. The outer space is the space for activity in the world, in which it is always a question of overcoming resistance and defending oneself against an opponent; it is the space of insecurity, of danger and vulnerability. And if it was only this space that existed, the existentialists would be right and man would indeed remain an eternally pursued fugitive. This is why he needs the space of the house. This is the area of rest and peace, in which man can relax his constant alert attention to possible threats, a space to which man can retire and where he can relax. To give this peace to man is the supreme task of the house. And in this way the space of security is distinguished from the space of threat.

These initially still very provisional definitions must be expanded in a number of ways, which, without anticipating our later discussion, we must at least suggest here in a preliminary way:

1. When we speak here in a comprehensive way of the house, this of course does not have to be a house of one's own in the sense of the one-family house. In modern urban conditions, it may just as easily be an apartment on one floor of a larger building. House and dwelling may be used interchangeably in this sense. Indeed, if necessary some modest corner would suffice. The appearance of this individual house or dwelling can take on many very different forms in various historical conditions.[10]

The essential thing is man's ability to dispose of a space of his own, which offers reliable protection against the rigours of the weather as well as the unwelcome approach of strangers. In these terms, Zutt, who has concerned himself with dwelling from the medical point of view, summarizes: 'When

10 How such a centre (even if moveable) is created in nomadic societies by temporarily setting up a tent and how this affects the present circumstances would require independent study.

the foreign approaches in a hostile and threatening manner, one seeks protection and security in the place where one finds familiar peace … In our usual dwelling we have the highest measure of spatial security.'[11]

2. While we have spoken so far in an abstract way of 'man' who needs a house, we should not be thinking of the individual human being in this context. Just as a single person is not enough to build a house, it is not enough for a single person to dwell in a house. We dwell plurally, we dwell with our family, with 'our own', but separate from the 'others', the 'strangers.'[12]

3. For the dwelling to transmit a sense of security, it needs not only the outward protection which fends off the intruder, but it must also be inwardly designed so as to meet the needs of those who dwell in it, so that a spirit of calm and peace radiates out from it. The question therefore arises of the homeliness [Wohnlichkeit] of the dwelling.[13]

4. While we have spoken so far of a sharp contrast between inner and outer space, between house and the foreign, in fact there are mediating structures that interpose themselves. When we walk out of the door of our house or overstep the borders of our land, we do not yet enter the foreign as such, but we enter the well-known street, the familiar village or the familiar town. And even when we leave these behind, at first we still remainin well-known areas before we gradually enter the entirely foreign. The house in a narrower sense therefore is part of a larger whole, in the homeland that is something like an extended house. House and home are closely connected. But when zones of familiarity form around the house and in a sense extend it, they do indeed create a more complex structure, but at the same time are unable to remove the unstable character by which the inner space of the house is distinguished from the outer world. So we are justified in leaving this structure aside for the sake of simplicity, and will restrict ourselves to the house.

Bachelard on the joy of dwelling

Bachelard, in particular, in his work *Poetics of space*, which has already been mentioned, has convincingly brought out the protective function of the house. The 'happy spaces', the 'beloved spaces' that he describes are

11 J. Zutt, 'Über Daseinsordnungen. Ihre Bedeutung für die Psychiatrie', *Der Nervenarzt*, vol. 24, 1953, p. 177 ff., p. 184.
12 See the present book, p. 281 ff.
13 See the present book, p. 172 ff.

the 'possession spaces', that is, those possessed by man and 'defended against adverse forces.'[14] These are the 'dwelt-in' rooms, in other words the various forms taken by the house, for 'all really inhabited space bears the essence of the notion of home.'[15] Dwelling and house, according to him, correspond to each other as long as we take the concept of the house far enough. As a welcome confirmation, as well as an extension of the conclusion reached so far, Bachelard's view will be presented in rather more detail, particularly since it is at the same time based on a wealth of evidence from French writers who are comparatively unknown to us.

For Bachelard, the primary function of the house is to protect and shelter. He speaks of the house's 'protective value.'[16] The house forms a 'protective centre' in human life.[17] It forms an ordered sphere in itself, in which the chaos of the world outside is defeated. 'In the life of the human ... the house thrusts aside contingencies.'[18] In contrast to the restlessly roaming life of the fugitive, the house enables a deeper stability in life. It is a persistent element. 'Its councils of continuity are unceasing. Without it, man would be a dispersed being.'[19] It is capable of gathering together what has been scattered and thus enables man to collect himself. Bachelard regards it as 'one of the greatest powers of integration' of human life.[20] The house thus provides a foothold in relation to all the attacks of the outside world. 'It maintains [man] through the storms of the heavens and through those of life.'[21] In particular it allows man to follow his imaginative dreams, which for Bachelard is its 'chief benefit.' 'The house shelters daydreaming, the house protects the dreamer, the house allows one to dream in peace.'[22] And from the dreams produced by the power of imagination there comes into being the 'oneiric house', that 'crypt of the house that we were born in',[23] in which the memory of the various dwellings in which one has lived, above all our first experiences of dwelling in the parental house, intensify

14 Gaston Bachelard, *Poetik des Raumes*, translated by Kurt Leonhard, Munich: 1960, p. 29 [*The poetics of space*, translated by Maria Jolas, Boston, Mass.: 1969, p. XXXV].
15 Bachelard, *Poetik des Raumes*, p. 37 [p. 5].
16 Bachelard, *Poetik des Raumes*, p. 29 [p. XXXV].
17 Bachelard, *Poetik des Raumes*, p. 71 [p. 39].
18 Bachelard, *Poetik des Raumes*, p. 39 [p. 7].
19 Bachelard, *Poetik des Raumes*, p. 39 [p. 7].
20 Bachelard, *Poetik des Raumes*, p. 38 [p. 6].
21 Bachelard, *Poetik des Raumes*, p. 39 [p. 7].
22 Bachelard, *Poetik des Raumes*, p. 38 [p. 6].
23 Bachelard, *Poetik des Raumes*, p. 48 [p. 15].

to become a primeval image of the house. 'Our house, apprehended in its dream potentiality, becomes as nest in the world.'[24]

The primeval sense of life transmitted by the house to man is, according to Bachelard, that of feeling at ease in a state of security. He feels comfortable in a quite direct sense in the warmth of his nest, and this gives him a quite elemental 'joy of dwelling' in which man feels his kinship with animals. He approvingly quotes a statement by Vlaminck: 'The well being I feel, seated in front of my fire, while bad weather rages out-of-doors, is entirely animal. A rat in its hole, a rabbit in its burrow, cows in the stable, must all feel the contentment that I feel.'[25] In this context he praises the warm 'maternal features of the house.'[26] In his confrontation with existentialism he stresses that this is the primeval experience of man, in contrast to which the menace and hostility of the outside world is something derivative and later in time: 'Life begins well, it begins enclosed, protected, all warm in the bosom of the house.'[27] In particular, the idea of winter with its snow and ice intensifies the 'intimacy value' of the house. In this context he quotes Baudelaire: 'Doesn't winter add to the poetry of the house?'[28] The dreamer 'asks the sky to send down as much snow, hail and frost as it can contain. What he really needs are Canadian or Russian winters. His own nest will be all the warmer, all the downier, all the better beloved …'[29]

On the other hand Bachelard warns against overlooking, in the 'dialectic of house and universe' that springs from this, the battle element that emerges from resistance against the forces of nature. Among the range of evidence from creative writers that he brings forward to support his account, one is particularly rewarding: it is by Henri Bosco, who describes a modest house in the Camargue in battle against the elements. Its importance in the present context demands that we repeat here a few sentences from the passages quoted by Bachelard. 'The house was fighting gallantly,' writes Bosco, 'it stood firm … [The roof] hunched over further and clung to the old rafters. … No doubt it was holding firmly to the soil of the island by means of its unbreakable roots … The already human being yielded nothing to the storm. … That night [the house] was really my mother.'[30] So

24 Bachelard, *Poetik des Raumes*, p. 131 [p. 103].
25 Bachelard, *Poetik des Raumes*, p. 119 ff. [p. 91].
26 Bachelard, *Poetik des Raumes*, p. 40 [p. 7].
27 Bachelard, *Poetik des Raumes*, p. 39 [p. 7].
28 Bachelard, *Poetik des Raumes*, p. 70 [p. 38].
29 Bachelard, *Poetik des Raumes*, p. 71 [p. 39].
30 Bachelard, *Poetik des Raumes*, p. 76 ff. [p. 44].

here it has become a 'dynamic community of man and house.'[31] Bachelard emphasizes: 'And faced with this pack [i.e. the forces of the universe], which gradually breaks loose, the house becomes the real being of pure humanity which defends itself without ever being responsible for an attack. [This house] is man's Resistance; it is *human virtue*, man's grandeur.'[32] So the house is not only an outward protection, but also, at the same time, a symbol of human life and here acquires an educational significance. It has become 'a fortified castle for the recluse, who must learn to conquer fear within its walls.'[33] Thus the house not only bestows warmth and comfort inwards, but also outwardly gives man the firmness and strength to hold one's ground in the world. 'Such a house ... is an instrument with which to face the cosmos. ... Come what may the house helps us to say, "I will be an inhabitant of the world, in spite of the world".'[34]

But the full development of the house involves not only its horizontal, but also its vertical extension, that is, in addition to the actual rooms lived in it must extend both in height and depth; it must have a cellar and a roof. 'Verticality is ensured by the polarity of cellar and the attic.'[35] 'A three-story [house], which is the simplest as regards essential height, has a cellar, a ground floor and an attic.'[36] The interior of the house reiterates what we were saying earlier about the symbolic meaning of above and below. Bachelard examines this structure too in detail. The steps that go down to the cellar are different from the ones that lead to the loft. But above all, with him it is the cellar by which the house is anchored in the deeper, but at the same time more uncanny underground of earth. Thus, on the model of another novel by the previously mentioned Henri Bosco, he develops the concept of a 'house with cosmic roots';[37] 'The house has become a natural being whose fate is bound to that of mountains and of the waters that plough the land.'[38] The houses in the great cities, he stresses elsewhere, are no longer genuine houses. 'In Paris there are no

31 Bachelard, *Poetik des Raumes*, p. 78 [p. 47 – the passage quoted by Bollnow has been omitted in the English translation. The original French text reads: 'Dans cette communauté dynamique de l'homme et de la maison, das cette rivalité dynamique de la maison et de l'univers ...'].
32 Bachelard, *Poetik des Raumes*, p. 76 [p. 44].
33 Bachelard, *Poetik des Raumes*, p. 77 [p. 46].
34 Bachelard, *Poetik des Raumes*, p. 78 [p. 46].
35 Bachelard, *Poetik des Raumes*, p. 50 [p. 17].
36 Bachelard, *Poetik des Raumes*, p. 58 [p. 25].
37 Bachelard, *Poetik des Raumes*, p. 55 [p. 22].
38 Bachelard, *Poetik des Raumes*, p. 56 [p. 23].

houses and the inhabitants of the big city live in superimposed boxes'[39] and 'quite unthinkable for a dreamer of houses, sky-scrapers have no cellars.'[40] These houses lack 'roots', and at the same time, as a result, they lack the deeper cosmic connection. But the real houses, in the deep structure of their dwelling functions, are more than can be understood by means of geometric ideas of space. Bachelard also sharply distinguishes the house as a concretely experienced space from the abstract mathematical concept of space: 'A house that has been experienced is not an inert box. Inhabited space transcends geometrical space.'[41] Space here takes on an emotional, human quality.

And yet Bachelard must immediately point out how quickly man strives once again to leave the security of his house. 'Why were we so quickly sated with the happiness of living in the old house?'[42] One could, to begin with, answer that man in the 'dialectics of house and universe', the 'dialectics of outside and inside'[43] in the house is taking hold only of one side, which again and again demands to be completed by the other side. But Bachelard, more profoundly, is referring not to a short-term departure from the house, in order to return to it once more, but as a definitive dissatisfaction with any house in particular. 'In reality something more than reality was lacking. We did not dream enough in that house.'[44] The house dreamed of in its perfection is not to be attained in any actual house. 'In the actual house, the day-dream of inhabiting is thwarted. A daydream of elsewhere should be left open therefore, at all times.'[45] This is aimed at the reciprocal relationship between house and distance, at that ultimate homesickness that draws people longingly out into the distance. 'Housed everywhere, but nowhere shut in', is how Bachelard formulates the 'motto of the dreamer of dwellings.'[46] In the context of Kunz's suggestion[47] that man can attain a final home only in the creations of the imagination born from his longing, we will put aside the question of whether this 'everywhere' already makes too much of the fixedness of dwelling.

---

39 Bachelard, *Poetik des Raumes*, p. 59 [p. 26].
40 Bachelard, *Poetik des Raumes*, p. 60 [p. 27].
41 Bachelard, *Poetik des Raumes*, p. 78 [p. 47].
42 Bachelard, *Poetik des Raumes*, p. 87 [p. 57].
43 Bachelard, *Poetik des Raumes*, p. 242 ff. [p. 211 ff.].
44 Bachelard, *Poetik des Raumes*, p. 87 [p. 57].
45 Bachelard, *Poetik des Raumes*, p. 92 [p. 62].
46 Bachelard, *Poetik des Raumes*, p. 92 [p. 62].
47 See the present book, p. 119 ff.

The anthropological function

After this confirmatory indication, let us return to our own object of study. The result of our discussion so far is what one might describe as the anthropological function of the house, its achievement in the general context of human life: in order to survive in the world and be able to fulfil his tasks there, man needs a space providing security and peace, to which he can retreat, in which he can unwind and become his normal self again, when he has worn himself out in battle with the outside world. The process of relaxation and recollection of oneself does not form part of this study, which is devoted to space. But it is important that this human process of becoming oneself has quite specific spatial prerequisites. Only as a dweller, only in possession of a house, only in having at one's disposal such a 'private' domain separated from public life can man fulfil his nature and be fully human. Man needs such a sphere of security in order to live at all. If his house – or, to put it more cautiously, the peace of his dwelling – is taken away, the inner subversion of the individual is unavoidable.[48]

A weighty objection to this statement appears to arise: particularly in our time, it has been the fate of many to be driven from their house and home. This is certainly a cruel fate. But should we therefore deny them the possibility of a final fulfilment of their human nature? That would be both cruel and unjust. And with the high degree of fluctuation of people today, does our relationship with our original homes still have the importance that it may once have had? Man can indeed change his dwelling-place (even if this in many cases may lead to psychological harm), and may find a new home after the loss of the old one. But even if the specific dwelling and home are changed, the fundamental importance of house and home are not affected, but rather the task of re-establishing the order of the dwelling and the security of the house in the new location becomes even more important.[49]

Here let us remember Goethe, who in one passage of *Faust* speaks of the 'fugitive', of the 'unhoused', the 'aimless, restless reprobate'[50]; for if

---

48 I have discussed the importance of preserving such a domain of one's own [Eigensphäre], especially in a time characterized by the intrusion of the public into even the most private realm, in more detail in *Maß und Vermessenheit* (Göttingen: 1962), p. 55 ff.

49 The catastrophic effect on our well-being of the present shortage in housing and the loss of one's own home, especially one's own hearth, as a root of criminal behaviour has been documented convincingly by Zutt. See also *Neue Geborgenheit*, p. 169 f.

50 'Flüchtling ... Unbehauster ... Unmensch ohne Zweck und Ruh', Johann Wolfgang von Goethe, *Faust erster Teil. Gedenkausagabe*, edited by Ernst Beutler, vol.5, Zurich and Stuttgart: 1948-71, p. 247 [p. 106].

the 'houseless' person is 'inhuman', in other words has fallen short of the actual nature of man, it follows conversely than man can only be truly human if 'housed.'

This anthropological function of the house can be discovered once again today; for after so many breakdowns of all apparently secure traditional orders, man today is suspicious of everything that appears secure, and anyone who defends the indispensability of the house in human life is easily stamped a petit bourgeois. Nevertheless, we must not understand this realization in the sense that man should hide away in his house and there lead an inactive and comfortable life. Then the dweller would really be the petit bourgeois who was mocked by the Romantics:

> Beatus ille homo,
> qui sedet in sua domo,
> et sedet post fornacem
> et habet bonam pacem[51]

No, man must go out into the world in order to fulfil his tasks there, as Schiller says:

> Man must go out into hostile life,[52]

and in the course of the world's business he must expose himself to the dangers necessarily associated with it. But when he has fulfilled his tasks in the world, then he must also have the possibility of returning to the shelter of his house. Both sides, dependent on each other in polar tension, are equally necessary; and on the equilibrium of the two sides, work in the outer space of the world and rest in the inner space of the house, depends the inner health of man. And for this reason man has the indispensable task of creating this secure space by building his house and defending it against attack.

---

51 'Das soll ein Reisen werden / durch Wald und grünen Plan. / Das heißt ein herrlich Leben! ... / Die Welt ist aufgetan.' Joseph Freiherr von Eichendorff, 'Wanderlied der Prager Studenten', *Heimweh. Neue Gesamtausgabe der Werke und Schriften*, edited by G. Baumann and S. Grosse, Stuttgart: 1957, vol. 1, p. 48.

52 'Der Mann muß hinaus ins feindliche Leben', Friedrich Schiller, *Das Lied von der Glocke. Sämtliche Werke*, edited by Eduard v. d. Hellen, vol. 1, Stuttgart and Berlin: n.d., p. 49.

The vulnerability of the house

All the same, it would be wrong to assume that a house could ever give ultimate security to man. 'Every home is threatened,'[53] Saint-Exupéry stresses. And Kafka, in his story 'The burrow',[54] describes the hopelessness of the attempt to construct an unassailable security system. Any effort to increase security demands complicated devices and at the same time creates heightened vulnerability. As soon as man fails to recognize this and takes the security in his house for something definitive, he does indeed become a contemptible petit bourgeois, and at some time or other, at the latest on his death, this illusion must collapse. This is why man in any house must at the same time preserve the inner freedom to leave the house again. He must know that there is something ultimate in him that cannot be injured even by the loss of his house. Today we call it his existence, in the concise sense of existential philosophy. But on the other side, knowledge of the vulnerability of the human dwelling and of the dangers of becoming established in one's house does not free man from the task of building his house with all the reasonable means of planning, to create in it the order of his life, and to defend it constantly in unremitting tough battle against the onslaught of chaotic forces. Only in such incessant fight can the island of security be maintained.

And one last thing: if it is the task of man to build his house, and to rebuild it time and again after repeated destruction, he would hardly be able to do so if he were not supported in this by ultimate trust in the world and in life. Despite all inevitable disappointments he must preserve the feeling that his efforts in some sense have been worthwhile.[55] In the troubled days of the First World War, Rilke composed a house motto which runs:

> In nineteen fourteen
> I was built,
> Have looked ahead, becoming,
> amidst storms of humans.
> Have trusted:
> who trusts, remains.[56]

---

53 'Jedes Heim ist bedroht', Saint-Exupéry, *Die Stadt in der Wüste*, p. 61 [p. 33].

54 Franz Kafka, 'Der Bau', in *Beschreibung eines Kampfes*, p. 173.

55 See Eduard Spranger, *Der unbekannte Gott*, Stuttgart: 1954, p. 24.

56 'Neunzehnhundertvierzehn / bin ich erbaut, / habe, von Menschenstürmen umweht, / werdend immer vorausgeschaut. / Habe vertraut: / wer vertraut, besteht', Rainer Maria Rilke, *Gedichte* 1906-1926, Wiesbaden: 1953, p. 343.

This makes a decisive point: without such ultimate trust in what the future brings, man would hardly be able to summon the strength to build a house; in view of the destructive forces threatening from all sides, it would appear senseless to him from the start.

Bachelard, above all else, has given strong emphasis to this side of the problem of space: 'Would a bird build its nest', he asks in one passage of his *Poetics of space*, 'if it did not have its instinct for confidence in the world?'[57] And what is true of the bird is correspondingly true of man. 'Our house', he continues, 'becomes a nest in the world, and we shall live there in complete confidence.'[58] Here we find in Bachelard the deeper background from which the sentence already quoted stands out. Without the background of such an ultimate trust in being and existence, no kind of human life, in particular no building and no dwelling is possible.[59]

57 Bachelard, *Poetik des Raumes*, p. 131 [p. 103].
58 Bachelard, *Poetik des Raumes*, p. 131 [p. 103].
59 See O. F. Bollnow, *Neue Geborgenheit. Das Problem einer Überwindung des Existentialismus*, Stuttgart: 1958, p. 139 ff.

2. Sacred Space

The return to mythological thinking

Even in these secular times the house still retains a certain sacred character, which is sensed by everyone who has ever begun to notice these things. However much talk there was, in days gone by, of a 'machine for living in' (Le Corbusier), in order to extend the will to protection characteristic of the machine age to the function of dwelling, one soon senses the inappropriateness of such an application. Human dwelling simply does not lend itself to being resolved in the rationalization of the modern technological world. Rather, there remain in it certain unresolvable remains of archaic life that are no longer understandable from a rational, purpose-oriented way of thinking. Today the house of the human individual is still a sacred area. Even someone who is used to dealing in a comparatively carefree manner with the property of others feels a certain inhibition about intruding uninvited into someone else's house. We find the legal expression of this special position of the house in the concept of breach of domestic peace, which is defined as 'unlawfully intruding in or remaining on private property.'[1] Here too it is noticeable that this offence is 'disproportionately' severely punished, at any rate more severely than would be comprehensible from a purely rational point of view. In the invulnerability of the dwelling – in relation incidentally to a general protection of the human 'intimate sphere', in the secrecy of the post and so on – there is a suggestion of a peculiarly sacred character.

In order to make visible this special sense of emotion which still today attaches to the house, it is appropriate to look back from our time, which is already largely alienated from religious feeling, to earlier forms of humanity, and see what ethnology and history of religion have to tell us about the original relationship of man, still in tune with mythology, with his house. Of course we cannot here pursue the widely branching individual research

---

1 E. Osenbrücken, *Der Hausfrieden*, 1857.

studies, and will keep essentially to the more recent summarizing accounts, though we will equally be able to pick out only a few features decisive for us out of the more complicated whole. Following the earlier work of Cassirer[2] and Van der Leeuw,[3] Eliade[4] has more recently successfully pursued these questions. It is of little importance in our enquiry whether we are considering the house inhabited by one individual or the temple as the house of a god. 'House and temple are essentially one,'[5] says the Dutch philosopher of religion Van der Leeuw; for the house too is in its origin a sanctified area. But it is also true in a further sense of the ordered human settlement, of the city as a whole. Everywhere, establishment and planning follows principles taken from mythological thought.

Sacred space

In his book *The sacred and the profane*, Eliade starts from the statement that for the religious individual there is no homogeneous space: '[it] experiences interruptions, breaks in it; some parts of space are qualitatively different from others.'[6] Here we must note immediately that in a certain respect the religious individual can be equated with the primeval man of mythological consciousness; for primeval man is necessarily religious. In contrast, modern secularized man has broken away from this basic condition. But even he has always broken away only up to a certain point, and certain remnants of the religious – to use this word in its original sense – are still preserved in him, for example what interests us here, namely a certain remaining sense of the dignity of the house. Thus even Eliade stresses that 'profane existence is never found in the pure state.'[7]

Eliade distinguishes, in respect of spatial relationships, in particular between a 'sacred, that is, power-laden, significant space' and a profane space. The profane space is, in contrast to the sacred space, homogeneous

---

2 Ernst Cassirer, *Philosophie der symbolischen Formen*, vol. 2, Berlin: 1923-9 [*Philosophy of symbolic forms*, translated by Ralph Manheim, vol. 2, New Haven: 1953-7].

3 Gerardus van der Leeuw, *Phänomenologie der Religion*, Tübingen: 1955 [*Religion in essence and manifestation*, translated by J. E. Turner, London: 1938].

4 Mircea Eliade, *Das Heilige und das Profane. Vom Wesen des Religiösen*. Rowohlts Deutsche Enzyklopädie, vol. 31, Hamburg: 1957 [*The sacred and the profane*, New York: 1959].

5 Van der Leeuw, *Phänomenologie der Religion*, p. 448 [p. 395].

6 Eliade, *Das heilige und das Profane*, p. 13 [p. 20].

7 Eliade, *Das heilige und das Profane*, p. 14 [p. 23].

and unstructured, as we know it from geometric space. We should perhaps distinguish more cautiously between this homogeneous mathematical space, which is an abstract construct, and profane space, here experienced as homogeneous, which appears homogeneous only in relation to sacred space, while nothing has as yet been stated regarding its own possible structure. What is essential here is only the distinction between the sacred and profane areas and the reference to the dividing 'breaks and cracks', which as such necessarily belong to the structure of original space. The non-homogeneity of which we spoke in our introductory remarks, as an essential distinguishing feature between experienced and mathematical space, here appears therefore in striking form as the sharp break between sacred and profane space.

The religious primeval experience which is Eliade's starting point consists in the experience that a special area develops within the great limitless space, a sacred space which is distinguished by the effectiveness of the numinous. We must perhaps (Eliade does not go into this) assume that such a sacred space or sacred area does not necessarily need to exist in a building artificially erected by man. It is also found in nature, in a sacred grove or on the sacred mountain or in other distinctive places. How these are distinguished from the other, profane space has been very sharply emphasized, for his part, by Van Leeuw, showing the non-homogeneity of original space in a new light. 'Parts of space', he writes, 'have their specific and independent value … They are "positions"; but they become "positions" by being "selected" from the vast extensity of the world. A part of space, then, is not a "part" at all but a place, and a place becomes a "position" when man occupies it and stands on it. He has thus recognized the power of the locality, he seeks it or avoids it, attempts to strengthen or enfeeble it; but in any case he selects the place as a "position".'[8]

Thus sacred spaces may be found in nature without any human involvement. Rather than other evidence, I will quote a wonderful account from Seneca, which is given by Van der Leeuw: 'If you ever have come upon a grove that is full of ancient trees, which have grown to an unusual height … then the loftiness of the forest, the seclusion of the spot … will prove to you the presence of a deity. We worship the sources of mighty rivers … and consecrate certain pools because of their dark waters and immensurable depth.'[9] Van der Leeuw's summarizing definition is as follows: 'Sacred space may also be defined as that locality that becomes

8 Van der Leeuw, *Phänomenologie der Religion*, p. 445 [p. 393].
9 Cited in Van der Leeuw, *Phänomenologie der Religion*, p. 447 [p. 394].

a position by the effects of power repeating themselves there, or being repeated by man.'[10] Even Christian churches are frequently found in the place of heathen shrines as a result of the sacredness of the place, which has been experienced even independently of the difference of religions.

Equally, however, it may be uncanny, squalid and menacing places that make us shudder with fear and that we therefore seek to avoid. Places of execution, for example, which have not served as such for centuries, have retained their eerie character, and the place where a murder was committed is still always passed with dark forebodings. Popular belief still has much to tell us on this subject. Among writers, Bergengruen knew a great deal about the uncanny power of certain places. One of his poems includes the lines:

> Everyone secretly shudders
> who passes that way,
> as though his soles
> had suddenly touched his own grave.[11]

The house as image of the world

The character of the sacred space, varyingly distinguished by sharp limits, is naturally evident to a particular degree in the shrines systematically designed by man, whether it be a temple, a city or only a single house. In this case too, man cannot arbitrarily choose the spot, but must respect the signs of the gods, in which the holiness of the spot is manifested. The gods must give a sign that a city, a temple, and so on is to be built in this place, and the gifted individual is able to recognize such a sign as a divine hint. This tradition is still handed down in the foundation stories of many Christian churches.

In all cases the building began with a certain area being cut out of the chaotic space and differentiated from the rest of the world as a holy area. In this connection Cassirer remarks in his *Philosophy of symbolic forms*: 'Hallowing begins when a specific zone is detached from space as a whole, when it is distinguished and one might say religiously hedged around.'[12]

---

10 Van der Leeuw, *Phänomenologie der Religion*, p. 446 [p. 393].

11 'Jeden schauert es verstohlen, / den sein Gang des Weges führt, / so, als hätten seine Sohlen / jäh das eigne Grab berührt', Werner Bergengruen, *Die heile Welt*, Zurich: 1950, p. 74. See my own account in *Unruhe und Geborgenheit im Weltbild neuerer Dichter*, Stuttgart: 1958.

12 Cassirer, *Philosophie der symbolischen Formen*, vol. 2, p. 123 [p. 99].

This is clearly expressed linguistically in the Latin word 'templum', which literally has the primary meaning of something 'cut out', although the word originally did not describe the building at all, but a place designated for the augur's observation of the flight of birds, and was only later applied to the structure built as a temple.[13]

The forms in which, in such primitive times, the building of the house – as of the temple, as of the city – took place are significant. Every building of a house is the establishment of a cosmos in a chaos. Here I rely above all on Eliade, whose account gathers together a rich selection of folklore. Every house, according to him, is an 'imago mundi', an image of the world as a whole. The world as a whole is mirrored in the house. And for this reason every house that is built, and even more so every temple that is built, is a repetition of the creation of the world, a reconstruction of the work done by the gods at the beginning of time. For this reason all human ordering of space is 'only repitition of a primordial act, the transformation of chaos into cosmos by the divine act of creation.'[14] This is true particularly of the human house: '[The house] is the universe that man constructs for himself by imitating the paradigmatic creation of the gods, the cosmogony.'[15] This is the basis of the deep reflective relationship between world creation and house-building: 'to organize a space is to repeat the paradigmatic work of the gods.'[16]

But conversely, this work created by the gods, this world, is dependent on the activities of men, it exists only if the divine act of creation is symbolically repeated by man. 'If the world is to be lived in,' says Eliade, 'it must be founded.'[17] House-building in its most profound meaning is thus a world-creating and world-sustaining activity, which is only possible with the use of sanctified rituals. This is why the rituals that have since ancient times been associated with the foundation of such a house are so revealing.

This building of houses takes place on the model of the cosmos, whose creation is after all to be symbolized in it. 'The creation of the world becomes the archetype of every creative human gesture.'[18] 'The house is an "imago mundi".'[19] It would here take us too far even to suggest how this has been adapted among various nations in a typically recurring manner.

13 H. Nissen, *Das Templum. Antiquarische Untersuchungen*, Berlin: 1869.
14 Eliade, *Das heilige und das Profane*, p. 19 [p. 31].
15 Eliade, *Das heilige und das Profane*, p. 34 [p. 56].
16 Eliade, *Das heilige und das Profane*, p. 20 [p. 32].
17 Eliade, *Das heilige und das Profane*, p. 13 [p. 22].
18 Eliade, *Das heilige und das Profane*, p. 27 [p. 45].
19 Eliade, *Das heilige und das Profane*, p. 32 [p. 53].

A few examples at random must suffice. Eliade reports of certain Indian tribes: 'The sacred hut in which their initiation takes place represents the universe. Its roof symbolizes the heavenly dome, its floor the earth, its four walls the four directions of cosmic space. The ritual construction of space is emphasized by the threefold symbolism of the four doors, four windows and four colours, which all represent the four points of the compass. The building of the sacred hut repeats the cosmogony, for this little building embodies the world.'[20]

But exactly the same is true in much more highly developed contexts within the Christian church. Sedlmayr for example summarizes the symbolism of the Byzantine churches as follows: 'The four parts of the church's interior symbolize the four points of the compass. The interior of the church is the universe. The altar is paradise, which was shifted to the east … On the other hand the west is the area of darkness, of horror, of death, the realm of the eternal dwellings of the dead who await the resurrection and the last judgement … The centre of the church building is the earth … The four parts of the interior of the church symbolize the four points of the compass.'[21] The interior of the church thus symbolizes the world as a whole, and each area of it, as can be traced in detail, has its own special significance. It must suffice here to place side by side this evidence from two entirely different contexts, in order to show the general principle of design.

The city

Quite similar relationships are found in the case of the city; for the city is nothing other than a house on a larger scale. So the same problems recur with its establishment as with the building of a house or a temple. The city too has after all not come into being out of a random collection of houses, but was deliberately founded. In this context it is not possible to examine more closely the wide-ranging group of questions with regard to the foundation of cities. We will merely refer briefly to one well-known example: the foundation of Rome, as it is handed down in Plutarch's account.[22] I will draw attention only to the most important points for our purposes:

---

20 Eliade, *Das heilige und das Profane*, p. 28, further evidence in Cassirer.

21 Hans Sedlmayer, *Die Entstehung der Kathedrale*, Zurich: 1950, p. 115. See notably Joseph Sauer, *Symbolik des Kirchengebäudes*, Freiburg i. Br.: 1924.

22 Cited in Otto Wilhelm von Vacano, 'Die Etrusker in der Welt der Antike', *Rowohlts Deutsche Enzyklopädie*, vol. 54, Hamburg: 1957, p. 28.

1. At first a round pit was dug, in which everything necessary for life was laid. This pit, which was called 'mundus', according to Eliade represented the navel of the world, but at the same time it is the 'image of the cosmos and the paradigmatic model for the human inhabitation.'[23] This pit was then sealed by a stone which was called 'lapis manalis', and which could be lifted only on three holy days, on which the 'manes', the spirits of the dead, would rise from it. Thus the pit unites the world of the living with that of the dead.

2. The builder then drove a plough drawn by a bull and a cow, digging a deep furrow at the borderline, where later the wall would be built. The plough was lifted only at the places where gates were to be placed, and Plutarch adds an explanatory remark: 'For this reason the whole wall, excepting only the gates, is held to be holy; but if the gates too should be considered holy, one would have a bad conscience about bringing things in and out through them which are necessary, but not clean.'[24] To what extent this was a recurring practice is shown by the report by Frobenius in his book on the cultural history of Africa, in which he describes in great detail the same practice in the establishment of African towns.[25]

3. Added to this are the axes of two main roads that intersect each other at right angles, corresponding exactly to the two basic directions that lay at the basis of the Roman technique of augury. This system of roads again has a sacred connection, and is the origin of the term 'Roma quadrata', referring to a Rome divided into four quadrants (but not itself square). This system of axes recurs, as we know, in every Roman camp, the 'castrum', where the circumvallation acquires a strictly rectangular form determined by the axial system. But here too we are looking at a type extending far beyond the Roman sphere of influence. In his book on the holy city[26] Werner Müller has prepared a rich range of material on the occurrence of this city type, which tempts one to further consideration.

As Brunner very interestingly points out, in Egyptian script there is a peculiar hieroglyph for 'city': a circle with a cross placed diagonally within it. Brunner comments: 'Undoubtedly this symbol represents the ground-plan for a city, in a circular form, with the mass of houses divided into four quarters by two roads intersecting each other at right angles at the central point.'[27] This is all the more interesting in view of the fact that the

23 Eliade, *Das heilige und das Profane*, p. 28 [p. 47].

24 Cited in Vacano, 'Die Etrusker in der Welt der Antike', p. 28.

25 Leo Frobenius, *Kulturgeschichte Afrikas*, Zurich: 1933, p. 177 and p. 179.

26 Werner Müller, *Die heilige Stadt*, Stuttgart: 1961.

27 H. Brunner, 'Zum Raumbegriff der Ägypter', *Studium Generale*, vol. 10, 1957, p. 618.

Egyptians themselves did not build their cities according to this plan, so that this ideal image of a city was in their minds without any connection with their everyday world.

In the same way the city of Rome, just like the house and the temple, is a reflection of world order and is incorporated by its order into the greater order of the world and the gods. In this context Vacano summarizes: 'This division of space, limiting and conveying sacred relationships, determines the standpoint of the individual as well as of the population in general. The city laid out "rite", according to cultic principles, is not primarily the housing for a community of dwellers and businesses, but the sanctified centre of a world directed and maintained by gods.'[28]

Conclusion

We cannot pursue these aspects further, highly interesting in themselves as they are. Here they have merely had the function of clarifying by means of a purer and more primeval case what has been preserved in a paler, but still effective form, in our own housebuilding, which can thus be helpful to us in the understanding of our own house; for our dwelling today is still rooted in these bases. It is not by accident that, more strongly than in other areas, the customs of the craft have been preserved that accompany the building of the house – the laying of a foundation stone, the topping-out ceremony and dedication of the house. Looking back from our own viewpoint we can perhaps recognize more clearly certain features noticed earlier in our analysis of house dwelling:

1. The house still remains the 'centre' of the world, but this centre stands out less clearly and is therefore more difficult to recognize. What was true then 'objectively' about the structure of the mythological world must now be taken over into the structure of 'subjectively' experienced and lived space.

2. The house still retains today a character of its own, which we can rightly comprehend only in the analogy with the sacred. From this viewpoint we understand the comparatively severe judgement of trespass, for it retains, even if only implicitly, the character of sacrilege. From this viewpoint we also understand the invulnerability of the right to hospitality, still retained today even if much more significant in earlier times. Everywhere, the guest

28 Vacano, 'Die Etrusker in der Welt der Antike', p. 27.

enjoys the protection of the house, and the master of the house watches carefully to ensure that he comes to no harm.

3. Thus the house is today still in a profound sense an invulnerable realm of peace, sharply distinguished in this sense from the troubled world outside. And even if there are no hostile demons any more, who threaten man outside his house and who must be restrained from intruding by magical means, the menacing character of this outside world has not yet disappeared, but has only taken another form.

4. Thus the house is today still an image of the world, a smaller world, whose order corresponds to that of the greater world outside. I will once again quote Bachelard: '[The house] is our first universe, a real cosmos in every sense of the world.'[29] 'It is the human being's first world.'[30] House and world correspond to each other. For the small child the house is still the whole world, and it is only because the child is rooted in the house that he can grow into the world. It is only because man lives in the house that he can then also be at home in the world, and dwell in the world.

29 Bachelard, *Poetik des Raumes*, p. 36 [p. 4].
30 Bachelard, *Poetik des Raumes*, p. 39 [p. 7].

3. The Homeliness of the Dwelling

So far we have been trying to develop the concept of the human built environment as the realm of sheltering and protection.

Human dwelling space has this special quality not only on the basis of consideration, when man realizes by a process of thought that no enemy can attack him within the walls of his own house, but he is directly, vividly present in the inhabited space. There is a perceptible character of the sheltering space. In this sense we speak of the homeliness [Wohnlichkeit] of the dwelling, of the cosiness or comfort that it conveys, of its homelike nature. Man is expected to feel at ease in this space, and we ask what is needed to give the character of homeliness to a space.

Not all spaces built by man have this character of homeliness, but they should not all have them; for not all are intended for the purpose of 'dwelling' in the strict sense, of feeling sheltered within them during one's stay. A church space is not homely, since it is intended to put us in a devotional mood. And a concert hall is not homely, since it is intended to concentrate our minds on listening to music, and so on. So it is quite a special quality of interior space that we call homeliness. But precisely this is the quality of the house in its actual sense. So we ask, what does homeliness mean and how is it created?

If we first glance at the terms that are available in the German language for this quality, the word 'Wohnlichkeit' [homeliness] does not take us any further, for all it means is suitability for dwelling. The word 'anheimelnd' [homelike] adds nothing new either, for it tells us only that a dwelling – or something else – has the necessary qualities for being a home. The word 'behaglich' [cosy] does take us a little further, for it suggests the concepts of 'Hag' [a hedge] and 'hegen', 'umhegen' [protect or cherish], that is, of protection by means of an enclosing hedge. The word "behaglich" can thus be narrowed down to the feeling of well-being in the house with its comfort and convenience.

The word 'gemütlich' [comfortable] adds another aspect. 'Gemüt' [disposition or nature] is primarily a formation from 'Mut' [courage], but soon acquires a narrower meaning in a more emotional sense. 'Gemütlich', therefore, is all conduct in which man abandons the exertion of his will and of active behaviour, and allows himself to relax in peace and quiet. In this sense he makes himself comfortable in his house, where there is a comfortable corner, a comfortable seat, and so on. Thus comfort represents an essential component of the domestic sphere in its contrast with the tension of life outside the house, even if it suggests the danger of degenerating into the negligence symbolized by dressing-gown and slippers.

A good old word, which has today unfortunately become hackneyed through overuse, is 'traut' or 'traulich' [cosy, intimate]. Today these two words have grown together so closely that it need not concern us that they are not linguistically linked to each other. 'Traulich' comes from 'trauen', to trust, and refers to the area to which one can entrust oneself with confidence.

Minkowski, in his essay 'Espace, intimité, habitat', examined this quality of the dwelling in the context of French linguistic usage as conveyed by the term intimacy, which however leads us beyond the spatial area of the dwelling into general human relationships.[1]

And so we return to the question of what it is that gives a human dwelling the quality of homeliness, of homelike-ness. We must note from the start that this is an objective question of what makes a dwelling-place suitable for dwelling, and that the sentimental aspects of feeling that are associated with many of these concepts must be excluded. We will perhaps be able to answer the question most easily if we think of the dwelling-places of friends, because our own have become too familiar to us and it is therefore harder for us to recognize their individuality. We will be able to isolate some features straight away, without, admittedly, already grasping at this point the entire nature of homeliness:

1. To start with, the dwelling space must give the impression of seclusion. If it is the task of the house to provide a refuge from the outside world, this must also find expression in the nature of the dwelling space. One cannot comfortably spend time in an entrance hall. Over-large windows, and walls made entirely of glass, which open the space to the outside world, suppress the homeliness of the space. The enthusiasm with which many currents of the new architecture adopted modern technical possibilities was at the expense of a house which would give the effect of protective enclosure and rest. While much was justified at the time in the battle against the degeneration of a bygone time, one must not, out of fear of a false

1 Minkowski, 'Espace, intimité, habitat', *Situation*, vol. 1, 1954, p. 172 ff.

'bourgeois' cosiness, destroy the true task of the dwelling, which is to be a space devoted to rest and peace. Even the window curtains which close off the space, above all at night, have a meaningful function here.

2. Furthermore, the size of the space also plays a part. Large spaces can easily appear unfriendly. A certain smallness of size seems to be rather advantageous, but excessive smallness can again be unsettling. The space must be so big that it can really be filled up by the life of the person dwelling in it. And that of course varies from one individual to another.

3. Another factor is the way in which the spaces are furnished. Bare, empty rooms have a chilling effect. A prison cell, despite its small size, does not have a homelike effect and is not intended to do so. An austere office room with its functional furniture does not have a homelike effect and is not intended to do so, because it is intended to put one in the mood for concentrated work. The furniture must fill the space in such a way that the impression is neither of emptiness nor of overcrowding.

4. A certain warmth is also part of homeliness. In winter, one cannot feel comfortable in an unheated room. One must be able to stretch out at one's ease, so furniture that invites one to sit in comfort is also part of the picture. The colour of the walls is also part of a warm atmosphere. Colours that are bright and warm at the same time lend the room an air of cheerful comfort.

5. One must also be able to see that the room has been lovingly cared for. But even though disorder and neglect have a disquieting effect, an excess of orderliness is also oppressive, because one is afraid of disturbing the order. The room must also show that it is lived in, and this means that certain signs of life – a book that has been laid aside, work that has been begun – should be recognizable in it.

6. The furniture in the room must also show that it has been lovingly chosen and cared for. Decidedly tasteless objects and cheap mass-production items are out of place. But this does not mean that particularly valuable pieces of furniture are necessary. A taste for so-called 'style in the home' and craftsman-made pieces is not sufficient to give the dwelling that homelike feeling that immediately captivates anyone who enters. Refugees who leave their goods behind and have to start again 'from nothing' have often shown in an impressive manner how, even with the simplest, indeed shabbiest, furniture an atmosphere of warmth and comfort can quickly be created. Even if this may be difficult to grasp, it is after all the charisma of a person that makes a room livable in.

7. Thus the dwelling becomes the expression of the individual who dwells in it, a piece of this individual which has become a space. So it can only be inhabitable to the extent that the person in question knows how to

dwell in it. One must be able to sense this even in a strange dwelling. The objects in it must be melted into the life of the dweller by the practice of being looked after. One cannot therefore buy a ready-made room setting, and what young couples acquire at the beginning of a marriage does not have to be tasteless in all cases, but it remains strange and cold until, after long use, by gradual acquisition of new objects and abandonment of old ones, or even through simple wear and tear, it slowly becomes assimilated.

8. Thus the dwelling must not only express an individual, but at the same time reflect a long past, if it is to give us a feeling of security and stability in life. This includes everything in it that has a 'history.' Even traces of wear and slight damage acquire a positive value in this context. In such a dwelling, gradual building is an expression of a life story; every object in it is a reminder of something, images and keepsakes, often inscrutably to strangers, keep a piece of the past alive. So the true dwelling is not artificially created, but gradually grows and takes part in the reliable security of slow growth.

9. But now a difficult question arises, which Minkowski was first to raise, very acutely, in the essay cited above: to what extent a single individual is at all capable of creating such an atmosphere of homeliness and comfort, of intimacy, as he puts it. And he stresses that this is not to be achieved by a single individual. Having already indicated that intimacy demands 'a female presence',[2] he develops this thought as follows: 'An intimate home [intérieur intime] is only one of the possibilities for expression of a human being, or more precisely a couple of human beings who strive after intimacy and know how to procure it for themselves. The dwelling of a bachelor could hardly appear intimate to us, and it will never be possible for a widower to preserve this intimacy that formerly held sway there. In such a case it inevitably vanishes away by degrees. It is equally true that one must be a couple, as human nature demands, to create intimacy around and between ourselves. And the [intérieur] now fills up with books and inconsequential odds and ends [bibelots], with joys and sorrows, with plans, with the effort to build up this life, like this dwelling, by creating there an important place for the climate of intimacy, which lies open to a small circle of sympathetic friends and close companions.'[3]

Here a decisive new thought has been taken for granted: for the single person, the bachelor, the true comfort of a dwelling is unattainable; and for one who has been left behind, alone, this comfort once again vanishes.

2 Minkowski, 'Espace, intimité, habitat', p. 183.
3 Minkowski, 'Espace, intimité, habitat', p. 180.

There may perhaps be exceptions, above all single women, who succeed in creating comfort in their dwellings, but in general we must say that it is only when humans live together that a common life story comes into being in the dwelling space that gives it its homelike atmosphere, that, in other words, it is the family that brings out the homeliness of a dwelling space. This realization is of wide-ranging importance; for it forces us to grasp the understanding of the house and of dwelling to a greater extent than we have done so far. Until now, we have seen the house only as a place of seclusion, of protective walls and a sheltering roof, that is, as a purely spatial formation. In a preliminary abstraction, we have been speaking of the single individual. But now we recognize that one cannot grasp the nature of the house at all adequately on the basis of the single individual. The community of the family living harmoniously in it is just as much part of it as the spatial enclosure by walls and roof. Dwelling is possible only in community, and a true dwelling-house demands the family. House and family belong inseparably together, in order to create human seclusion – as far as it is attainable at all. We shall return to this.[4]

The sentences quoted here from Minkowski touch on a further profound thought, which we must now particularly stress: the homeliness of the dwelling does not only create a sheltering living space for the people that live there together. It creates at the same time a point of attraction and becomes fruitful for others too. Thus we read in the sentences quoted that this home 'lies open to a small circle of sympathetic friends and close companions.' And Minkowski continues: 'For intimacy always keeps the door open, evidently not for anyone at all. Thus intimacy secures its importance in life; it demands a certain education of the heart and the mind.'[5] The liveable dwelling of another person not only captures us in its spell, but it also transforms us, as we are guided back to ourselves in the atmosphere of its intimacy.

4 See the present book, p. 281 ff.

5 Minkowski, 'Espace, intimité, habitat', p. 185.

4. Door and Window

The door

So that the house does not become a prison to man, it needs openings into the world, which link the interior of the house in an appropriate way with the outside world. They open the house to dealings with the world. This task is fulfilled in the house by the door and the window. Both are connecting parts that place the world of inside to the world of outside. But they fulfil this task in very different ways.

We will begin with the door. The one basic characteristic of the door originates from what may be called its semi-permeable character. Just as in chemistry there are certain vessels whose walls allow specific substances to permeate, but retain a certain residue, so it is with the door: the person who belongs to the house can pass freely in and out of it, and it is part of the freedom of his dwelling there that at any time he can unlock the door that has been locked from the inside, while the stranger is locked out and can only be admitted by special permission.

Man can lock the door of his house from the inside, but he is not for that reason locked into his house. If that were the case, his house would immediately become a prison to him, and the consciousness of being locked in settles on a person with a tormenting and almost unbearable pressure. He begins to rattle at the doors of his prison, even though he is convinced of the senselessness of his actions. Just as McDougall has written of a flight response which instinctively stirs even in the small child when one holds it tight and hinders its freedom of movement, the person who is locked in rebels against being deprived of his freedom. This explains all the severity of the prison sentence.

But he who locks his own door preserves his freedom, indeed in doing so he positively experiences his freedom in a particular way; for he retains the power to open the door again at any time, when it suits him. Simmel in his day referred in his profound essay 'Bridge and door' to the great importance of the door, stressing precisely this function. 'It is absolutely essential for humanity' he writes, 'that it set itself a boundary, but with freedom, that is, in such a way that it can also remove this boundary again, that it can place itself outside it.'[1] But this freedom lies in the fact that man can open his door and leave the room through it, if he wishes.

But while the person dwelling in the house can freely pass through the door, it excludes the stranger. It is only with the dweller's permission that another person can enter the house, and the former acquires an inner independence by being able to close his house to others and thus remain unreachable by them. It is also to be considered an aspect of this protection (and not one merely conditioned by building considerations) when in northern European log cabins the door is so low that the person entering must first bend down low; for this means, according to the explicit information provided by the inhabitants, that when he wants to enter this space, he must first enter into a state of defencelessness, where the person in the room could easily overpower him. A similar precaution is also found in many examples of the design of approaches to medieval castles. I will mention only in passing that the German word 'Schloss' for a castle comes from the possibility of 'verschliessen', locking up.

The consent that is required for entering a house thus distinguishes friend from foe, or merely stranger. In southern countries, houses are closed to strangers even more strictly than with us, so that contact between individuals is more likely to take place in the neutral area of the street. But conversely, if anyone is once admitted to the house, he is in future under the protection of the house, enjoys the right to hospitality, and nothing bad must be done to him in this house.

The lock

The means for closing one's own door with safety is the lock, or in more modest circumstances, the bolt. This, in its original powerful form, consists of a bar which is entirely pushed across to secure the door against break-ins.

Josef Weinheber, who in his calendar book *O Mensch, gib acht* has so splendidly described many a human household appliance, in that work also speculated about the nature, the deeper significance of the bolt.

1 Georg Simmel, 'Brücke und Tür' (1909), *Brücke und Tür. Essays*, edited by Michael Landmann, Stuttgart: 1957, p. 4 ['Bridge and door', translated by Mark Ritter, 1994; now *Simmel on culture*, edited by David Frisby and Mike Featherstone, London: 1997, p. 172].

Why [he asks] are not the gates
open by day and night?

So that traffic could pass through them in total freedom. He sees in the need to lock oneself in only the expression of a peculiar defect, a 'sign of our weakness' or 'a mark bearing witness that we are in general uncertain.' It is fear, and in particular the fear of other people, that led us to invent the bolt.

That we may peacefully sleep,
we who are always consumed by fear,
you watch over us and ours.

But Weinheber sees a reversal of the true human relationship in the fact that one always sees in other people only the dangerous enemy. 'If we but loved better', he objects, then the bolt too would be unnecessary, because then we would have nothing bad to fear any more from other people.

Thus the change of direction with which Weinheber allows his deeply thoughtful poem to die away is significant:

Still you help our fears.
Help our happiness too sometimes!
Go, my girl, push back the bolt –
the beloved one comes![2]

For the bolt serves not only to keep the interfering, hostile visitor at bay, but also, just as much, to admit the welcome visitor to the intimate realm of the house. It serves, in fact, to allow the door to become a partly open, discriminating connecting element between the inner space and the outer world. And thus, in a figurative sense, the door opened wide can also become the symbol of man's inner readiness to receive, which is expressed in the moving inscription on the city gate of Siena: 'Cor magis tibi Sena pandit' [Siena opens its heart to you even wider than its gate], and in the well-known German Advent song: 'Make the door high, make the gate wide!' Further to Weinheber's poem, however, we must ask whether it is right to attribute the use of the bolt so exclusively to insecurity and fear.

---

2 'Warum (so fragt er) sind nicht die Tore / offen bei Tag und Nacht?' 'Auf daß wir ruhig schliefen, / wir, stets von Furcht verzehrt, / bewachst du uns und Unsres.' 'Noch hilfst du unsern Ängsten. / Hilf manchmal auch dem Glück! / Geh, Mädchen, schieb den Riegel / – der Traute kommt – zurück!', J. Weinheber, *Der Riegel. Sämtliche Werke*, vol. 2, Salzburg: 1954, p. 329 ff.

While it is certainly right in primitive conditions, we must ask whether the need for security has not meanwhile become so sublimated that it is no longer a question of the protection of external life, but of the interior, intimate sphere of human life. In that case it would, independently of all external threats, be the need to be alone with oneself that leads us to retreat into our houses and lock ourselves in.

The threshold

Going through the door means crossing the threshold, which is the term usually used for the lower beam of the door. The threshold, even more precisely, therefore indicates with even greater certainty the border between inside and outside. Crossing the threshold is therefore often used in high-flown speech, the part for the whole, for entering the house. One greets an honoured guest at the threshold of one's house.

So far, we have looked at the door predominantly from the point of view of someone who is at home within his dwelling under its protection. The circumstances are quite different for the person who, coming from outside, enters the space through the door; for by doing so he enters into the other person's living space – or, if we adopt the analogous case of the temple ultimately meaning the same as the house, into the deity's area of power. This is the origin of the high cultic significance that the threshold had in earlier religions, much of which has been preserved in the customs of rural areas.[3] Special veneration is due to it. One bows before it, piously touches it with one's hand, and in particular avoids the ominous action of kicking it with one's foot, or carries one's bride in one's arms over the threshold. For this reason Van der Leeuw stresses throughout his *Phänomenologie der Religion*: 'The threshold too was the sacred boundary possessing its own special power.'[4] In the same vein, Eliade has recently also referred to the great importance of the threshold as the border between the sacred and the profane, and has thus contributed significantly to the understanding of today's customs. 'The threshold, the door', he says, 'show the solution of continuity in space immediately and concretely; hence their great religious importance, for they are symbols and at the same time vehicles of passage

---

3 See L. Weser-Aall, *Handwörterbuch des deutschen Aberglaubens*, 7 vols., edited by v. H. Bächtold-Stäubli, and Pauly-Wissowa, *Realenzyklopädie der klassischen Altertumswissenschaft*.

4 Van der Leeuw, *Phänomenologie der Religion*, p. 449 [p. 396].

from one space to another.'[5] Religions, therefore, also have much to tell us about special guardians and protectors of the threshold, which hinder the intrusion of hostile powers, and according to still current superstition, all sorts of spirits gather there which besiege the house and must be held at bay by various magical means.

The gate as a place of transition at the same time also acquires at this point a deeper symbolic meaning: it is the place of transition to a new life, as for example is meant by the demand in the Gospel: 'Enter through the narrow gate.'

The window

The window is a different matter from the door, and here again it is various functions of life that are combined in this simple component of the human life environment. Here, where we are primarily concerned with the relationship between inner and outer space, I will disregard the simplest task of the window, which is to illuminate the inner space. This is an unrewarding aspect in this context, and in this respect the window could of course be replaced by artificial lighting.

The window's most straightforward tasks, then, include the opportunity to observe the outside world from the inner space. Long before man had learnt to manufacture larger glazed windows, there was at least the spyhole, through which one could survey the surroundings of the house on the approach of a possibly threatening stranger. This is already indicated by the earlier Germanic words, later superseded by the Latin loan-word, such as 'Augentor' [eye-gate] (that is an opening to the outside, intended only for looking through, not for actually moving through) for the side openings of the house formed by gaps between walls and roof-beams.[6] In terms such as 'Windauge' [wind-eye], 'Ochsenauge' [ox-eye], 'Bullauge' [bull's eye or porthole] and the rest, in other Indo-Germanic languages too, the window is interpreted as the eye of the house, and in addition, it may also be the case that the windows themselves – for example, as openings in a wall made of woven willow – originally were often formed as eyes. Reversing this comparison, Keller in one passage calls the eyes his 'dear little windows.' Such spyholes after all are still often used in urban flats, and the apprehensive housewife quickly glances through the little hole in

5 Eliade, *Das heilige und das Profane*, p. 16 [p. 25].
6 See *Trübners Deutsches Wörterbuch.*

the door before she opens it to the visitor announcing himself from the outside.

The unilateral permeability of the opening in the wall, already noted in the door, is also quite noticeable in the window. The ability to see without being seen, this basic principle of careful security procedure, is realized in its purest form in the window. While earlier we considered the function of the bolt as that of an instrument of human fear, the bolt in this respect requires to be supplemented by the spyhole, if we do not want to be blindly exposed to the possible preparations for attack by an enemy. But, just as earlier with the bolt, it should here be pointed out that in a further development, the observation of the outside world, originally born of fear, gives way to a more general pleasure in observation. Langeveld pointed out how deeply the desire for a hiding-place lies in the child, a place from which he can observe the world around him, while himself remaining concealed and unobserved. Dreaming in such a hiding-place, he senses the joy of a delightful concealment.[7] What we can here observe so directly and vividly in the child is also correspondingly true of a deeply grounded need in the human adult. Even if the spyhole has long ago become a wide window, he feels the need, in his secluded space, to keep an eye on the world outside. From a window he sees the world spread out before him in all its brightness, but the world does not see him, for he is hidden in the darkness of the room. Curtains of fabric or net have been used extensively to heighten the window's opaqueness, while it is typical of the modern style of living that it uses large areas of glass to open the house up to the outside world. But conversely, when man is exposed to the gaze of strangers in a brightly lit room at night, he feels insecure and likes to close the curtains and shutters.

Orientation in the environment

But when the spyhole widens into a window, which no longer focuses on a single potential enemy, but fully admits the whole picture of the surrounding world, the function of the window immediately changes. It now opens up the inner space to the world as a whole. Through the window, the small dwelling space is placed within the large world, and the window makes it possible to orient oneself in this world. Through the

7 M. J. Langeveld, 'L'"endroit secret" dans la vie de l'enfant', *Situation*, vol. 1, 1954, p. 124 ff.

window one looks out into the open air, one sees the sky and the horizon (or at any rate a part of the outside world, in which the latter, if not actually visible itself, is invisibly present). So through the window the human inner space is observably and clearly positioned in the great order of horizontal and vertical, which in a totally closed space is only indirectly given by the floor and the objects that stand on it.

From this need for further orientation comes the uncanny feeling of underground shelters. One feels trapped, constrained, in such spaces. Recent newspaper reports have stated that in such underground spaces American military forces have at least been able with the help of large pictures to give the illusion of an unobstructed view of the landscape, in order to remove the oppressive atmosphere of a long stay. A similar policy of building modern concert-halls without windows from the start, which is of course perfectly possible with artificial means of lighting and ventilation, has as its object the avoidance of the frequent descent of darkness and its repeated elimination. It is not a romantic custom that impels people to cling to windows. It is from a need for freedom that we demand windows, and resists the sense of enclosure in a windowless space.

Of course it is different where it is a question of temporary enclosure, for example of the feeling of seclusion and security radiated by the living room when it is lit by night, while the family sits around the lamp with closed shutters. Here we do not feel at all constrained, because we are always aware that it is a temporary state, which has to do with the general rhythm of day and night, and that the world will open up to us again with the dawn of a new day. The opening of the shutters in the morning is always at the same time a joyful opening up to renewed contact with the world. The impression of space of, for example, the Pantheon in Rome, when the outside world seems to be cut away and the sky looks in from above through one great eye, is to be comprehended in this sense: man feels entirely collected within himself, because the view of the visible world is forbidden to him, and nevertheless a piece of infinity always remains present.

The transporting effect of the window

And one last aspect of the distinction between window and door must be added here, although it might perhaps have found its suitable place at an earlier point: one goes through the door, but one looks out of the window. This simple and apparently all too obvious statement actually says a great deal about the difference between the two openings of the house to the outside world. One actually goes through the door and is then outside the house. With the window (the 'eye-gate'), however, one only looks out with one's eyes, but stays inside. But this means that the world is present in very different ways in the two cases: with the door, the world is palpably there, one needs only to go out in order to reach some point or other in person. With the window, however, one sees the world through the glass sheet, and this glass, even if it is apparently invisible (or almost invisible), changes the world in a very decisive manner.

Indeed the opened window itself, even without the separating sheet of glass, has a similarly transporting effect.

When we look through the window, the world recedes into the distance (for the path to it – as we are always aware in the deep recesses of our consciousness – leads us through turning away from the window, on to the door, to which the path is usually longer). Window-frame, mullion and transom emphasize this effect, for they transport what is seen through the window, they cut a specific section out of the surrounding world and make it into an 'image.' To that extent, the window idealizes the part of the world that is cut out and isolated in this way.

Rilke, who in his poems has repeatedly endeavoured to capture the transporting and idealizing effect of the mirror,[8] attempted to interpret the nature of the window from this viewpoint in his French cycle of poems 'Les fenêtres.'[9] The window is for him the 'measure of expectation', 'ô mesure d'attente', which raises us out of the world only for a period suitable for us. To this extent it is the 'grasp by which the great too-much of the outside brings itself into line with us.' In its framing effect it is the form brought to it by man, 'our geometry' as Rilke says, through which what is seen in the window is cut out of the endlessly flowing surroundings and is lifted to the level of pure pictorial quality. What is seen through the window seems to be removed from chance: 'Tous les hasards sont abolis.' It becomes an image, 'il devient son image', and is to that extent removed to a timeless, ideal sphere: 'Tu la rends presque éternelle', says Rilke of his beloved appearing in the window.

Thus it is an inexhaustible secret that is revealed by the thoughtful observation of the window. And just as for Rilke in the last passage quoted above it is the beloved other person whose ideal image appears in the frame

8 See O. F. Bollnow, *Rilke*, Stuttgart: 1956, p. 250 ff.

9 Rainer Maria Rilke, *Gedichte in französischer Sprache*, Wiesbaden: 1949, p. 85 ff.

of the window, so also the motif of the person in the window has, time and again, with its profundity stimulated the artist to portray it. The human figure, gazing pensively out of the window, absorbed in the contemplation of the landscape, preoccupied by the endlessness of the landscape and yet again taken out of the landscape by the distance of his gaze, and thus removed from the direct pressure of reality – this is how he has been seen above all by the Romantics. We may perhaps be reminded of the verses of Eichendorff:

> The stars were shining so golden,
> I stood at the window alone,
> and heard from the far distance
> a post-horn in the silent land.[10]

But this would lead us beyond the sphere of the present inquiry, which must for now first search in the simplest possible way for the meaning of door and window, these openings in the house, for the understanding of human dwelling.

10 'Es schienen so golden die Sterne, / am Fenster ich einsam stand / und hörte aus weiter Ferne / ein Posthorn im stillen Land', Eichendorff, 'Sehnsucht', *Heimweh*, vol. 1, p. 35.

5. The Bed

Hearth and table as the middle of the house

We started from the premise that space specifically experienced by man, in contrast to unstructured space, is built up around a specific centre and that this centre again is not to be determined as an abstract mathematical point, but for its own part forms a definite space, a heart-space as we may call it: that is, a closed space of shelter and security as opposed to the threatening expanse of the outside world. And we found this sheltering space to begin with in the house, built by human labour, with its protective walls and its sheltering roof and its doors and windows, mediating components which enable contact with the outside world. But the house with its various rooms, with its loft and cellar, is itself again a comparatively extensive and spacious structure, itself richly structured, so that the question recurs as to whether one cannot determine the centre of living space even more precisely within the house.

If we go back to simple country conditions and in particular keep in mind the ancient world, we find a common centre of the house of this kind. In a quite literal sense this is the hearth, which in those days stood in the spatial centre of the house and also had a directly sacred significance: the hearth as altar. In the Germanic realm too, the hearth originally stood in the centre of the house. The smoke escaped through the opening in the roof above it. The hearth fire, which did not go out even at night, but was carefully tended under the ashes, was thus the central point of domestic life.

Even today, the hearth has retained some remnant of this sacred significance. House and hearth are often linked together in everyday speech. 'One's own hearth is worth gold', says a common German proverb, and Schiller too speaks of 'the shrine of the hearth' that must be defended. The hearth becomes synonymous with the household. Even if, in a figurative sense, we speak of a 'Krankheitsherd' [the focus of a disease], this denotes the basis and actual seat of the disorder. But to the extent that in modern dwellings the kitchen has become a subsidiary space, the hearth too has lost its position as centre of the house, until finally, in the form of the modern electric cooker, it has even lost its outward symbol, the visible flame.

To a certain extent, the dining table has replaced the hearth. This is now the place at which, and around which, the whole family gathers at regular times of day. The table too has preserved its symbolic significance in many proverbial phrases. Thus, to have one's feet under the table is today still considered the expression of the dominance of the master of the house, in particular the father of the family, in contrast to his still dependent children.

The bed as centre

Hearth and table in this way became symbols of the family's common centre. But to the extent to which the communal life of the family breaks up and that of the individual components gains independence, both lose their function as central points, and the question arises as to where the individual is to find a corresponding centre within the house, to which all his various paths within and outside the house are related. Now I believe that this centre is best designated as the bed; for the bed is the place from which we rise in the morning to go to our daily work, and to which we return in the evening when our work is done. The course of every day (in the normal state of affairs) begins in bed and also ends in bed. And it is the same with human life: it begins in bed, and it also ends (again, assuming normal circumstances) in bed. So it is in the bed that the circle closes, the circle of the day as well as that of life. Here, in the deepest sense, we find rest. From here, therefore, we derive the task of investigating the significance of the bed for the structure of human life, and in particular of the space lived and experienced by humanity.

And here we notice to what a small extent the bed seems until now to have stimulated human thought. Who among the poets has given it its due praise? Who among the thinkers has tried to discover its significance for human life? We can find only a few examples, and even these are difficult to find, because they mostly occur concealed in other contexts. It is a rare exception when Weinheber, to whom we will soon return in more detail, praises the bed with genuine emotion:

> Holy household bed!
> Whoever thinks of you falls silent.[1]

1 'Heiliger Hausratt Bett! / Still wird, wer dich bedenkt.' Weinheber, 'Das Bett', *Sämtliche Werke*, vol. 2, p. 281.

This lack of attention is clearly due not only to the inconspicuousness of this silent piece of furniture, but also to its secrecy. It belongs to an 'intimate' area of life which is not much discussed. Apart from furniture shops, where it is placed shamelessly on display, it belongs to a private area which, as such, is again separated from the rest of the house. The bedroom too is usually out of bounds to visitors. And so it is characteristic that language has produced a number of alternative names to help us avoid direct reference to the bed. It is known as the 'pit', the 'sack', etc. Trübner's German dictionary includes circumlocutions such as 'to go to Bethlehem' or 'to Bettingen' (from 'bed'), 'to Liegnitz' (from 'liegen', to lie), etc. The bed is the only common piece of furniture to be provided with such an abundance of circumlocutions, and this is already an indication that it belongs to an area which people do not like to specify explicitly.

Indications from linguistic and cultural history

Once again, links with linguistic history provide a first indication of the function of the bed in our lives. The word 'bed' is presumed to have an original Indo-Germanic meaning as 'a sleeping-place or hollow dug out of the ground.'[2] In this sense, there is of course also a river-bed and a flower-bed. This is interesting for our purposes in so far as it gives us the word 'bed' in its original meaning, directly linked with that of 'room', which, as we found earlier, meant a sleeping-place carved out of the forest thicket, a clearing. This seems to suggest a deeper inner connection: the bed, so to speak, repeats on a smaller scale the same function that the sleeping-place in the clearing performed on a larger, that is, the creation of a surrounding space of safety, a hollowed-out space in which one can move freely. It is also significant that the word 'Weile' or 'while' is closely connected with this basic meaning. Linguistic scholars link it with the Old Norse words 'hvila', a bed, and 'hvild', rest. The bed is therefore the place where, in the actual sense, one spends a while, whiles away the time, that is, where one habitually stays.

This is not the place to go into more detail about the complex cultural history of the bed.[3] We will take the living customs of modern European culture as our starting point, without closer differentiation. But it is important to keep in mind that a bed as we understand it today, a wooden

2 *Trübners Deutsches Wörterbuch.* I draw attention once again to the relevant dictionaries.

3 I regrettably had no access to Mary Eden and Richard Carrington, *The philosophy of the bed* (London: 1961) and had to rely on more easily available reference works.

frame containing a mattress, is a new concept. It was late in arriving in central and northern Europe from the south. Most peoples outside Europe, for example the cultures of the Far East, do not know it at all. Even the old Germanic tribes slept on animal pelts, and only later did they place benches for sleeping against the walls of their dwellings. But since then the southern form of bed has become so well established that since the Middle Ages a bed without a frame was only in use among the poor or penitent. And let us remember, only briefly in passing, that the need to create a special space of total separation in the house, in the form of the bed, led to the development of various characteristic forms of bed. It was often screened off by curtains, or a special bed area was explicitly created by means of a canopy fixed to posts, or indeed the bed was placed in a lockable cupboard or bunk.

Characteristic of the human desire to create an unshakeably firm basis within the world in the bed is the custom, apparently widespread in earlier times, of built-in, that is, immovably fixed beds. Homer's account of the bed of Odysseus provides a fine example. When, on his return home, Penelope attempts to test him with the remark that she has had his bed moved to a different place, Odysseus replies:

> 'Penelope, ... you exasperate me! Who, if you please, has moved my bed elsewhere? Short of a miracle, it would be hard even for a skilled workman to shift it somewhere else, and the strongest young fellow alive would have a job to budge it. For a great secret went into the making of that complicated bed; and it was my work and mine alone.'[4]

And he describes how he took the stem of an olive tree, rooted firmly in the ground, and after lopping off its crown and carefully smoothing the stem, created from it the main post of the bed, and constructed the rest of the sleeping space around it. Immovably rooted in the ground, the bedpost is here the firm axis of the world, to which the hero returns after long wanderings, a magnificent symbol of this fixed point of reference.

Security in the bed

Everywhere, the bed, with its warmth and comfort, gives us a sense of peace and security. Job says, 'My bed shall comfort me, my couch

---

4 *Odyssey*, book 23, verse 183 ff. [translated by E. V. Rieu, Harmondsworth: 1946, p. 357].

shall ease my complaints.'[5] According to Trübner's dictionary, 'It is the proverbial place of security', and he quotes the Swabian proverb, 'He who is afraid is not safe in his bed', that is, even in this most secure of places he does not feel safe. There have been strong men who simply fled to their beds when the difficulties of life threatened to overwhelm them. On the medical side, Fraenkel too stresses 'that even in psychologically healthy people a terrifying experience is best worked off by a day of bed rest.'[6] When we pull the covers over our heads, we experience something similar to what is falsely attributed to the ostrich. But it is easy to pass over such forms of self-deception with mere mockery. The problem lies deeper. It is linked to the vital function that the bed has to fulfil as a space of security in human life. Thomas Mann quotes the passage in Tolstoy's memoirs in which Tolstoy speaks of the pain he experienced 'when the end of childhood was signalled by the fact that he moved from the care of women to be with his older brothers on the lower floor.' He writes: 'It was difficult for me to separate myself from my accustomed life (accustomed for an eternity). I was sad … less because I had to separate myself from people, my nurse, my sisters, my aunt, than from my little bed, with its curtain, its pillows, and I was anxious about the new life I was entering.'[7] Here the bed becomes most profoundly the place in which the reliable permanence of life is concentrated.

This great significance of the bed as providing inner peace even in the lives of adults has been emphasized most aptly in verse by Weinheber:

> Sickness, pain and struggle
> come to you: take care!
> And you will relieve the cramp,
> drip healing into the blood;
> give us who go astray
> and sway in the wind
> a blissful slender feeling
> that we are secure.[8]

---

5 Job 7:13.

6 Albert Fraenkel, 'Über das Bett als Therapeutikum', *Pathologie und Therapie der Zirkulationsstörungen*, Leipzig: 1930, p. 69 ff., p. 76.

7 Thomas Mann, 'Goethe und Tolstoi', *Leiden und Größe der Meister*, Frankfurt a. M.: 1957, p. 58.

8 'Kranksein, Leiden und Kampf / kommen zu Dir: Machs gut! / Und du lösest den Krampf, / träufelst Heilung ins Blut; / gibst uns, die von dem Ziel / abirrn und schwanken im Wind / selig ein schmales Gefühl / daß wir geborgen sind.' Weinheber, *Sämtliche Werke*, vol. 2, p. 282.

So it is in the bed that the distresses of life are dissolved into a 'slender feeling', in the restrained words of the poet, of security, 'slender' in so far as this security is won only for the duration of a night, after which follows a new day with new dangers.

But the same characteristic which is expressed here in poetic form by Weinheber is at the same time confirmed from the point of view of the observations of phenomenological psychology. Thus Van den Berg says of the healthy person (as opposed to the quite different situation of the invalid), 'For him, the bed is the attribute of night. He finds himself received by it with the same sweetness every night, and he summarizes his thoughts in the sentence, "For the healthy sleeper the world is silence, silent expectation that all will be well".'[9] Similarly, Linschoten remarks, 'It is the characteristic of security that makes it possible for me to fall asleep [in bed].'[10]

The upright posture

So we must now go on to ask how it comes about that the bed, of all things, is given this particular importance as a place of ultimate security in the environment shaped by man. It cannot simply rest on the fact that the bed is the place for sleeping, since to be able to sleep, one must already have a sense of security. It must have something to do with the earlier process of lying down; for the human being lies in bed, even though he otherwise maintains an upright posture in life, with various modifications. In order to understand this, we must take account of the relationship between standing (or walking) upright and simply lying down. This contrast between standing and lying is known to animals, but only in the upright posture of humans – that is, in the transition from four-legged to two-legged walking – does it appear in its full clarity (but we will not linger here on this difference). To understand what it means when a human lies down in a bed, we must first try to grasp what it means when he stands upright.

When we lie down in order to sleep, this is not just a movement within space where space stands still and we move in it, but there is a basic change in the relationship between man and space, and at the same time (in the sense of our introductory observations) between man and experienced space

9 J. H. van den Berg, '"Garder le lit", essay d'une psychologie du malade', *Situation*, vol. 1, 1954, p. 68 ff., p. 83 ff.

10 Johannes Linschoten, 'Over het inslapen', *Tijdschrift voor Philosophie*, 1952; German translation 'Über das Einschlafen', *Philosophische Beiträge*, vol. 2, 1955, no. 1 and 2, p. 274.

itself. This change rests on the profound difference between standing, or maintaining an upright posture, and lying down. Standing always requires a continuous strain, in order to resist the force of gravity. Here we might distinguish in detail between the four-legged stance of the animal and the upright posture of man, as well as the various forms of standing, sitting, bending down, etc., in man – but we will not discuss these differences further. We will speak in a general sense of man's upright posture. We must linger a little over this concept; for on closer observation only the upright posture can in the strict sense be called a 'posture.' When standing, man must hold himself upright in the literal sense, that is, he must make a continual effort to remain upright, and this is always an individual effort in opposition to the natural forces of gravity. Standing upright is thus actually a continually renewed keeping of oneself upright, which must be wrested anew at every moment from the forces of gravity.

This posture is to be understood not as something merely corporeal, but it determines and permeates the whole relationship of man with his world. This concept has been very convincingly presented by Erwin Straus in his seminal work on 'the upright posture.' In this posture, man frees himself from his direct dependence on the world around him, and the upward direction at the same time includes the symbolic significance of this concept. 'The upright posture', Straus emphasizes, 'points upwards, away from the ground. It is the opposite direction to the binding, confining force of gravity. In standing upright we begin to free ourselves from the direct power of physical forces.'[11] So it is in the upright posture that man realizes his own freedom and freely opposes himself to the world around him. In it, he gains a clear distance from the things of the world. The space around him becomes the field of his free perspective. 'There is a great deal of space around the upright man,' Straus points out.[12] And as a result of this distance, the world becomes an object towards which he can behave with freedom. 'In standing upright,' Straus continues, 'man attains status in the world; he gains the possibility of being independent of the world, to shape himself and the world.'[13] Thus the relationship of tension between man and world characterizes man in his upright posture.

11 Erwin Straus, 'Die aufrechte Haltung. Eine anthropologische Studie', now in *Psychologie der menschlichen Welt*, p. 244 ff., p. 226 ['The upright posture', *Phenomenological psychology. The selected papers of Erwin Straus*, translated by Erling Eng, London: 1966, p. 137 ff.; the original German citations could not be located in the translation].

12 Straus, 'Die aufrechte Haltung', p. 230.

13 Straus, 'Die aufrechte Haltung', p. 226.

The concept of posture thus acquires a special sense, which goes far beyond the physical. Linschoten, to whose work on falling asleep, already mentioned above, we will need to return in more detail, has presented this concept clearly when he writes: '"Posture" refers not only to the position of the body, but also to the behaviour of the person, which we may call an inner posture.'[14] In addition, in his book on human nature,[15] Hans Lipps has developed the concept of posture in a general sense, expanding even further what Linschoten interprets as an 'inner posture', and I myself, in my book on 'the nature of moods' have tried to categorize this concept in a comprehensive anthropological connection.[16] Unlike the mood, which comes upon the person and permeates his entire world, posture is quite generally a certain inner formation which man has given himself, and which then reacts to his relationship with the world, to other people and in general to the questions of life. Unlike the unreflective 'behaviour' in the world, posture always presupposes an explicit behaviour towards oneself and thus an inner freedom, in which he can himself confront his natural condition. And this in itself makes possible a clear distance from the world. Here there is an essential difference between man and animals. The animal has no posture, because it still has 'the unbroken relationship with its nature.'[17] But posture always presupposes self-awareness and thus the distance, the tension in relation to the world. Having 'posture', Lipps says, 'means superior distance; one safeguards oneself in it.'[18]

Lying down

The understanding of posture now becomes decisive for the understanding of what happens to us when we lie down. For there seems to be a natural connection according to which the inner posture can be kept upright only together with the outer posture, that is, man can only have inner posture in the tension of his physical posture, but in the position of lying down he loses the possibility of inner posture. In this context, although he is referring to the next stage, going to sleep, Linschoten writes: 'Going to sleep means giving up one's posture. This is true not only of the body, but

14 Linschoten, 'Über das Einschlafen', p. 279.
15 Hans Lipps, *Die menschliche Natur*, Frankfurt a. M.: 1941, p. 18 ff.
16 O. F. Bollnow, *Das Wesen der Stimmungen*, Frankfurt a. M.: 1956, p. 154 ff.
17 Lipps, *Die menschliche Natur*, p. 19.
18 Lipps, *Die menschliche Natur*, p. 23.

also for the person as a whole.'[19] But this loss of posture does not only take place in the process of falling asleep, but is directly noticeable in merely lying down. So we must distinguish between the two conditions, which are usually linked in literature without distinction. Certainly Straus is correct in pointing out on one occasion that 'only in wakefulness can man stay upright',[20] but this does not mean, conversely, that man must immediately fall asleep if he abandons the upright posture. The person lying down already has a different relationship with the world from that of the one standing upright. Indeed this is true to a certain degree even of merely sitting. One needs only to let oneself fall into a comfortable chair to notice how the tension of the posture falls away from one, and how one becomes more 'peaceful' and reacts less actively to the stimuli of the environment.

This means in our context that someone lying down has lost the relationship of tension with the world, which is exactly what we have identified as characteristic of the inner posture. In this connection, Vetter writes: 'The transition from the upright posture to being horizontal with the ground is an abandonment of the general confrontation which man adopts in being awake.'[21] Here, admittedly, being awake is equated with the upright posture, while we are for the time being concerned with the conditions in which one is lying down, in particular in bed, although not yet asleep. But even for these conditions, most of what has been noted in the literature about falling asleep is valid. This includes, for example, Linschoten's observation: 'Everything that the upright posture means to us: the confrontation between person and world, the process of straightening up and grasping for what is above us, or of access to the distance, the tangible nearness of things around us, the clarity of the space in which we find ourselves, the free choice of place, all this is abandoned when falling asleep.'[22] And similarly, Straus writes: 'that we, in lying down to sleep, stretching out, give ourselves up completely to the world; we stop asserting ourselves towards the world.'[23] This is true, as we have noted, to a great extent from merely lying down, even though, of course, falling asleep represents a further step towards the abandonment of confrontation.

It follows from this (to return to our specific problem), that the person lying in bed has a different relationship with space, or rather, he has a different space from one who is moving in an upright posture. This is true

19 Linschoten, 'Über das Einschlafen', p. 279.
20 Straus, 'Die aufrechte Haltung', p. 225.
21 A. Vetter, *Die Erlebnisbedeutung der Phantasie*, Stuttgart: 1950, p. 118.
22 Linschoten, 'Über das Einschlafen', p. 275.
23 Straus, 'Die aufrechte Haltung', p. 225.

even in quite an external sense: if, in the ordinary world of the person moving in an upright posture, the distance of things and their arrangement relative to each other is determined by their attainability, that is, by the (virtual) movement that would be necessary in order to grasp them, then for someone lying in bed they move into a much greater distance, because he can no longer reach them without leaving the bed. And this always demands a substantial inner effort. I will here refer once again to Van den Berg's work, already mentioned, in which this alteration of the world around us is described as follows: 'The world has reduced itself to the dimensions of my bedroom, or rather, of my bed. For even if I only place my feet on the floor, I am under the impression of entering an unknown zone. To go to the lavatory becomes a kind of unfamiliar excursion ... When I return from there, at the moment when I pull the covers over my head I have a sense of being back at home.'[24]

This is also true in a more general sense. Not only are objects apparently taken away, into a distant world, which is not only difficult for me to reach, but which also no longer has anything to do with me inwardly; but also, the challenges posed to me by this world impinge upon me only in a confused manner, as though from an uncertain distance. They no longer directly concern me, and the cares that assailed me only a short time ago already weigh less heavily upon me. Even the telephone rings differently when I am lying in bed. I no longer feel obliged to be constantly ready to answer every call; I can simply let it ring, and am pleased when it stops ringing of its own accord. And this is the situation in general.

I am no longer consciously reacting to a world that objectively confronts me, but feel in harmony with warm and pleasant surroundings. Just as in the physical sense I am not forced into resistance by some hard object, so too I no longer need to exert my will-power. I am again at one with my world. And from this comes the feeling of a boundless security which surrounds me in bed. 'You drip healing into the blood', says Weinheber, and this exactly describes the state of affairs. Lying in bed, I find the state of security that allows me to abandon myself and really fall asleep.

From this point we experience most deeply the necessary function of the bed in the whole of human life. Certainly sleep also comes outside the bed. It can overcome us in other circumstances when we are in a state of exhaustion. But this is only the sudden breaking off of attention, because we no longer have the strength to remain awake; it is not the true sleep that releases us, to which we peacefully abandon ourselves in a feeling of

24 Van den Berg, '"Garder le lit", essay d'une psychologie du malade', p. 70.

pleasant well-being. The creation of the outward conditions for this deep, genuine sleep, that is, a realm of perfect security, is the task of the bed. The bed is a space of protective seclusion of this kind, and to that extent it is the ultimate heightening of the security of the house.

6. Waking up and Falling Asleep

The alteration of our conscious attitude while lying down thus necessarily leads to the deeper problems of sleep and the transitional processes from the waking to the sleeping condition, going to sleep and waking up. Lying down when tired is often only a preliminary step to falling asleep, and therefore the two processes have often not been distinguished from each other in the examples cited so far. In our considerations about the position of lying down, it has been presumed that one cannot comprehend the alternation of waking and sleeping as though the nature of our self remains unchanged from one state to the other, or that the stability of experienced time is interrupted every night only by sleep, and in the morning is simply picked up again where it was interrupted by sleep the night before. Rather, the self is transformed in these processes, and with it, simultaneously, the world around it. Every night man descends into a greater depth in which his conscious self is dissolved in a more comprehensive medium, and every morning this self – together with the world around it – is built up again anew. This may at first appear to be a rather daring statement, an airy speculation, and yet it is nothing but the conclusion which necessarily results from the specific experiences of humans every day when going to sleep and waking up.

The processes of going to sleep and waking up thus acquire a particular philosophical significance; for one may hope to bring to light in them connections that are once more covered up in the usual waking consciousness. Thus the question arises for us: what actually happens when one falls asleep and when one wakes up again? These processes take place in man every day entirely as a matter of course, and yet it is enormously difficult to determine anything reliable about them. For to a great extent they resist systematic observation. On the one hand, it is part of their nature that consciousness is not yet, or no longer, present. They lie on the edge of twilight consciousness. It is essentially only our memory that, when full consciousness is reached, is capable in retrospect of capturing the blurred shadows, that is, bringing into consciousness what was unconsciously experienced earlier. But this succeeds only to a limited extent, and this fixing is further hindered by the fact that these are very rapid processes, whose individual phases follow each other with exceptional rapidity, seem to flow into each other and can only with difficulty be distinguished from each other. Therefore, methodical caution directs us to abandon our individual observations, carried out for this purpose; for these could too easily be influenced by systematic questioning and initial expectations. It is safer to rely on the statements of others, even though these, because of the fleeting and inconspicuous nature of the processes we are discussing, are rare, and successful only in the case of a few sensitive observers. We are grateful for every one of these statements. Once we have disentangled their individual elements, it will be possible to distinguish their basic theme and to review and confirm the evidence by means of our own observations.

a. *Waking up*

We will begin, appropriately, with the process of waking up; for this has the advantage that after this process we immediately find ourselves in a state of full consciousness and can still recall it while our memory is fresh. Let us look at two statements of a phenomenal sensitivity, which reciprocally support and happily complement each other. One is the poetic description by Marcel Proust in the opening pages of his *A la recherche du temps perdu* [In search of lost time],[1] and the other the psychological observations of Graf Dürckheim in his 'Untersuchungen zum gelebten Raum' [Investigations into experienced space],[2] already mentioned, which he already places in the context, decisive for us, of the question of experienced space.

In what follows, we will also attempt to restrict ourselves, when looking into these very complex processes, to this one aspect: the question of what they have to tell us for the understanding of experienced space.

The uncertain sense of existence

If we take both descriptions together for purposes of comparison, we find that man, in the moment of waking up, does not immediately find

1 Marcel Proust, *Der Weg zu Swann*, Berlin: 1926.

2 Karlfried Graf Dürckheim, 'Untersuchungen zum gelebten Raum', *Neue Psychologische Studien*, vol. 6, Munich: 1932, p. 383 ff.

himself in his familiar space. Rather, at first he finds himself in a condition of total non-spatiality. It takes several steps for space to build up, and it is only the result of these intermediate steps that he at last finds himself again in his usual space. Parallel to this, another simultaneous process takes place: he does not yet find himself as this specific, individual ego. This too is a gradual process – and one which takes place in strict correlation to the building up of the spatial environment. This however gives the process a special significance in our context; for we will hope to gain an insight into the processes in which space is built up for people in general, and to take apart the layers in which this building up takes place.

The one feature that is striking here is the extraordinary brevity of the process. Graf Dürckheim speaks of 'moments', Proust of the 'few seconds' for which this process lasted.

Proust describes the first moment of waking up as follows: '…when I awoke at midnight, not knowing where I was, I could not be sure at first who I was; I had only the most rudimentary sense of existence, such as may lurk and flicker in the depths of an animal's consciousness; I was more destitute of human qualities than the cave-dweller; but then the memory … [would] draw me up out of the abyss of not-being, from which I could never have escaped by myself.'[3] Beyond the identification of a certain being-somewhere and being-someone there is a still undifferentiated sense which Proust describes as 'the sense of existence such as may lurk and flicker in the depths of an animal's consciousness.' It is only memory that gradually lifts man out of this uncertainty.

In the differentiation of these stages I will follow the description, more detailed in this respect, of Graf Dürckheim. He writes, in the passage cited: 'Everyone remembers moments of awakening in which "all orientation" is lost. By this term we do not mean orientation as knowing where one actually is, but we are thinking of those singular cases when one awakes, perhaps in an unfortunate position, and for a moment simply loses all sense of direction. One does not know what is up and what is down, or rather, there is no up or down; one does not yet have it. There is no sense of direction of the subject and thus no spatial certainty of any kind. These are moments of a strangely characterless, non-centred suspension-in-the-void. It is a total state of weightlessness, bodilessness, spacelessness, neither fixed in itself nor flowing in any direction, without consciousness of space and, significantly, no actual sense of self-awareness.'[4] Proust too

3 Proust, *Der Weg zu Swann*, p. 10.
4 Dürckheim, 'Untersuchungen', p. 400.

points out that it is predominantly in cases where one has fallen asleep at an unusual time in an unaccustomed position that these experiences make a particularly forceful impression. What emerges more clearly from Dürckheim's account is the more precise definition of what is meant when we say that we do not yet know 'where' we are. This simple 'sense of existence' to which Proust refers is not only a not-knowing the point in space where one finds oneself, but beyond this, the total lack of spatial direction. We do not know what is up and what is down, and in this sense it is a 'a strangely characterless, non-centred suspension-in-the-void.' And characteristically he also refers here to the lack of an actual sense of self-awareness. So, at the beginning, the first stage of awakening, we are in a state which can best be described as a still uncertain, still non-spatial and strange sense of oneself.

The building up of near space

Then comes the second stage, which is sharply distinguished from the first only by Graf Dürckheim. It is still not as yet the specific determination of place, but before that a general determination of direction that forms here. First, because of the sensation of lying on a base, is the orientation of above and below, through becoming aware of one's own position in space. In the writer's own words: 'The first thing that generally frees us from this state [of uncertainty] is the sudden experience of the "ground", the experience of a sudden finding of oneself and the simultaneous separation of the base [on which one lies] and the body that rests upon it. We have achieved an awareness of position.'[5] We know where we are, and in this sense are in an initial manner oriented in space.

The first step towards structuring spatial orientation, then, is the experience of above and below, that is, the realization of a vertical axis, and it is only from this point that the further orientation in space is built up. The next step is the position of the limbs, and around them the first parts of the surrounding room. Proust writes, for example: 'My body, still too heavy with sleep to move, would make an effort to construe the form which its tiredness took as an orientation of its various members, so as to induce from that where the wall lay and the furniture stood, to piece together and to give a name to the house in which it must be living.'[6] Dürckheim pursues the first steps of this building-up process in even more detail. 'At this moment,'

5 Dürckheim, 'Untersuchungen', p. 400.
6 Proust, *Der Weg zu Swann*, p. 11.

the passage just quoted, in which man has recaptured his awareness of position, continues, 'as a rule the whole orientation in space clicks into place. At times, however, a special phase intervenes, a state in which one does not yet move, although one already has the belowness, the ground; one does not yet have the direct aroundness. One is already there "oneself", but as though rooted to the spot. The zone of movement immediately around us remains uncertain. One does not yet "have" the position of the wall, what one's freedom of movement is, or what sort of base one is lying on. So the lack of motion which is characteristic of the state in question continues … But with the determination of direction which is already vaguely present here, but linked only to awareness of position, there also goes along a certain centredness and with that a fragmentary sense of self which was not previously present.'[7] Sometimes, in his opinion, full orientation in space comes at this point. Then the process has taken place too quickly for the purposes of our observations. But what is particularly important for us is the other cases, where the process becomes further fragmented and a further preliminary stage intervenes, where certainly a general determination of direction in the area of the body is present, but since the body is unmoving, it has not yet built up the immediate zone of spatial environment around it.

So at this stage, given the individual body, even if lying motionless, a certain structuring of spatial direction is also given, but not, as yet, any structuring of the space around the individual.

For this, even if the processes are seamless, a further step is necessary, and if we follow Dürckheim's description further, this happens with the first spontaneous movement. With this movement the given space expands from the area of the body outwards to its 'environs': 'But only when a spontaneous movement reveals the environment to us, often at a stroke bringing it back into a familiar space with a sudden ordering of the whole – when, for example, a tentative movement suddenly reveals the conditions around us – then the capability of focused and oriented movement returns. Only then does a complete sense of self return, to which a sense of direction and, therefore, centredness and determination belong.'[8] The first movement of one's own, while still lying in bed, thus opens up to us a certain surrounding space. According to this account, the process of waking up ends here. Dürckheim actually speaks of a 'clicking into place', a sudden process with which, when the development has reached this point, the whole spatial orientation is back again. It is always important in this

7 Dürckheim, 'Untersuchungen', p. 401 ff.
8 Dürckheim, 'Untersuchungen', p. 401.

process that throughout the different stages, the formation of actual self-awareness goes hand in hand in indivisible unity with the building up of the surrounding space. The building up of the outward space and the building up of the inner self thus continually correspond to each other.

The identification of place

But just at this point, where Dürckheim rather hastily passes on, Proust amplifies with some much more detailed observations. He links the inexact building up of the space around us with an immediate localization in a particular place. Uncertainty about where we are can occasionally torment us when we awake from sleep. This is the moment when, to put it concisely, the question unavoidably arises: just where am I? Probably everyone is familiar with the experience to which Proust alludes and which was also touched on earlier by Dürckheim: one feels uncertain, and asks oneself in this preliminary attempt at orientation, where is the wall? Particularly when waking up in an unfamiliar room, perhaps in a hotel room when on holiday, one asks oneself, is the wall on the right or the left? Is there free space to the right or the left? In fact, whereabouts in the room is the bed? It is no longer a question of the building up of near space, of which we were speaking at the previous stage, but the recognition of this particular surrounding space serves to identify this particular room, and thus to identify my present situation in life itself. Only with this recognition have I at the same time finally recovered myself. If memory does not set in quickly enough, I must try to orient myself by touch. I stretch out my arm to see if it encounters the resistance of a wall. I do not yet know if I am in a familiar or a strange room, and it can take long periods of uncertain thought before I rediscover a connection to the place where I fell asleep the night before.

Proust describes this experience very vividly: '[The body's] memory … offered it a whole series of rooms in which it had at one time or another slept; while the unseen walls kept changing, adapting themselves to the shape of each successive room that it remembered, whirling madly through the darkness.'[9] The memory that once again builds up the space, Proust says, is 'not yet of the place in which I was, but of various other places where I had lived, and might now very possibly be.'[10] Proust, whose exceptional sensitivity was particularly responsive to these borderline experiences of waking consciousness, describes how changing images pass in front of

9 Proust, *Der Weg zu Swann*, p. 11.
10 Proust, *Der Weg zu Swann*, p. 10.

him: soon his mother would come to say goodnight to him – it was the bed of his childhood – or he had overslept, had to hurry in order to be in time for a meal – at a later age when visiting friends in the country. Just when 'he gets drowsy in some even more abnormal position; sitting in an armchair, say, after dinner: then the world will fall topsy-turvy from its orbit, the magic chair will carry him at full speed through time and space, and when he opens his eyes again he will imagine that he went to sleep months earlier and in some far distant country.'[11]

Only in total wakefulness, as soon as, for example, one recognizes the particular room by touching its wall, does this turmoil cease, 'and the good angel of certainty had made all the surrounding objects stand still, had set me down under my bedclothes, in my bedroom, and had fixed, approximately in their right places in the uncertain light, my chest of drawers, my writing-table, my fireplace, the window overlooking the street, and both the doors.'[12] Admittedly, as long as darkness persists, this ordering of the environment succeeds only to a partial extent. Proust speaks cautiously of an 'approximately right place.' The light of day is needed for a final determination. Only broad daylight, 'as with a stroke of chalk across a blackboard, its first white correcting ray', brings the approximately ordered to its definitively correct place: 'that pale sign traced above my window-curtains by the uplifted forefinger of day'[13] had 'put to flight' the dwelling built up in the darkness.

Only when localization in space is complete are we ourselves again in the fullest sense. So regaining one's space means at the same time regaining oneself. Hence the decisive importance of space for the constitution of the self. The widespread presumption of an identity of the ego as fundamental to the building up of a world of experience is practically reversed. One cannot take hold of oneself, because one is in a state of constant transformation. Only by localization at a particular point in space can the ego gain the strength to hold itself fast as something identifiable. Thus space is the indispensable precondition for the formation of an ego that can develop freely from itself.

It is therefore very aptly that Lipps speaks of awaking 'to oneself' in a pointed sense when one awakes from sleep: 'That in doing so one assures oneself of the reality of one's immediate, tangible surroundings, that one knows one is not dreaming, this alone does not yet allow one to come to

11 Proust, *Der Weg zu Swann*, p. 10.
12 Proust, *Der Weg zu Swann*, p. 15.
13 Proust, *Der Weg zu Swann*, p. 263.

oneself. But it is that … in that situation one takes possession of oneself again. That one is able to sort oneself out in one's own mind.'[14] This alone completes the process of waking up from sleep.

b. *Falling asleep*

Falling asleep is the same process in reverse. While waking up leads us out of the darkness of a state which is difficult to bring into the bright light of consciousness, falling asleep leads us back from this brightness into the mysterious darkness. But falling asleep is very much more difficult to observe than waking up, for while with the latter process one immediately finds oneself in the full clarity of consciousness, and is able to hold fast the memories, still fresh, or rather the experiences which are still fading away (in the sense for example of Husserl's retention), when falling asleep one sinks into sleep, and usually several hours pass before waking up again, so that the intervening time of sleep prevents the memory from keeping hold of these processes. It is therefore necessary to make use of those exceptional cases, advantageous for our purpose, in which, for whatever reason, we wake up again at the very moment of falling asleep, and can therefore be certain of the process that has just been completed, even as it is still fading away.

Again we will be better advised not to rely on our own observations, but rather on the evidence of others, which report the facts of the matter independently of our formulation of the question. Here we are in the fortunate position of being able to rely on Linschoten's excellent and very detailed investigation,[15] from which we will try to extract what is important for our purposes, namely the insight it provides into the building up of experienced space.

The return to the unconscious mind

Linschoten interprets falling asleep as 'the becoming still of the reflecting "spirit" and the return of the experience of the unconscious mind [Seinsgrund].'[16] Falling asleep means the renunciation of activity,[17] although this statement immediately needs to be clarified; for the task of

14 Lipps, *Die menschliche Natur*, p. 46.
15 Linschoten, 'Über das Einschlafen', see note 109 above.
16 Linschoten, 'Über das Einschlafen', p. 71.
17 Linschoten, 'Über das Einschlafen', p. 266 ff.

activity is itself another action by a human being, even if it is an action of a particular kind.[18] It is an act of letting go, of surrender, in which we abandon ourselves to sleep.

The surrendering of activity means at the same time a suspension of reflexion, of the 'spirit' or intellect, in the special sense of Klages, with whom Linschoten here largely associates himself, and also the re-creation of a stream of experience not interrupted by acts of conscious reflection. This is the state in which we glide from waking to sleeping. 'The sphere of experience', says Linschoten, 'is rounded off, becomes free and flowing, the pure stream of experience is no longer interrupted by the separating reflexive actions.'[19] The thread initiated by the consciousness is dissolved, but at the same time the 'images' – again in Klages's sense – awake to a life of their own.

Darkness and silence emerge as essential elements in this state. But Linschoten rightly points out that one cannot simply say that darkness and silence result in sleep. It is not a causal connection, but one of nature, that links them.[20] Therefore one cannot either say that when sleeping we give up our connection with the world. It is not an isolation from the world, but the world itself becomes a different one. The world itself is transformed for the sleeping person into, as it were, a sleeping world. And what happens in man, this transformation of consciousness in sleep, is mirrored in this sleeping world and can perhaps be more easily grasped from this world than by direct personal observation. Proust, again, supplies a fine confirmation of this experience of the world which itself seems to be sleeping. He writes, in the passage already extensively quoted: 'often I would be awake again for short snatches only, just long enough to … open my eyes to settle the shifting kaleidoscope of the darkness, to savour, in an instantaneous flash of perception, the sleep which lay heavy upon the furniture, the room, the whole surroundings of which I formed but an insignificant part and whose unconsciousness I should very soon return to share.'[21] The world itself falls asleep and takes the sleeper captive. He himself dissolves and becomes a part of the sleeping world.

The same individual processes can be observed here that we already know from waking up, only of course in reverse: our spatial orientation is lost. We no longer know where we are. Claudel, for example, describes it thus: 'The night takes away our evidence, we no longer know where we are … Our

18 Linschoten, 'Über das Einschlafen', p. 276.
19 Linschoten, 'Über das Einschlafen', p. 89.
20 Linschoten, 'Über das Einschlafen', p. 80.
21 Proust, *Der Weg zu Swann*, p. 8 ff.

gaze is no longer bounded by the visible, but is imprisoned by the invisible, homogeneous, direct, indifferent, solid.'[22] Man slips away from the space spread visibly around him. At the same time, time vanishes; falling asleep, we live in a kind of timeless time, a time that loses itself in the present moment. Even the knowledge of our own body slips away. Linschoten describes the process: 'Thus the body dissolves when falling asleep, arms and legs lose their places, we lose knowledge of the position of the body', and so on.[23] And at the same time we lose the possibility of an active opinion. The world escapes from our grasp. But at the very same time, the individual ego also dissolves. 'When falling asleep I no longer remain with myself, I become anonymous and exist only in the objects that show themselves to me.'[24] Lévinas is also very aptly quoted: 'Waking up [in the night] is anonymous. It is not my wakefulness during the night, in sleeplessness. It is the night itself that is awake. It is awake. In this anonymous wakefulness I am entirely at the mercy of existence; all the thoughts that fill my sleeplessness are suspended in nothingness. They are unsupported. I am, as it were, more object than subject of my anonymous thought.'[25] It is a strangely impersonal condition, in which man merges into the singularly empty world of the night, dissolves in it without a centre of his own.

The feeling of security

These processes have been described. Now we must ask what they mean for our purpose, that is, the understanding of experienced space. We will go back again to the special character of this world that is falling asleep. Even when falling asleep, as we have said, the world is still there. And not only that, but it must have a certain character so that we can fall asleep in it, a character of protectiveness and trustworthiness, to which we can surrender ourselves without reservation. 'We succeed in falling asleep', Linschoten stresses, 'only in the tranquillity of a peaceful and well protected environment. To fall asleep, I must feel safe, or rather, I must experience the security of the situation in its enclosing and protecting character. I must be shielded from hostile intrusion, in order to relax and sink into the oblivion of sleep. This is why we always find the characteristics of comfort and security in the sleeping situation. Darkness and silence too have a function here.' In short, 'it is the characteristic of security that makes sleep possible

22 Cited in Linschoten, 'Über das Einschlafen', p. 84.
23 Linschoten, 'Über das Einschlafen', p. 278.
24 Linschoten, 'Über das Einschlafen', p. 283.
25 Cited in Linschoten, 'Über das Einschlafen', p. 283.

for me.'[26] Only in the consciousness of security can we abandon ourselves to sleep. And in order to produce this security, we are again helped by darkness and silence, which cut us off from the distant world and form, as it were, a more narrow world around us. Further, we need a certain warmth, which allows us to give way to a pleasant feeling of comfort. Space itself becomes a protective covering that draws itself together around us.

All these exterior circumstances may favour security. But they are not enough on their own. Darkness and silence may also have a disturbing quality, and one may listen with anxious attention for the slightest sound. We have already cited the proverb which says that he who is afraid does not feel safe in his bed. In order truly to abandon oneself to the feeling of security, man must feel something in his own being, a trusting attitude to the world and to life. He must supply from his own self the conditions that enable him to fall asleep.

This again is important for a discussion of existentialism. Because for the existentialist the world has become a threatening place, he cannot fall asleep, or at least not with a good conscience, but only against his own will, from sheer exhaustion. For the existentialist must always be on his guard against the threat that may overtake him at any moment. Linschoten too stresses this from a different viewpoint: 'Woe to him who imagines that he can live only in activity! He must live in fear of falling asleep … he is afraid of losing the secure hold of wakefulness.'[27]

But falling asleep is letting oneself fall, surrendering to the sleep that overcomes one. We literally 'fall' asleep. 'The floor subsides, the world vanishes, and as we fall asleep we slip back into unconsciousness.'[28] But to allow oneself to fall in this way, we need trust, trust in the future, trust, as we have already learnt, that all will be well. 'Now sleep confidently', runs a line of one of Bergengruen's most beautiful poems,[29] for only the confident person is capable of genuine sleep. To summarize: the hope that looks confidently towards the future, not a specific individual hope, but a general hopeful trust in the future, is therefore the necessary precondition of sleep.

Deep sleep

Thus falling asleep at last leads to full sleep. Of this we know no more, for consciousness is extinguished in it. But if we carefully continue to consider

26 Linschoten, 'Über das Einschlafen', p. 273 ff.
27 Linschoten, 'Über das Einschlafen', p. 263, see also p. 81.
28 Linschoten, 'Über das Einschlafen', p. 267.
29 Bergengruen, *Die heile Welt*, p. 203.

the gladdening experiences of falling asleep as well as the corresponding sensations of awakening from refreshing sleep, then we will have to think of sleep as a condition of perfect non-spatiality, or rather, perhaps, as a state in which space no longer confronts us as a connection with objectively ascertainable objects, but in which the tension between self and world has entirely disappeared. And this state would at the same time be understood as one of a final sense of security. We no longer need to make the effort of asserting ourselves. We feel as though taken up into a deeper existence. The unconscious mind 'Seinsgrund' which was mentioned in a statement cited earlier merges with the state of pure being 'Seinsgrund' itself.

In the sense of security in which we surrender to sleep, we are defenceless, open to any attack. Thus Shakespeare speaks of 'innocent sleep.'[30] But it is precisely from this that one fears to do any harm to a sleeping person.[31] It is reverence for vulnerability that lays itself protectively around the sleeper.

But as we have already stressed that it is not one-sided causal relationships, but reciprocally operating connections, so it is not only the external circumstances supplying security that make sleep possible, but sleep for its own part also has a healing and soothing effect on us. This is why, after the troubles and cares of our waking existence, we long for release in sleep. We praise sweet sleep, gentle sleep, even sacred sleep. Sleep is praised as happiness, although the sleeper himself knows nothing of his own happiness, but even the falling away of the torments of waking life appears to us as happiness. 'Sleep is sweet to me,'[32] cries Michelangelo, in despair over his life, tormented by the futility of his efforts. But this happiness is mostly only a negative one, a state of numbness in which we forget the cares that torment us. Michelangelo continues significantly, 'but above all I praise being stone', that is, reaching a state of total lack of feeling. Homer too writes of sleep, 'for sleep makes him forgetful of all things, of good and evil, when once it has overshadowed his eyelids.'[33] And Shakespeare speaks similarly, in the passage already cited, of

> Sleep that knits up the ravell'd sleeve of care,
> The death of each day's life, sore labour's bath,
> Balm of hurt minds, great nature's second course[34]

30 Shakespeare, *Macbeth* in Schiller's translation, *Sämtliche Werke*, edited by Eduard v. d. Hellen, vol. 9, Stuttgart and Berlin: n.d., p. 37.

31 See Schiller, *Wallenstein's Tod. Sämtliche Werke*, edited by Eduard v. d. Hellen, vol. 5, Stuttgart and Berlin: n.d., p. 362.

32 Michelangelo, translated by Rainer Maria Rilke, *Gesammelte Werke*, vol. 6, Leipzig: 1930, p. 214.

33 *Odyssey*, book 20, verse 85 ff.

34 Shakespeare, *Macbeth* in Schiller's translation, *Sämtliche Werke*, vol. 9, p. 37.

But such a merely negative concept hardly does justice to the more profound nature of sleep. Goethe's words in *Egmont* lead us closer to its positive character: 'You loosen the knot of strenuous thought, mix all the images of joy and pain; unobstructed flows the circle of inner harmonies, and swathed in agreeable delirium, we sink and cease to be.'[35] Here, sinking away is no longer merely perceived as the fading away of painful feelings, but as a gladdening experience in its own right, in which we feel ourselves drawn into the 'circle of inner harmonies.' And this perception probably corresponds more closely to the experiences which emerge from a more precise description of the process of falling asleep.

Several times already the thought of sleep has been reminiscent of a return home, 'a return to the unconscious mind [Seelengrund].' And after all it was the interrelation of forward and back that led us in the first place, even if by indirect paths, to the problem of sleep. As confirmation, I will give a further piece of evidence, again taken from the work of Linschoten. The Hegel student Erdmann writes that the sleeper is at rest 'because he is happy and at peace, that is, because his soul has returned to itself from the drudgery of life, because it has returned home and no longer has to deal with foreign matters, because it has composed itself away from distractions, and in this composure resembles the deep ocean, which, because the storms have fallen silent, offers a surface as clear as a mirror.'[36] Here we notice particularly the concepts heaped upon each other: returned, returned home, at peace, no longer dealing with the foreign. In the interpretation of sleep, this leads to a more profound question, which touches on the problems that arose earlier in connection with wandering.

In the general understanding, sleep is considered as a pause for recuperation between the times of our existence dedicated to sleep, a pause that is necessary in order to be able to work again after exhaustion. Sleep thus only has meaning to the extent that it prepares and strengthens us for renewed wakefulness. This is entirely compatible with the fact that in a state of world-weariness, sleep is valued positively as a means of forgetting one's sufferings. But now we are assailed by definitions that touch on the praise of sleep as a means of oblivion, but nevertheless perceive the relationship between waking and sleep quite differently, in fact practically reverse it:

---

35 'Du lösest die Knoten der strengen Gedanken, vermischest alle Bilder der Freude und des Schmerzens, ungehindert fließt der Kreis innerer Harmonien, und eingehüllt in gefälligen Wahnsinn, versinken wir und hören auf, zu sein.' Johann Wolfgang von Goethe, *Egmont. Gedenkausagabe*, edited by Ernst Beutler, vol. 6, Zurich and Stuttgart: 1948-71, p. 99.

36 J. E. Erdmann, *Psychologische Briefe*, Leipzig: 1882, p. 116, cited in Linschoten, 'Über das Einschlafen', p. 92.

wakefulness is seen as a life in foreign parts, as an alienation of man from his actual nature. Thus sleep appears to man as the aim of wakefulness, and the actual point of life. This indeed would be a very sweeping conclusion. But we hesitate to complete this final step. Even Linschoten, who called falling asleep 'the return of experience to the deepest "Seelengrund"', shrinks back here: 'Sleep is unquestionably a resting-point. But is it actually life? the purpose of mankind?'[37] This opens up the whole problem of a romantic return to our origins.

The double movement of life

The spatial double movement of life in striving forwards and returning, with which we started, without at first suspecting its full consequences, is here intertwined with the deeper double movement of waking up and falling asleep, which can no longer be understood in spatial terms. The Romantic attitude consists in the preference for the movement that leads one home to one's origins, that is at the same time the path towards the unconscious mind of the soul and the depth of sleep. But however many reasons arise for such a return from a superficial life and from being lost to vain activity – this is the whole problem of the critique of contemporary culture – it would be an absurdity to wish to return home without having first gone away, and life would be extinguished by doing so. A return home makes sense only as a counter-movement, when it has been preceded by a great wide-ranging movement away. And this second movement must therefore, if one can speak at all of a precedence, be described as the first.

So we here encounter once again the double movement of which we have already become aware in our discussion of wandering and of the house. As man needed to strive forwards from the house in order to carry out his work in the world, he must also, over and over again, urge himself forward in the freshness of the morning to waking, active life, in order to allow himself to surrender to sleep on completing his work. These two movements belong inseparably together, like breathing in and out. But it is only in the movement which ranges widely into the distance that man opens himself up to the full breadth of space, while in falling asleep he again withdraws from it. So in order to understand adequately what it is to return home, we must first turn our attention to the other side and to the path that leads from the narrowness of the house into the expanse of the world and from the self-consciousness of sleep into a powerfully active life.

37 Linschoten, 'Über das Einschlafen', p. 91.

IV
ASPECTS OF SPACE

1. Hodological Space

Distance

Having so far preoccupied ourselves essentially with the character of space in general, we must now probe more deeply into its inner structure. For this too, it will be expedient for us again to start with a comparison with mathematical space. As is well known, we can very successfully understand the space that surrounds us in mathematical terms. We can measure it precisely, report the distance between individual points in metres and centimetres, and represent the whole, true to scale, in a plan or map. This is how the ground-plan of a building is produced, with its walls, windows and doors, and if applicable the individual pieces of furniture in it, or the map of a city with its streets and squares, or a country with mountains, cities and rivers, and finally the globe as the image of the entire sphere of the earth. Everywhere the relationships between positions, in particular distances, are precisely represented, and if one needs them, we can read them from the map. The map, as a true-to-scale image, enables orientation in the terrain.

And yet every map-user, such as the wanderer in the mountains, soon experiences the limits of such a geometric representation of space; for the distances experienced in real life when one traverses space do not coincide with the distance as the crow flies, or with carefully measured road distances, or, more generally, they do not coincide at all with the distance between two points expressed in metres, but in addition to this they depend very strongly on the accessibility of the destination in question, on the greater or lesser difficulties to be overcome if one wishes to reach it, and on the energy to be expended in doing so. The ascent from the valley to the mountain is already different from the 'same' path in the reverse direction from the mountain to the valley. In particular we must consider that the straight line by no means represents the shortest connection between two points, that detours may be necessary or appropriate in order to reach a destination. The actual distance in real life must take these detours into account. So it may happen that places that are geometrically quite close are difficult or even impossible to reach, that is, they are far away or even infinitely far away, while others, geometrically much further away, are very much easier to reach. So the concrete nearness and distance of things cannot be reckoned according to a geometric standard.

Perhaps we can consider the relationships in terms of the following, somewhat abstractly exaggerated question: how great is the concrete (experienced) distance between a place on a wall of my dwelling which borders on a neighbouring house, and the corresponding place on the other side of the wall in the other dwelling? Abstractly, mathematically seen, it would be a few centimetres, according to the thickness of the wall, but in concrete terms it is much further; for to reach this point, to see this wall from the 'other side', I would have to leave my room and my house, go through my front door into the street, go along the street to the neighbour's house, and finally find myself on the 'other side' of my wall. But even apart from the difficulties that we would encounter in trying to find 'the same place' with the help of a map, presumably the occupants of the neighbouring house would not understand my purpose, and would respond with such surprised expressions to my request that I would rather not ask them at all. This means that the place in the neighbouring dwelling, of whose existence I can of course be sure in the abstract, is infinitely far away in terms of experienced space, for in those terms it does not exist at all.

The cave-like character of the living space

Similar considerations force themselves upon us when we try to understand objectively the given space in a dwelling (I will restrict myself for the purposes of simplification to the two-dimensional plan). We need not reflect on whether the original dwelling of mankind was a cave. In experienced space, the dwelling today is in any case still a cave in a mountain (and perhaps all the more so, the more modern cities develop into artificial cement mountains). The dwelling has an opening, through which alone it is in contact with the surrounding space. This is the door through which one enters. From here the possibilities of movement unfold like a system of lines of force, which extends from within, across the corridors and stairs, into the rooms. But everywhere they come up against their limits at the walls of the dwelling. Here the space ends. What lies outside these walls is no longer attainable from within. It is, in practice, not available; for what is offered to the gaze through the window has, as we have seen, no longer any direct reality. So a dwelling within a house is really not essentially different from a cave into which I might enter, in which people might also live. But what is quite noticeable about a cave – that it has a limit from the inside, where the hollow meets the rock, and that behind it is not another space, but a non-space, namely the amorphous mass of the rock, something in which there is simply no space – is also the case with apartments within built houses. This becomes clearest when there are several apartments in a block of rented apartments, branching off from a common staircase. For the concrete experience of space, it is no different from a system of caves carved into the rock. Whether they touch each other in objective space, or are separated by a layer of non-space, many metres thick, is of no importance for this concrete experience.

An example that very finely clarifies these relationships is given by Kusenberg in his tale of fantasy 'Die Himmelsschenke' [The celestial inn].[1] He writes of a building which was at the same time a church and an inn. According to the entrance through which one entered the building, it was an inn or a church, and each time totally so, so that when one had entered one of the two buildings through the corresponding door, one found it to be so spacious that it seemed to take up the whole of the space enclosed by the outer walls, and could hardly understand how there could be room for more spaces within the same walls. In a grotesque account, it is now explained in detail how the individual circles of life suddenly interpenetrate, how customers of the inn suddenly turn up in the church, or choirboys and churchgoers in the inn. But this is more to do with the creative development of the story. Nevertheless, the fantasy is based on a quite concrete experience of space and once again very aptly clarifies the peculiar cave-like character of the living and dwelling space in the house.

It is simply only abstract geometrical thinking that divides the rooms of a house with their measurement on a floorplan so that (apart from the necessary thickness of the walls) they precisely fit together. This does correspond to the architect's perspective, but not that of the occupier. The latter rather brings the individual rooms and spaces, according to their accessibility and inner links, into a network of concretely experienced relationships, but he takes no account of how they fit together 'in themselves.' The famous 'secret chambers' in old castles already suggest that for someone living in a complicated building it is not possible at all to visualize fully the geometrical-spatial relationships, and that it is always possible to omit such secret rooms from the ground-plan without danger

1 K. Kusenberg, 'Die Himmelsschenke', *Mal was andres*, Hamburg: 1954, p. 59 ff.

of discovery. Kusenberg's story too indicates the discrepancy between geometrically available space and experienced space. This demonstrates the difficulty generally found in visualizing concrete living space from a mathematical floorplan. It never becomes clear from such a two-dimensional scheme, and if, guided by a necessary requirement for rational clarity, we nevertheless seek after a floor-plan-like representation, we soon get into difficulties.

There can of course be events which suddenly bring the dwelling next door much closer to me. This may happen if, for example, the inhabitants of the other dwelling come to my attention by hammering or other disturbing noises. Then I detect who is disturbing my peace, and it is then that the concrete sense of distance returns. The neighbouring dwelling thus comes closer when it intrudes on my area of life because of the disturbance.

But a totally revolutionary change would take place if I knocked a hole into the wall, or had a connecting door built between two previously unconnected spaces; for this would basically alter the whole scheme of distance. I well remember another example from my own experience: a hole in a fence separating two properties, intended for children to pass through, in order to spare them a long journey by way of the street, not only brings the two houses spatially much closer together, but also the 'private', 'secret' link between the properties, outside the public access, links the two families much more closely than they had been before.

The relationships between the storeys of a house are similar. I remember the alarming indignation I felt in my childhood when I discovered that, on a holiday visit, my noise had awakened my grandfather, sleeping in the room above mine. It had never occurred to me that such a thing was possible; for to me, the two rooms were much too widely separated for the sound from one to penetrate to the other – through several rooms, then up the stairs and into my grandfather's bedroom. It was a shift, a real discovery, when it suddenly became clear to me that the sound could take a different and much more direct path through the ceiling than the one determined by my own experienced distance.

Hodological space according to Lewin

In this connection the concept of hodological space and hodological distance, introduced by Lewin and subsequently adopted by Sartre, appears to be highly enlightening and useful. Coming from the Greek word ὁδός, a path, it denotes the space opened up by paths, in the sense in which we wrote earlier, when discussing paths with reference to Linschoten, that the path opens up space, and the distances to be covered on these paths. One could, if it were not linguistically too unfamiliar, even speak of a 'path-space.' This hodological space is from the start contrasted with abstract mathematical space. In mathematical space the distance between two points is determined only by their respective coordinates; it is thus an objective quantity, independent of the structure of the space lying between them. Hodological space on the other hand means the change that in concretely lived and experienced space is added to what we had already designated the accessibility of the respective spatial destinations. Here the straight line as the shortest distance between two points is replaced by what Lewin calls the 'distinguished path.' At the same time, the 'distinguished path' can be something highly differentiated. This depends on the various demands placed by us on the path. Lewin formulates it as follows: 'The distinguished path may for example be interpreted as the "cheapest", the "fastest", the "least unpleasant" or the "safest" path.'[2] So these are specific minimum demands: the shortest time, the least effort, and so on. One can also formulate distinction as a maximum demand, if one perhaps seeks the most enjoyable path, for example when looking in a holiday resort for the footpath that offers the greatest number of beautiful views within a given period of time.

Thus the distinguished path in a particular terrain is not determined once and for all, but depends on the extreme condition on which it is based. The most convenient path is not necessarily the shortest, and this again is not necessarily the fastest, and so on. This depends on the determining factors in each case. Lewin stresses: 'Structure, direction and distance in the living space are only to be determined relative to the underlying processes or the decisive principles of choice.'[3] Relationships are still comparatively simple where plainly insuperable obstacles are present, such as strong walls, which force us to make a particular detour. But they become substantially more complex where it is a question of larger or smaller respective obstacles. To choose a very simple example, if I want to reach a point located on a newly ploughed field, I will first look for the point closest to this destination on the edge of the field, so that the difficult part of the path is as short as possible. If on the other hand the difference in the easiness of access is smaller, then the distinguished path will always be closer to a straight line. And so the determination of the hodological path, mathematically speaking, is a variation

---

2 K. Lewin, 'Der Richtungsbegriff in der Psychologie. Der spezielle und allgemeine hodologische Raum', *Psychologische Forschung*, vol. 19, 1934, p. 249 ff. and p. 265.

3 Lewin, 'Der Richtungsbegriff', p. 285.

problem. But if all non-homogeneous factors are absent, hodological space, as already mentioned, passes into the borderline case of Euclidean space, and the distinguished path is the connection in a straight line.

It is in these terms too that Lewin also determines hodological direction and hodological distance. Hodological direction does not coincide with the direction determined by the geometrical connecting line, that is, that in which I would see the object if it were not covered by something else, but it is the direction that I must take with my first step if I want to reach the point in question on the hodological path. It can diverge considerably from the geometrical direction, if I can only reach the destination in question by a detour. Similarly, hodological intervals are also different from geometrical intervals. They are determined by the length of the distinguished path that I must traverse from one point to another. Lewin shows, among other things, that the axiom of the triangle is valid here too: the sum of the distinguished paths from A to B and from B to C is greater than or equal to the distinguished path from A to C, and the equality sign arises when B lies on the distinguished path from A to C.

As Lewin explicitly stresses, the distinguished path is to be determined not only from objective relationships, but depends equally on the mental state of the person in question. 'The geometry of living space, including the directions in it, depends on the state of the person in question.'[4] If, for example, I am afraid of meeting a person who is disagreeable to me on the path which in itself is the shortest, I will make a detour and strike out a new path, which now becomes the distinguished path. If, on the other hand, on another occasion I am in a great hurry, I will put up with the risk of a disagreeable encounter, and so there is a shift in what is considered the distinguished path at any one time. It will change again according to one's state of tiredness or freshness. And with this, distances also change. While in the freshness of morning a destination is quick and easy to reach, 'for tired feet every path is too long.'[5] But our choice of paths itself may vary. In a state of physical exhaustion I will avoid the accustomed time-saving shorter path because of its difficulty. In the same way, someone suffering from a heart condition, as Plügge points out, will avoid the differences in height that represent an effort for him, even at the cost of considerable detours,[6] and so on.

---

4 Lewin, 'Der Richtungsbegriff', p. 286; see also p. 254.

5 'für müde Füße jeder Weg zu lang', Georg Büchner, *Leonce und Lena. Werke und Briefe*, Frankfurt a. M.: 1940, p. 130.

6 H. Plügge, 'Über das Befinden von Kranken nach Herzinfarkt', *Wohlbefinden und Mißbefinden. Beiträge zu einer medizinischen Anthropologie*, Tübingen: 1962, p. 231 ff.

Sartre's continuation

From this point, Sartre, in a meanwhile considerably altered philosophical position, has taken up the concept of hodological space and thus awakened Lewin's almost forgotten approach to new life. Thus Sartre stresses in a direct reference: 'The real space of the world is the space which Lewin calls "hodological".'[7] And elsewhere: 'The space which is originally revealed to me is hodological space; it is furrowed with paths and highways, it is instrumental and it is the location of tools,'[8] adding, quite in the spirit of our earlier observations: 'There are barriers and obstacles in my hodological space.'[9]

Sartre however extends even further the concept of hodological space, and in a very interesting way. His reference to its instrumental character already appears to go beyond what Lewin had in mind. We will return to this. But for the moment let us consider another thought. Man 'situates himself', in Sartre's linguistically rather harsh phrase, through the system of paths that start out from his place of residence. But these paths, beyond what has already been argued, are particularly related to places which have become significant through the presence of other persons. 'An individual', says Sartre, 'is not situated in relation to locations by means of degrees of longitude and latitude. He is situated in a human space.' It is the presence of the individual in question 'which allows the unfolding of the "hodological" space in which he is situated.'[10] When, for example, thinking about his cousin in Morocco, he designs in his thoughts what might be called the road to Morocco. And thus the situation of man in the world is determined by the multiplicity of paths that link him with the other persons who are present in his mind.

While this thought is rewarding, we should remember that it causes a not inconsiderable shift in Lewin's original thought, increasing its content but also diminishing its conciseness. With Lewin it is a case of a specific path in the terrain, unequivocally fixed through a certain minimal demand, which can clearly be visualized. But with Sartre this thought pales into a somehow uncertainly envisaged relationship with a spatially distant person (or thing). The specific path by which one might meet this cousin

7 Jean-Paul Sartre, *Das Sein und das Nichts* [*L'être et le néant*, Paris: 1943], translated by v. J. Streller, K. A. Ott and A. Wagner, Hamburg: 1962, p. 404 [*Being and nothingness*, translated by Hazel E. Barnes, London: 1957, p. 308].

8 Sartre, *Das Sein und das Nichts*, p. 420 [p. 322].

9 Sartre, *Das Sein und das Nichts*, p. 427 [p. 328].

10 Sartre, *Das Sein und das Nichts*, p. 392 ff. [p. 279].

in Morocco, and the question as to which of the various possibilities might be chosen for a journey, play no part here. In this way the preference for a specific 'distinguished path' disappears, and thus the thought loses its specifically hodological quality as understood by Lewin.

The hodological structure of the landscape

Before we decide upon a fundamental extension of the concept, it will be appropriate to visualize somewhat more graphically, by means of some examples, Lewin's perhaps somewhat abstractly expressed (in terms of its ability to be mathematically formulated) principle of the hodological, in its application to the structure of the landscape.[11]

Such an extreme example of a landscape structured according to the hodological principle is discussed by Lewin in an early essay (and therefore prior to the conceptual framework developed later): the landscape of war, as he describes it very vividly from his experience of the First World War, from the situation determined by the static warfare of the time. Lewin distinguishes the particularity of this landscape from a normal 'landscape of peace', which extends uniformly into the distance. 'This landscape is round, without front or back.'[12] In contrast, the landscape of war is distinguished by two significant characteristics: it is directed unilaterally, that is, oriented throughout towards the 'front', and it is limited by the same 'front.' Everything relates to this, but behind it there is nothing.

The landscape manifests this orientation as soon as it is approached, that is, when one comes from the hinterland: 'It knows a front and back, namely a front and back not related to marching, but to the area itself. Neither is it a question of the consciousness of the threat that increases in moving forward, and finally of inaccessibility, but of the alteration in the landscape itself. The area at the "front" seems to end there, to be followed by a "nothing".'[13] 'At the "front" the area seems somewhere to

11 I will not discuss the complication raised by Lewin, that the distinguished path can be unequivocally determined only in a totally 'through-structured' space, since in general I am selecting from the wealth of ideas in his essay only what will directly lead us further in the present context.

12 K. Lewin, 'Kriegslandschaft', *Zeitschrift für angewandte Psychologie*, vol. 12, 1917, p. 440 ff.

13 K. Lewin, 'Kriegslandschaft', *Zeitschrift für angewandte Psychologie*, vol. 12, 1917, p. 440 ff.

come to an end; the landscape has borders.'[14] And moreover the structure of the landscape increases as one approaches the front. Roughly parallel to the border, a particular 'danger zone' forms, not uniformly but with specific 'danger points', which for their part change according to the state of action. This zone compresses itself towards the front into a 'position.' We are not too concerned here with the details of this landscape. What is important is that an extreme case clarifies something that will recur in other cases, and will be more easily recognized in these other, perhaps less pronounced cases, after it has previously been clarified by means of such a borderline case.

It is similar in deeply carved valleys in high mountain regions. Concrete space is structured according to the traffic possibilities on the roads and paths, and these themselves follow the course of the valleys, as do the waterways. The continuous traffic artery is determined by the base of the valley, the side roads by the side-valleys, which in each case come to a dead end at the end of the valley. The high mountains, like the front discussed earlier, take on the character of a border, to which the upward course of the paths relates. These borders, apart from a few mountain passes, are totally impassable to motorized traffic. The village lying only a few kilometres away as the crow flies may be several days' journey away. It already belongs to a different world and may lie at a practically inaccessible distance for the valley-dweller. This is best illustrated by the lack of cultural exchange between neighbouring alpine valleys.

A corresponding situation is found in a coastal landscape by the sea. Even though the border is here not pronounced, and the orientation takes on a different character, this too is a case of a half-landscape, bordered by the coast. Here one lives in relation to the sea, and though this does not signify a simple nothingness, it is still an area of basically altered possibilities of access, which is accessible to the fisherman, but not the land-dweller.

The relationships are different again, but still comparable, when a great river divides a city in two. Here too the river is a border, and only one bridge (if we restrict ourselves to this simplest of cases) allows a connection. All traffic routes come together into it and emanate from it, so that (as with the alpine valleys) a major detour by way of the bridge is often necessary to link two points lying opposite each other on the banks of the river. So, despite the bridge, total merging does not succeed, and the two halves of the city remain distant from one another despite their spatial proximity. In

14 K. Lewin, 'Kriegslandschaft', *Zeitschrift für angewandte Psychologie*, vol. 12, 1917, p. 440 ff.

many cases, even after centuries, one side remains unable to shake off the character of inferiority.

The situation is of course similar with the borders of countries, which can be crossed only at certain customs frontiers, above all at times when the crossing demands greater formalities. This becomes particularly noticeable when national borders are redrawn after a war; for then it is perceived that not only is a region being newly divided, but countless traffic routes of importance in people's lives, in fact a whole hodological system, is cut up and must be rebuilt with great effort according to the new circumstances.

And finally a last example to show how little our actual experience of a landscape coincides with its representation on the map: a journey by boat on a river; for the river is after all to a particularly striking extent a 'hodological path', in Lewin's phrase. I am thinking – if I may refer to my own experiences – of the Rhine journey from Mainz to Koblenz, one I have often taken in days past. It is often difficult to reconcile the structure of the landscape, as it appears from the boat, with the 'real' image as given on the map. This impression is particularly strong if we climb up the hill and see the same Rhine in front of us that we have just left behind. It is surprising that the loops of the Rhine are 'in reality' much more strongly curved than one would have expected from the boat journey. The Rhine we experience from the boat seems more straight. Not that we perceived it as simply running in a straight line; after all, we see how the course of the river turns left and right, but while the boat is moving into the loops, these seem to weaken and seem to be less curved. Basically, therefore, the image is formed of a direction of movement which is practically straight-lined. The banks move past, with the villages and mountains lying behind them, and there is certainly something exciting about it when an outstanding landmark, such as a tall chimney, comes into view from various angles.

Incidentally, something similar is also true of the country road and the railway line. It is also rather confusing when one sees the same city, now on the left, now on the right, from the car window, and this perhaps leads us to the general rule that a hodologically distinguished path, if one moves on it in the terrain, tends to create the impression of a straight line.

2. Space of Action

The extension of the hodological concept of space

However rewarding the concept of hodological space has proven to be, in making transparent a certain inner structure of experienced space, it only reveals certain aspects of it convincingly and cannot simply be equated with experienced space itself. We must therefore attempt to avoid the danger of one-sided observation, by accepting other, no less important aspects of experienced space and thus extend our understanding of its inner structure.

Such an extension, as has been indicated, has already been implicit in the manner in which Sartre adopted the concept of hodological space and equated it with that of specific experienced space. An extension of this kind seems to me not quite appropriate, for this, on the one hand, blurs the clear features so convincingly revealed by Lewin with his concept of hodological space, when on the other hand the peculiarity of what was really new, what may be observed from other points of view, is not emphasized clearly enough. It therefore seems to me more suitable to hold fast to the idea of hodological space as conceived by Lewin in its original strength, but for precisely that reason to distinguish it as a special aspect from the more general concept of experienced space and to look out for other aspects that may make visible the greater wealth of this concept.

Such an extension seems necessary to me in two respects. Hodological space describes the system of paths by which I can reach individual points in space. Thus it is comparable to a network of lines of power which flow through this space. But in the physical sense too these lines of power refer to charges or masses from which they emanate. Likewise, in experienced space paths with their directions and distances relate to the destinations to which they lead. Every path is the path to something or towards something, and only in this respect is it a path. But these destination points of paths have a significance to man, for whose sake he strives towards them – or flees from them, for there are not only places to be striven after, but also places of danger and discomfort, so that escape and exit routes must also be included in the system of paths. The totality of paths that start out from wherever an individual resides determines, as Sartre correctly saw, the situation of man in concrete space. However, the individual destinations do not stand side by side in an unconnected fashion, but form an ordered whole of things and individuals in space. Thus experienced space represents a meaningfully structured totality of these places and points that are laden with significance. And it is this well-ordered human space as a system of such places and points that we must now analyse more precisely in its individuality.

To this however we must add a second point of view, which also leads us beyond the concept of hodological space: it is only outside the house that we speak meaningfully of paths. Paths link individual locations of human activity, houses and places of work. But within the house we do not speak of paths, even when domestic activity involves walking. The many steps taken daily by a housewife in the kitchen are not paths (and only an inappropriately rationalizing observation could consider the idea of measuring these steps in order to find the most appropriate arrangement of workplaces). Even the considerable movements undertaken by the farmer in order to till his fields are not paths. Paths are only means of access to the workplace. A messenger, in particular a postman, is probably the only worker for whom paths are part of the nature of his work. Otherwise, however, paths link places of human activity and rest. The concept of the path can be transferred to what happens in these places only in a very forced and ultimately inappropriate sense.

And one more consideration must be added here: the concept of hodological space has developed out of human activity which corresponds to meaningful behaviour on the paths: walking or driving. We are here considering a comparatively extensive movement in the landscape, whose individual places I seek out while walking or driving. It is from here that the structure of this space develops. The structure of the space which I occupy when working or in my free time is quite different. Here too there are differences of greater or lesser accessibility. I look for objects, when I need them, in their places. I grasp them in my hand. And sometimes I must remove myself from my current position in order to take them in my hand. So a combination is created of a distance to be covered with my feet and with my hand. But no one (unless in an irrelevant abstraction) would say that my hand takes a path. And while I always move on a horizontal place in the network of paths, so that the network can be represented cartographically on the surface, the grasping and holding by hands is always at the same time a reaching in all directions, including up and down, so that from the start a three-dimensionally extended space is built up.

Clearly quite different conditions prevail here, and with them we encounter an entirely different aspect of spatial construction. For lack of a better term, I would like to call this space the space of action [Tätigkeitsraum]. I mean by this quite simply the space occupied by man when engaged in meaningful activity, working or resting, dwelling in it in the widest sense.[1]

In a linguistically somewhat awkward analogy, one might also speak of an ergo-logical or simply an active space. The concept of a space of action [Handlungsraum / Aktionsraum] has meanwhile established itself in the literature, and therefore I would like to retain it, without differentiating in detail from the usage not uniformly adopted by the various authors. We must now turn to the consideration of the individual character of this space of action.

The tangibility of objects in space

A suitable starting point is provided by Heidegger's analysis of human spatiality in *Being and time*, which, despite being restricted by the different direction of the questions raised in this book, clearly discusses the decisive features of this space. I will follow it, without keeping in detail to the structure required by the total context of the book. The concept of what is 'ready-to-hand' which Heidegger applies to the original condition of things, or, in his phrase, of equipment [Zeug], is well chosen in this respect, for it refers from the start to a space. That a thing is 'ready to hand' after all signifies that it is available for my use, that it is thus accessible and I need only reach out to take it in my hand and use it in the way I wish. For this easy accessibility, at the same time, a certain spatial proximity is necessary. It must be conveniently graspable. A book for example, which is ready at the library for me to collect, is certainly accessible to me, but it is not yet ready to hand. For this, I must first have collected it and placed it in the proximity of my workplace. Thus what is ready to hand, understood in the

---

1 Thus, in connection with a differentiation made by Dürckheim, activity space is frequently limited to the space present in completing the action, while what is here understood by this term is called purposive space. In the present context, this distinction appeared superfluous. The designation of historic space introduced by Straus, which he distinguishes from presential space (see p. 237), also seems unfortunate to me, because the concept of the historic is accompanied by new, fateful points of view which lead us beyond the purely rational structuring of activity space.

strict sense, is bound to a certain close area, without my being able to name its exact limits. This already distinguishes the narrower region of space of action from the more widely ranging path space.

But for a thing to be lying ready to hand for me, it must at the same time lie (or stand) in its right place, where it belongs and where I will find it without having to search too much. At this particular place the object is in a certain spatial relationship to me. It lies in a certain direction, which I must reach towards and if necessary walk towards, and it lies at a certain greater or smaller distance, determined by its easier or more difficult attainability. In the same sense we could also speak of the place to which the thing belongs, in order to denote the functionality of its task in life. 'Place' is from a purely linguistic point of view an even more appropriate term, as it clearly expresses the connection with the activity of ordering, namely 'to place' (along with 'replace', 'misplace', 'displace', and so on). Every object has its place or position in the human environment.

One could imagine the relationship in a greatly simplified mathematical model in such a way that the place of the object in relation to me would be determined by polar coordinates, by a direction to be measured as an angle and a distance to be measured in length. But we must note here that direction and distance are to be understood in a hodological sense and will not correspond to an equivalent geometrical definition. With rarely used objects a searching look may be necessary, which as such would correspond to the geometrical direction, although to get hold of the object might require us to reach into different directions. But the more familiar an object is to me, the more it really is ready to hand, the less such finding aids are necessary, and I will reach out, without my hand needing to be guided by my eye. Thus, for example, my bunch of keys is in its place in my pocket. I can take hold of it any time that I need it. In this way it has direction and distance, without my being able to determine these, even approximately, in geometric terms.

The importance of this sentence becomes clear particularly when something is not in its place and I must first make an effort to search for it. Immediately a state of disorientation sets in, for example when, on inspection, I cannot find my ticket where I thought I had put it, and look wildly around for it.

So the ready-to-handness of a thing in its place is something quite different from its mere availability in a place in space which can be geometrically determined. It is no merely theoretically perceptive attitude in which I perceive it in this place, but it has its specific significance in the practical activity in this place; I am linked with it by a 'life reference.'

Thus we define the space of action as the totality of places which include the objects of use around the working individual. Here no object stands alone, but the individual places are ordered into a significant whole, in which each individual object is related to other things with which it belongs. The book stands on the bookshelf, and the bookshelf is on the wall of the study, the washing is in the wardrobe, the pliers are in the toolbox, and so on. Each individual thing is in a spatial proximity to other things, with which it is linked by a meaningful connection. Heidegger speaks of the 'region' [Gegend] in which the place of these things is found, where 'region' of course does not refer to the terrain of the landscape, but the overarching area of the things linked together by the fact that for practical purposes they belong together. It is to this 'region' that I turn first when I am looking for a particular object, perhaps the 'region' of the desk in the case of the inkwell, in order to find it successfully by inspecting this 'region' more closely. And this 'region' in its turn exists in a larger connection. And thus, from the individual object in the place where it belongs, to the areas of these 'regions', a spatially ordered arrangement gradually builds up, of ever larger areas, that of the house, the workplace, the city, and so on. Thus space is structured as a totality of places and areas that belong together.

The ordering of space

The individual object however has its place where I look for it and find it, in so far as a place is assigned to it by someone. The place is thus already the result of human creation of order. The manner of assignation can again vary greatly in detail. Things are, to quote Heidegger, 'as equipment essentially fitted up and installed, set up, and put to rights.'[2] Thus there are very different forms of lying ready, keeping, and so on. I can put a book in order on the bookshelf for later use, or I can lay it on my desk ready for use in the near future. I can put my bicycle in the shed, store the potatoes in the cellar, keep provisions in the larder. There are various possibilities here which are connected with the temporal distinction between immediate use and use at a later time. And then there arises the further distinction that there must be not only places for laying objects ready for immediate use, but also spaces for storing them for later use: larders, stockrooms, warehouses, libraries, and so on.

2 Martin Heidegger, *Sein und Zeit*, Halle a. d. Saale: 1927, p. 102 [*Being and time* (1962), translated by John Macquarrie and Edward Robinson, Oxford: 1967, p. 136].

These relationships become particularly clear where I am not already in an ordered environment, but have to create order for objects, assign places for them, through my own actions, for example when I am moving into a new room or filling a newly acquired chest of drawers. Ordering space means that, with conscious deliberation, I assign a place in a space or a container to every object, to which from now on it belongs, and to which I will always return it after I have removed it to make use of it. This ordering must be done appropriately, so that all available space is used, and that things that belong together are in fact placed together, that things which are used frequently are preferably placed in the most accessible places, and so on. Thus human ordering always gives a strange sense of satisfaction, because here the world, in the ordered area in question, has become clearly comprehensible and manageable as a result of this activity. From this example we can immediately apply the concept of ordering to the way in which people build up their spatial environment in general through purposeful activity. In this way, the system of places and positions in which we live becomes an ordered world.

But this order created by humans is continually, necessarily, lost through human activity, through 'life' itself, and then requires a specific effort to restore it. If, after making use of an object, I do not immediately return it to its place, but carelessly leave it lying where it was used, then it lies around 'somewhere or other', in some arbitrary place. This 'lying around' is, as Heidegger has observed, 'must be distinguished in principle from just occurring at random in some spatial position',[3] but, as a sign of disorder, it is a disturbance of my order and as such it is from the start related to my order. What is lying around will soon be in my way, that is, it is taking place away from other things, and hindering me in my movement. I must then make order again, that is, make space for myself by tidying up, or new ordering.

The process of new ordering is a very significant one for the understanding of concrete space. We are re-creating space for ourselves. This means that space, such as the space of a certain room in which I live and work, or the space of a particular container in which I keep things, is not always immediately available in an objective sense, but disorder decreases space, so that soon we can no longer move, and order once again creates new space. Ordering shows us a newly found distance, liberating and in extreme cases even a little empty and cold. The size of the space thus essentially

3 Heidegger, *Sein und Zeit*, p. 102 [p. 136].

depends on human activity. So one can adapt Mephisto's phrase for this context: method will teach you space to win.[4]

The comprehensibility of living space

The concrete space of human life is organized by purposeful activity in such a way that everything has its assigned place. This spatial order is created only in the smallest detail by the individual. For the most part, we find it already present as a supra-individual order, into which we are born. But this too has come into being as the result of a purposeful human activity. This space of human operation has therefore rightly been referred to as purposeful space [Zweckraum]. It is in this purposeful form that the world becomes comprehensible to us, and only because of it can I move meaningfully in space. Purposeful space is necessarily at the same time a comprehensible space.

This connection was already very clearly seen in his day by Dilthey. In one passage he writes: 'Any place planted with trees, any room in which seating is placed in order, is understandable to us from childhood, because human setting of purposes, ordering, assessing of value as something common … has assigned its place to every object in the room.'[5] And in another passage: 'Everything by which we are surrounded is understood by us as a manifestation of life and intellect. The bench in front of the door, the shady tree, house and garden, have their nature and their significance in this manifestation.'[6] Dilthey too here speaks of a place which human activity has assigned to every individual object. Things have been placed together by man in their spatial proximity according to the plan of a discernible inner order. Spatial location at this particular place here acquires its deeper significance. From the outset it guides my understanding of things in their meaningful connection. The bench in front of the door is different from one in a public area, and the chairs around the family dining table are different from those ranged in rows in a lecture hall.

Dilthey thus understands this ordered space as the embodiment of human intellect. The whole designed human life space is therefore for him, as he understands the Hegelian concept, objective intellect, or as we would say today, with the sharper distinction made by Nicolai Hartmann, objectivized

4 Editor's note: the original phrase here is 'Method will teach you time to win' [Doch Ordnung läßt Euch Zeit gewinnen].

5 Wilhelm Dilthey, *Gesammelte Schriften*, vol. 7, p. 208.

6 Dilthey, *Gesammelte Schriften*, vol. 8, p. 79.

intellect. And as such, spatial order then becomes a common medium, in which we can safely move and in which everything is 'understandable to us from childhood.'

Room to manoeuvre

Before we pursue these perspectives further, we need to consider an addition and partly a correction of the discussion up to this point. We will refer again to the simplest case of an ordered connection of places. However convincing the image in which the individual places in the space join together to form a whole, on the other hand the space is not identical with the whole composed of these places. The places are places for the things that belong there. But they need not always be taken up by those things. Sometimes these places will stand empty. We do not find in them what we expected to find. The tool is not lying in the place where it belongs, and in the storage areas, such as the potato cellar, nothing is to be found. I return disappointed. Or else the places are still free. This is something different. Here I still have the opportunity to place something or other there. I constantly need a free place when I want to put something down or lay it ready for later use. All this means that the totality of places is not by any means to be considered as that of a volume of space composed of parts that constantly remain together.

But beyond this, my living and operating space is still basically something different from the totality of the full and empty places around me. At the same time, I need space to move between these things and to deal practically with them, in fact to have any interaction with and among them. This does not mean that I, as a physical creature, myself also need a certain place – although the word is now subject to a certain shift in meaning: it is no longer a place in the sense of the assigned position, but place in the sense of the volume of space taken up. As long as I look at the relationships in this way, I see myself simply as a thing among things (which in a certain sense is what I am). But what is different is the manner in which I have something ready to hand, grasp it, do something with it, or perhaps only look at it; because for this I need a space for my own actions, a space out of which I reach, a space for my movements (not seen from outside in an objectivizing way, but seen from within and carried out from within) to be allowed full play. Here the word 'space' acquires a quite different sense, namely the one that has become familiar to us in our preliminary linguistic observations as the free hollow space of human dwelling. It is only here that we come across the transcendental side of the problem of space. Heidegger presented it in the context in question by distinguishing between the 'spatiality of the ready-to-hand within-the-world' and the 'spatiality of being-in-the-world',[7] where the nearness and direction of things to their places correspond to the new characters of 'dis-stance' [Entfernung] and 'orientation.' Sartre also has something similar in mind when he says in the passage already quoted that man 'situates himself' in hodological relationships, for here too 'situation' does not mean the objective spatial position, but the relationship with the world, developed from within. Thus the totality of ordering of places on the one hand and my room to manoeuvre on the other together, in exact correlation, determine my space of action.

Extending the concept of the space of action

Earlier we looked at the space of action in so far as it is totally shaped in purposeful human action. What is ready-to-hand in the strict Heideggerian sense, the things in daily use, are not only put in their place by the order-creating individual, they are also previously constructed by him, through the skill of a craftsman or a technician. The bringing together of these objects of use with the totality of spatial order creates a totally organized and therefore also totally comprehensible space. This is the work-space in the narrower sense, the space not only in which we work, but also which is totally constructed by human work. This is the space of the craftsmen's and technicians' world. This is most clearly realized in the interior of the house and in organized workplaces, workshops and factories, as well as link roads and means of transport, and most purely, as we may say in a careless but understandable abbreviation, in the world of the city. In this space I move with total safety, everything here is ready to be grasped and available for use, from the door handle to the handle of the cigarette machine. I know how to use everything correctly. Where in the interior of this space there are still limits to this meaningful order, they are conditioned as 'disorder' by human negligence or failure.[8]

But this space is not the whole space. This does change to a certain extent when we step out of the urban-technical area into the landscape. At

---

7 Heidegger, *Sein und Zeit*, §§ 22 and 23.

8 I will not discuss here the other limits I come up against if I move out of the space of my traditional culture and into the equally functionally structured space of another culture, in this context from home into a foreign land.

first, certainly, the basic structure is preserved. We stay on the paths that we have laid out, between the gardens we have planted, between the fields that we have tilled, and so on. Nature too is included in human ordering of space. The landscape too has been cultivated. And even if the preset nature of the terrain and the inherent laws of organic growth set certain boundaries to the human urge to design, basically the same ordering arrangement of places and positions is preserved in which space becomes comprehensible. The landscape too has become culture, has become a human working and dwelling space.

It is only at the limits of human development, already difficult for us to attain today, that the truly untouched landscape opens up, to which the preceding definitions no longer apply. It is no longer shaped by the human urge to design. Perhaps one can still speak here, outside the region of structured paths, of a hodological space, even when one must first carve out one's own path according to the conditions of the terrain. But beyond the attainable destinations lie other points, steep mountains for example, to which no possible path still leads. And furthermore, here there are no longer any fixed places for available objects. The definitions of a space of action shaped by individuals are therefore missing. But does the landscape on that account cease to be a space? We can answer this question only by saying that we are here entering into a different space. Different human behaviour corresponds to a different space, whether it is the geographical space of the explorer, already extensively theorized, the aesthetic space of the individual who observes and perceives, or simply the endless expanse as the scope of the human appetite for adventure. And from these other spaces a new light immediately also falls upon the narrower space of daily life in the civilized world.

3. Day Space and Night Space

The relationship between the two spaces

In describing the space of action, we concentrated above all on the rational factor that results in a structure of space created by man and thus comprehensible by man. But in doing so, in a methodologically conditioned one-sided emphasis, we have isolated only one specific aspect of space, and thus, for the time being, put to one side other aspects that we must now make equally part of our considerations. That such quite different aspects exist had already struck us quite forcefully when we considered falling asleep and waking up; for we realized then that here space does not simply disappear and become restored, but in the darkness of night a quite different space appears, which was concealed during the daytime and has quite different characteristics of its own, and because of these other characteristics is capable of surrounding the sleeping person in a sheltering manner, as has been described.

Only by means of such experiences do we come to notice how much, in our everyday ideas of space, we are guided by a quite specific space, that is, the clear and visible space of daytime, and that many qualities that we are accustomed to ascribe unquestioningly to space as such are by no means attached to space in general, but are only specific characteristics of day space. This includes above all the assumption, which up to now we have silently taken for granted, but which in reality is not at all justifiable, that we can see in space. Only in a visible world, for example, is there a horizon and a perspective, such as we had, apparently quite naturally, assumed to be part of the elementary basic structure of space. But if one can no longer see, then both horizon and perspective disappear. For this to happen, one does not even have to be totally blind. Every evening, with the onset of darkness, the visibility of objects in space disappears. And yet we remain in the space. Only, this space has a totally different character. To distinguish it from the bright space of daytime, we will call it night space, and must now turn our attention to the new aspects that accompany it.

In juxtaposing the two kinds of space, we are immediately struck by how strongly day space is perceived by sight, and so is primarily a seeing space. Sight takes the lead here, and the other sense, touch and hearing, are only additional factors, while at night they take over the lead and sight is not quite eliminated, but is driven back except to a very small extent. Therefore we must obviously investigate the share of the individual sense in the building up of total space, and to distinguish between the corresponding forms of space, seeing space, hearing space and touching space. (We can here ignore the senses of smell and taste.) Thus psychology has in fact turned to the research of these different spaces of the senses, and the results are of the highest importance to us too. However, we will not concern ourselves for the time being with these artificially separated partial spaces, which can be separated only in the abstract, but first of all we will consider experienced space in general, as it is modified in different circumstances. This is the difference here between day space and night space with the transitional forms that insert themselves between them, and only as a construction to aid our train of thought will we occasionally refer to the different spaces of the senses.

Day space

Day space has precedence for the experiencing of space. Our familiar perceptions of space are taken from day space, and if we wish to recognize night space in its individual essence, we must first distinguish it from day space. And here it will at first be through exceptional phenomena that we characterize night space, that is, the removal of elements that are linked with visibility. Only afterwards will we be in a position to discover the positive aspects of night space. So our considerations must necessarily begin with day space, in order to distinguish it from night space, and in doing so we can restrict ourselves to the features that are decisive in the distinction between the two kinds of space.

The essential feature of day space lies in the fact that we can 'oversee' it in its entire extent. Not only do I have individual objects, but I have always incorporated them in the totality of space. If for the moment we use the abstraction of the visual plane, that is, the projection of all spatial phenomena on a level vertical to the line of vision, disregarding their distance, then the individual objects appear clearly distinguished from each other, with defined contours. However, the visual plane is always filled up with colours and brightness. It is always given as a continuum, that is, it has no holes. Even the 'blind spot' in the eye, which ought to appear as a gap in the field of vision, or some defect in vision, is always compensated for.[1]

But the visual plane has been introduced here only as a preliminary simplification. In reality, I see things from the outset in their full spatiality, that is, also taking into account depth of vision. It is not a question here of how the experience of depth of vision comes about genetically. We are concerned only with the purely phenomenal, in which depth of vision has always been given. What initially appeared as a continuum in which gaps are compensated for, now becomes our ability to see past the nearer objects into the space of things lying further off. Here the continuum that creates the closedness of the visual plane becomes a free space which separates the nearer objects from the more distant ones. What is peculiar to day space and that which distinguishes it from other forms of space is that the intermediate space between things, that is, this apparent nothingness, is perceived in it.

The perceptible deep structure of vision space is based on the link, not to be analysed here in detail, between perception and movement[2] that is, on the way in which the gaze at the distant space shifts when I look past the objects in front. The physical precondition for this possibility is the rectilinearity of the ray of light, the fact that one must in any case bear in mind that it is only in optical space that rectilinearity (and the concept, based upon it, of a level surface) has any meaning. It is only on the possibility given by the ray of vision of bringing three points into alignment [visieren], that the 'orderliness of the visible'[3] is based, as Lassen has called it and from which he derives the essential kinship between space and appearance. For him, this means that space, as we understand it from the start, is the space experienced by the eye, and that the other senses, above all the sense of touch, co-operate, but do not produce space on their own.

This observability of visible space has been clearly stressed by Minkowski in his *Lived time*, where he distinguishes between a day and a night space, a light and a dark space: day space opens itself out to me to its whole extent when I open my eyes. I see objects with their sharp contours, but I also see the gaps that separate them. I see not only the objects but also the empty space that lies between them. There is clearly distinguished mass as well as open space. The decisive thing here is the observability which

1 See Harold Lassen, *Beiträge zu einer Phänomenologie und Psychologie der Anschauung*, Würzburg: 1939, p. 80 ff.

2 See Viktor von Weizsäcker, *Der Gestaltkreis*, Leipzig: 1940.

3 Lassen, *Beiträge zu einer Phänomenologie*, p. 59 ff.

brings everything together into a unity. 'Everything in this space', says Minkowski, 'is clear, determined, natural, unproblematic.' It is also the 'intellectual' space which is characterized by light, brightness, clarity and certainty. Minkowski adds that this bright space is from the start given as a common space, which I share with other people. 'Bright pace is at the same time a socialized space in the widest sense of the world.'[4] If I do not wish to be totally at the mercy of this communal sense, I must create private areas for myself in it, hiding-places which belong to me alone and to which I can retreat from public space.

Twilight spaces

Before we turn to night space with its total darkness, let us glance at the transitional phenomena mentioned above, in which the clarity and observability of day space, and with it the given fact of the horizon, are gradually lost. These include twilight, fog and other related phenomena. I will refer to these collectively as twilight spaces.

a. The forest

Among these fading, horizontal spaces I would like, in preparation, to include the forest, although here, strictly speaking, we cannot speak of a twilight (or only in the very restricted sense of a certain forest darkness, merges with the dissipated rustling of the trees). In contrast to the other transitional phenomena, we are not dealing here with an obstacle to visibility in the form of intervening media, such as fog or darkness. Things are entirely recognizable in their forms; it is rather the obstruction of vision by the things themselves, by the tree-trunks and bushes, the branches and leaves, which enclose us in their own realm, almost as if in a kind of inner space. The gaze penetrates only so far into the forest and then loses itself among the tree-trunks.

To this extent, the forest takes up a kind of intermediate position between the inner and the outer space. On the one hand, despite its genuine extent, it is not a free space. It has no view and it has above all no horizon with its clear demarcation. Man is enclosed in the shelter of the forest. But this

4 Eugène Minkowski, *Le temps vécu. Études phenomenologiques et psychopathologiques*, Paris: 1933, p. 393 [*Lived time. Phenomenological and psychopathological studies*, translated by Nancy Metzel, Evanston: 1970, p. 429].

enclosure is very different and in a certain sense more material, because it is after all no mere obstruction of the view by fog and other intangible media (of which we will speak later), but an obstruction of the ability to move itself, by tangible material things such as trees and bushes. But on the other hand there are no solid walls to designate an impassable boundary. Man is enclosed in a narrow space, though this has no firm, assignable boundary. He can to a certain extent move freely. He can walk through the forest. But as soon as he enters it on one side, he finds no escape from the imprisonment of his gaze and he does not gain freedom, for the narrow, observable area moves with him, like his shadow; he cannot get rid of his constriction, but remains enclosed in it. This paradoxical character of the forest is expressed by a modern French writer quoted by Bachelard: 'A characteristic of forests is to be closed, and at the same time, open on every side.'[5] Hence its uncannily oppressive character.

What is confusing here is that in this 'world without frontiers'[6] no direction is distinguished above another. For this reason we easily lose our orientation if we cannot allow ourselves to be guided by the paths leading through the wood, and even these do not reliably guide us, because we are at the mercy of their unobservable twists and turns, and cannot maintain a clear direction in them. Even on these paths, we are walking as though blind. So we can easily get lost in the forest. This can be positively disturbing. We never attain the protective field of free vision. An enemy may lurk behind any bush. Twilight, that is, semi-clarity, is part of the nature of the forest. Individual objects lose their sharp contours and dissolve into a medium that flows through everything. And again this is linked in the area of the audible with the rustling of the trees, in whose uncertainty the individual voices come together in a fading total impression.

Eichendorff expresses this in continually new ways in the sense of the Romantic notion:

> In the forest, in the rustling,
> I do not know where I am,[7]

---

5 Gaston Bachelard, *Poetik des Raumes*, translated by Kurt Leonhard, Munich: 1960, p. 282 [*The poetics of space*, translated by Maria Jolas, Boston, Mass.: 1969, p. 185].

6 Bachelard, *Poetik des Raumes*, p. 215.

7 'Im Walde, in dem Rauschen, / ich weiß nicht, wo ich bin,' 'In der Fremde', Joseph Freiherr von Eichendorff, *Heimweh. Neue Gesamtausgabe der Werke und Schriften*, edited by G. Baumann and S. Grosse, Stuttgart: 1957, vol. 1, p. 34.

he says in the sense of this Romantic-pantheistic idea of being taken up into a comprehensive whole. But this effect can, where the Romantic optimistic enthusiasm for life has got lost, also rise to the point of uncanniness, and the forest is then perceived as a mighty, threatening force, which (as the tropical primeval forest devours many a site of an earlier culture) once again destroys all human structuring of space.

> The forest has much force,[8]

says Bergengruen, who still has a strong sense of these elementary forces.

b. Fog

This disappearing of individual objects into a common whole, which was already preparing itself in the forest through the confusing multiplicity of forms that shift behind each other, is completed where the gaze is no longer obstructed by tangible individual things, but by the atmospheric conditions as a whole. This comes across particularly impressively in fog; for fog shows us a totally altered world compared with the observable world of daytime. In fog, things lose their tangibility, they glide into the incomprehensible and acquire by this very process a newly menacing character, stronger than that which we have already perceived in the forest. They emerge from the fog and disappear again, and both suddenly, without my having noticed their coming or going. I cannot therefore prepare myself inwardly for their approach; suddenly they stand before me and are dangerously close. In this world there is no gradual shading off of distances, but there is only – as with the forest, but to a much more striking extent – a quite narrowly bounded close zone, behind which a white nothingness immediately opens up. Significantly, in East Friesland they speak of a 'little world' when they speak of fog; the restriction to this small close zone is clearly expressed in this phrase. Therefore, whatever I meet in the snow immediately strikes me in the vicinity of a directly threatening touch, a direct collision. The ordinary 'fore-sight' with which I allow things to approach me has here become impossible, and must be counterbalanced by a correspondingly greater alertness.

Hermann Hesse once described this experience movingly as an experience of human loneliness: 'It is always wonderfully moving to see

8 'Der Wald hat viel Gewalt', Werner Bergengruen, *Die Rose von Jericho*, Zurich: 1964, p. 9 and p. 14.

how the fog separates everything neighbouring and things that apparently belong together, how it surrounds and closes off everything and makes it inescapably lonely. A man passes you on a country road, he is driving a cow or a goat, or pushing a cart, or carrying a bundle … You see him coming and bid him Godspeed, and he thanks you; but hardly has he passed you, and you turn and look after him, than you see him at once becoming indistinct, and disappearing without trace into the grey.'[9] Loneliness becomes all the more oppressive because the other world is still audible, but no longer visible: 'You hear, right next to you, people and animals that you cannot see, walking and working and uttering cries. All this has something fairytale-like, strange, other-worldly about it, and for some moments you perceive the symbolism of it with frightening clarity. Just as one object is mercilessly strange to another, and one person to another, whoever he is, and just as our paths always cross only for a few steps and a few moments, and attain the fleeting appearance of belonging together, neighbourliness and friendship.' Hesse introduces the thought in the well-known lines:

> Strange to wander in fog.
> Lonely are bush and stone,
> no tree sees the other near,
> everyone is alone …
> Strange to wander in fog.
> To live is to be lonely.
> No man knows the other,
> everyone is alone.[10]

Perhaps it is a particular interpretation of Hesse's when he lays so much stress on human loneliness. If we keep to the directly given fact that emerges so clearly from his lines, it is rather the strangely oppressive feeling of being suspended in empty space. And this again is the more oppressive the lighter, the whiter the fog becomes, so that beyond all possible sense of danger a feeling of loss of one's own nature, of a floating in empty space,

9 'Seltsam, im Nebel zu wandern! / Einsam ist jeder Busch und Stein, / kein Baum sieht den andern, / jeder ist allein ... / Seltsam, im Nebel zu wandern! / Leben ist Einsamsein. / Kein Mensch kennt den andern, /jeder ist allein.' Hermann Hesse, 'Im Nebel', *Gesammelte Dichtungen*, vol. 1, Frankfurt a. M.: 1952, p. 635 ff.

10 'Seltsam, im Nebel zu wandern! / Einsam ist jeder Busch und Stein, / kein Baum sieht den andern, / jeder ist allein ... / Seltsam, im Nebel zu wandern! / Leben ist Einsamsein. / Kein Mensch kennt den andern, /jeder ist allein.' Hermann Hesse, 'Im Nebel', *Gesammelte Dichtungen*, vol. 1, Frankfurt a. M.: 1952, p. 635 ff.

forces itself upon us. Even more oppressive than the silence of infinite space of which Pascal spoke,[11] emptiness here becomes directly defiant.

c. Falling snow

In a similarly nightmarish manner, Stifter describes in *Bergkristall* the journey of two children through the densely falling snow, which makes the surrounding world disappear for them: 'Around them', he writes, 'was nothing but the dazzling white, … which drew an ever smaller circle around them, and then passed into a light fog, falling in streaks, which devoured and concealed everything else, and in the end was nothing but the inexorably falling snow', and then, a little later: 'Again there was nothing around them but white, and all around there was no intervening darkness to be seen. There seemed to be a great abundance of light, and yet one could not see three steps in front of oneself; everything was, so to say, wrapped in one white darkness, and because there was no shadow, no judgement could be made about the size of things, and the children could not tell if they were going upwards or downwards, until a steepness grasped their feet and forced them to go upwards.'[12]

It is once again the feeling of floating in empty space, similar to the space of fog, and yet in a peculiar way after all different from it. Stifter speaks of a 'great abundance of light' and of 'one white darkness.' The skier in the mountains knows this experience. It is the great excess of brightness, the 'white darkness', combined with the impossibility of recognizing anything with certainty, which puts man at the mercy of the oppressive nothingness, far more than the black darkness of the night was ever able to do. It is the total dematerialization of the surrounding world. We have the feeling of having to tumble into nothingness, because we see nothing fixed around us that we could hold onto. We feel as though floating and falling into nothingness. At the same time certain stages can be distinguished, according to whether it is a case of disembodiment in the dimly falling snow or whether at the same time an actual fog appears, which is turned by the intensive sunlight from above into the white abundance of light that has been mentioned.

It is again an entirely horizonless space, and as is shown very clearly here, this means that the basis of human orientation, the distinction between vertical and horizontal is, not actually entirely removed (for it

11 See the present book, p. 111.

12 Adalbert Stifter, *Bergkristall*, in *Bunte Steine*, Munich: 1951, p. 188 ff.

remains in the sense of weight), but made disturbingly uncertain. One sees no differences of height, one sees no boundary between heaven and earth, and only when the foot, feeling its way carefully forward, becomes aware of greater differences in height, does one notice from the change in muscular sensation that the ground is rising.

d. Twilight

The conditions are similar to those of fog when twilight comes and the night finally thickens into total darkness. The two phenomena are often combined, for it is precisely at twilight when fog begins to rise to a greater degree. Only, this fog, rising out of the twilight and disappearing in the darkness, has quite a different character from the fog that is flooded by full, bright light. It is not so much the feeling of a devouring nothingness, which somehow sucks a person in, so that he has the sensation of falling into a void, but on the contrary something, as it were, assuming materiality and menacingly intruding on him. Where the border between perception and deception of the senses become blurred, an intangible, constantly changing, nightmarishly threatening world comes into being. Every bush, blurred in the half-darkness, turns into a menacing shape. Everywhere there lurks a danger always present in its intangibility, and we are seized by a feeling of deep anxiety.

In Goethe's 'Erlkönig' this nightmarish effect of twilight finds its poetic expression.[13] The 'streak of fog', the wind whispering among dry leaves, the grey old willows are enough to build up such an uncanny and dangerous world. This menacing power of the twilight is well formulated by Goethe in various poems. For example, in the 'Chinese-German book of seasons and hours' he writes:

> Twilight descended,
> soon all that is near is distant …
> Everything turns into uncertainty,
> creepy fog rises;
> reflecting deep black uncertainty
> the lake lies still.[14]

---

13 Johann Wolfgang von Goethe, 'Erlkönig', *Gedenkausagabe*, edited by Ernst Beutler, vol. 1, Zurich and Stuttgart: 1948-71, p. 115 ff.

14 'Dämmrung senkte sich von oben, / schon ist alle Nähe fern ... / Alles schwankt ins Ungewisse, / Nebel schleichen in die Höh; / schwarzvertiefte Finsternisse / widerspiegelnd ruht der See.' Goethe, 'Chinesisch-deutsche Jahres– und Tageszeiten', *Gedenkausgabe*, vol. 2, p. 53.

What is important here above all is the shrinking and at the same time the retreat of the surroundings into a 'little world': 'Soon all that is near is distant …' The immediate surrounding area narrows around the individual, because what had until now seemed near has moved into the distance. Or, even more pointedly, in 'Welcome and farewell':

> Soon stood, in robe of mist, the oak,
> A tow'ring giant in his size,
> Where darkness through the thicket broke,
> And glared with hundred gloomy eyes.[15]

The 'hundred gloomy eyes' of darkness is an apt expression of this uncanny feeling that overcomes us from the twilight world. We feel helpless, at the mercy of a gaze which sees us, which however we ourselves cannot locate anywhere.

> The night a thousand monsters made

the poem continues. These are the creations of human fear.

However we must not overlook the fact that this very twilight can appear quite different to the individual, and very much less threatening. Matthias Claudius, for example, in his well-known 'Evening song', speaks of 'the cover of dusk' in which the world is 'intimate and sweet.' The reduction of the world to a narrower region through the falling away of the more distant zones is felt here too, but to the extent to which these disappear in the darkness, there also disappears with them the hostile menace of the world, while the narrower surrounding area, now no longer threatened by outside forces, is perceived as a sheltering cover, one which practically belongs to us. It is a world falling asleep, which invites man too to fall asleep.

Man may therefore react with entirely opposite feelings to these spaces. At first it was the sense of the uncanny, the frightening, even the nightmarishly menacing, that overcame men in fog and twilight. These are the spaces of fear, in which man is tormented by a feeling of uncertainty and lostness. And yet this twilight may acquire some quality of an enclosing 'intimacy.' And this feeling is then completed by night.

---

15 'Schon stand im Nebelkleid die Eiche, / ein aufgetürmter Reise, da, / wo Finsternis aus dem Gesträuche / mit hundert schwarzen Augen sah.' 'Die Nacht schuf tausend Ungeheuer'. Goethe, 'Willkommen und Abschied', Gedenkausagabe, vol. 1, p. 49.

But how is it possible that the same circumstances, or, at most, different ones to a greater or lesser extent, can have such opposite effects? This is clearly the effect of people's different attitudes. With the process of falling asleep, we noticed that man must let go of himself in order to sink into sleep, to some extent abandoning the alert attentiveness of daytime. So he is at first gripped by crippling fear when day space, with its observability and the possibilities based upon it of cautiously secure self-confidence, slips away. Man feels insecure, and thus the sense of vulnerability which has been described comes into existence. Darkness is lack of light, and thus lack of the possibilities of purposeful action in the world. Only when man renounces orientation in the bright world of daytime and insecurely entrusts himself to darkness can that orientation develop in its own nature. And then there grow the deeper experiences of the night space that shelters man. We must therefore turn to this space in its full individual nature.

Night space

a. Moving through the night

The process by which the familiar visible space is modified by changing atmospheric conditions is completed by night. If we now juxtapose the two extremes, the dark space of night is distinguished from the clear, observable, but also sober and problem-free day space by a totally altered structure. I do not mean the abstract construction of a pure space of touch and hearing, as it may be realized in the world of the blind, but the concrete experience of space, as it is given to all of us at night and as we repeatedly encounter it in the regular change to the bright space of day. Perhaps only a creature which knows the bright world of day is capable of completely comprehending the individual character of dark space.

In order to provide a graphic image, I will clarify it in terms of a walk on a country road by night. This space too retains a degree of visibility. Just as noises reach my ears, the barking of dogs on a distant farm, the steps of a person approaching me, there are also certain residues of visibility if I am walking on the road by night: perhaps the stars above me, or the overcast light of the moon behind clouds, the lights of a settlement in the distance; and I also recognize the path a few steps ahead of me, distinguishing it from the darker grass beside it. In general, however, it is only a vague proximate zone that is recognizable to me here. Even the few lights that I can glimpse are at no precise distance. For this reason it is difficult to assess how far away an emerging light may be, how far I may still have to go in a state of weariness.

This at the same time determines my altered movement in the darkness. Because I cannot 'oversee' this space, I do not have in it the free space for natural unconcerned movement. And when it is so dark that one cannot 'see one's hand in front of one's eyes', we can move in this space only by carefully feeling our way. At every moment we fear to stumble over an uneven patch in the road or somehow painfully bump into something. To the extent to which we can still stride out confidently, it is conditioned by 'blind trust' in the solid nature of the road. In the same way I move even in my own house in darkness in comparative freedom, because I know the position of all the objects from the daytime, and movement between them has become a practised habit. All the more frighteningly – and often more painfully – am I surprised when an object blocks my way in a place where it does not belong, and I bump into it. But as soon as I move into an unknown space, perhaps off the path in a forest, I can only move along carefully, feeling my way with my feet and securing myself with my hands, listening to every unexpected noise to determine where it comes from. I must exercise attentiveness everywhere, because the normal 'fore-sight', that is, the overview of the space lying before me, is missing.

Yet, it would be wrong to look at night space merely as a deprivation of day space caused by a lack of full visibility and the possibility of localization. Rather, night space has its very own character, which needs to be recognized.

b. The descriptions of Minkowski and Merleau-Ponty

Minkowski, whom we have already cited when characterizing day space, was probably the first to try to develop the individual character of night space. We will first examine his observations. The darkness that determines night space is not, according to Minkowski, simply a lack of light, but has a positive character of its own. It is 'more material' than brightness. The space of darkness does not 'spread out before me', like the clearly recognizable space of daytime, 'but touches me directly, envelops me … even penetrates me, completely passes through me, so that one could almost say that while the ego is permeable by darkness it is not permeable by light.'[16]

Space therefore no longer has the character of a free space, in which I can move freely in a certain circumference, but it encloses me more narrowly.

16 Minkowski, *Le temps vécu*, p. 393 [p. 429].

It lies, as it were, directly on the surface of my body, 'it directly touches me.' But on the other hand it is not something foreign. I feel myself to be almost protectively enveloped by this space. 'It penetrates me and totally permeates me.' The self thus merges with the darkness. Man mingles with his space.

And to this is linked the second characteristic. In contrast to the sober clarity of the bright space, this dark space is 'opaque' and thus full of secrets. 'In dark space everything is obscure and mysterious.'[17] One feels the presence of the unknown. Thus, darkness is by no means an absolute nothingness, on the contrary it is full of surprises and secrets. A light, a shimmer may break through the darkness, a rustling may begin, and as it is entirely filled with these patterns and noises, they also fill me.

In this space there is no distance, no extension in the actual sense, and yet it has a depth of its own. But this depth is different from the dimension of depth of day space, for it is not linked to height and breadth; rather, depth, resisting all quantification, is the only dimension of this space. It is a dark and unlimited covering, in which all directions are the same. And while the bright space of day (according to Minkowski) is from the start a common space, in this dark space man remains alone. The gaze, as the means of silent agreement, the smile as a sign of closeness, is lacking. Night does not show, it can only speak or be silent.

Minkowski first develops his findings about dark space with reference to the world of the mentally ill. Schizophrenics, according to him, have in fact only one such dark space. But this night space also exists in the world of the healthy, but with them it has become one form of space which rhythmically alternates with the other form, that of bright space. This results in the question of the mutual relationship of day and night space. Minkowski starts from the observation that I, while sitting in my room, still know that space continues beyond the walls of the room. This space, not visible from my room, is equated by Minkowski with night space, which has in a certain way retreated behind the boundaries of the bright area. Bright space, by his account, is surrounded by dark space, and dark space lies behind bright space. If it is perhaps not a totally convincing notion that the uncertainly understood space beyond the boundaries of the visible can be equated with the quite concretely experienced dark space, it is certainly accurate to say that the relationship between the two spaces can be grasped not so much in the sense of a symmetrical correspondence, but rather the dark space forms in some indeterminate way, which is still difficult to comprehend,

17 Minkowski, *Le temps vécu*, p. 394 [p. 429].

the basis from which day space can develop (even though comprehension must begin in bright space).

The question of the precedence of night space over day space has been taken up by Merleau-Ponty with direct reference to Minkowski, in his *Phenomenology of perception*. Here he describes the transition from the world of day to that of night, as follows: 'When, for example, the world of clear and articulate objects is abolished, our perceptual being, cut off from its world, evolves a spatiality without things. This is what happens in the night. Night is not an object before me; it enwraps me and infiltrates through all my senses, stifling my recollections and almost destroying my identity. I am no longer withdrawn into my perceptual look-out from which I watch the outlines of objects moving by at a distance. Night has no outlines; it is itself in contact with me and its unity is the mystical unity of the "mana". Even shouts or a distant light people it only vaguely, and then it comes to life in its entirety; it is pure depth without foreground or background, without surfaces and without any distance separating it from me.'[18]

This on the one hand entirely corroborates Minkowski, to whom only partial reference is made. All the more important then is the direction in which he pursues the thought already expressed by Minkowski. This includes above all the way in which he picks up the concept of 'mana' to denote the mystical participation in night. It is 'pre-logical' forms of thought that emerge in the night space, and to that extent the Romantics were totally right when they felt closer in the night to the origins of life. The extinguishing to a great extent of personal identity is then only the necessary consequence of the discontinuation of the division between subject and object. It also corresponds to this primeval sense of life that animistic ways of thinking turn up here again, and what we encounter as a belief in ghosts and a fear of ghosts is only the consequence of these.

This alteration in spatiality becomes even clearer in sleep and dreaming; for when we awaken in a night space, then 'spatiality without things' at first appears to be something alarming, as a lack of the familiar security of things, and in the face of this we will at first maintain our attentive observation of the daytime, until we succeed in finding that mystic unity in which night space comes to life from within. During sleep, however, man has finally abandoned the level of conscious thought and surrendered entirely to the more profound depths of his life. Only here is the experience

18 Maurice Merleau-Ponty, *Phénoménologie de la perception*, Paris: 1945, p. 328 [*The phenomenology of perception*, translated by Colin Smith, London: 1962, p. 283].

of night space complete. 'During sleep, on the other hand', Merleau-Ponty stresses, 'I hold the world present to me only in order to keep it at a distance, and I revert to the subjective sources of my existence. The phantasms of dreams reveal still more effectively that general spatiality within which clear space and observable objects are embedded.'[19] In this connection he speaks of a 'primary spatiality' [spatialité originaire][20] as it is also accessible to us in the mythical and pathological experiences of space. 'Primary spatiality' does not here mean, as might be suggested by the unclear phrase 'spatiality without things', something like an a priori spatial structure, which is innate before all individual perception, but the form of spatiality that corresponds to an original state of the human subject and out of which the other modifications of spatiality first develop.

19 Merleau-Ponty, *Phénoménologie de la perception*, p. 328 [p. 283].
20 Merleau-Ponty, *Phénoménologie de la perception*, p. 334 [p. 289].

4. Mood and Space

The sense of narrowness and expanse

When we were considering twilight space and night space, it became clear that space is more than the unchanging field of objective realization and purposeful behaviour, that it is, rather, closely connected with the emotional and volitional aspect, in fact with the whole psychological condition of mankind. In this area of expertise, Lewin had already pointed out that hodological space depends not only on the outer conditions of the terrain, but also on the psychological state of the person. This also applies in a more general sense to experienced space as a whole.

In this connection we will again refer to our earlier observations on the narrowness and width of space. We attempted to understand these from the point of view of the room to manoeuvre of human life: narrowness is that which hinders the development of life, and width is that which opens it up to an adequate area of development. But we saw straight away that what is narrow and what is wide can never be established by means of an objective and generally valid standard. What seems wide to one person is perceived by another as only just adequate or even as restrictive. Where one retreats into a narrow cell to work, another needs a spacious hall in order to expand his mind. Where one loves the view from his window and moves his desk near to the window, so that his gaze can sometimes roam pensively into the distance, the other will turn it away from the window, because for him only a closed space enables him to maintain sufficient mental composure. But even in the same person, the need for space varies according to his psychological state and his needs at the time. In a state of deep melancholy he will creep into the narrowness of a cave, in a state of joyful high spirits, conversely, he needs the space for development of a freely opening expanse. Thus Bachelard, for example, explains in his analysis of the dwelling functions: 'The two extreme realities of cottage and manor … take into account our need for retreat and expansion … To sleep well we do not need to sleep in a large room, and to work well we do not have to work in a den.'[1] And for other people perhaps it is different again.

Conversely, the character of the space surrounding the individual has an effect on his mood. So we have a reciprocal influence: the psychological state of the person determines the character of his surrounding space, and conversely the space then affects his psychological state. Every concrete space in which we find ourselves, whether interior or exterior space, as such already has a particular character of mood, has its human qualities, so to speak, and these again, among other things, as the simplest determinants, condition the experiences of narrowness and width of a particular space.

The concept of mood space

To characterize these relationships it will be best to adopt the concept, first introduced by Binswanger, of mood space [gestimmter Raum],[2] even though it should be added to avoid misunderstandings that this mood space is not a space among other possible spaces, but just like hodological space and space of action, an aspect of how we look at space. Mood is a characteristic of just about every space, even if it is more strongly in evidence in one case and less so in another. Less ambiguously we could perhaps say that we are looking at space in terms of its mood character.

Mood, as Heidegger in his day introduced it as a basic philosophical concept,[3] and as I have since tried to develop and expand it on the same basis,[4] proves to be a suitable point of departure through the fact that it still lies before the formation of a distinction between object and subject. Mood is itself not something subjective 'in' an individual and not something objective that could be found 'outside' in his surroundings, but it concerns the individual in his still undivided unity with his surroundings. But for this very reason, mood becomes a key phenomenon in the understanding of experienced space.

What is repeatedly important here is reciprocity. Space has its particular mood, both as an interior space and also as a landscape. It can be cheerful, light, gloomy, sober, festive, and this character of mood then transfers

1 Bachelard, *Poetik des Raumes*, p. 95 [p. 65].

2 Ludwig Binswanger 'Das Raumproblem in der Psychopathologie' (1933), *Ausgewählte Vorträge und Aufsätze*, vol. 2, Bern: 1955, p. 174 ff., and especially the section 'Der gestimmte Raum', p. 195 ff.

3 Heidegger, *Sein und Zeit*, p. 134 ff. [p. 172 ff.].

4 O. F. Bollnow, *Das Wesen der Stimmungen*, Frankfurt a. M.: 1956.

itself to the person staying in it. In particular it is atmospheric conditions that have a cheering, bright, oppressive, etc., effect on man. And in the same way man himself is governed from within by a certain mood, and is inclined to transfer this to the surrounding space, where the concept of transference should only be used in a temporary sense for the preliminary clarification of this direct sense of belonging together and agreement. One speaks of a mood of the human temperament as well as of the mood of a landscape or a closed interior space, and both are, strictly speaking, only two aspects of the same phenomenon.

To start with, I will attempt, quite informally, to gather together some contributions to this question.

The sensual-moral effect of colour

I need not stop to pursue in detail the influence of atmospheric conditions on the experience of space; for these connections are directly known to everyone from their own experience. Even the simplest spatial factor, even the mere distance at which objects appear to us to be in space, changes with weather conditions. On bright evenings, after a rainfall or, even better, when rain is imminent, the distant mountains or houses seem to move much nearer to us. Suddenly they are 'within our grasp' and at the same time gain a much greater degree of sculpturality. As is well known, this phenomenon can be used to predict the weather: it is always a bad sign when distant objects are too near. In a mist, on the other hand, particularly when seen against the sun, objects move away. Mountains retreat further and further back and finally disappear entirely in the atmospheric mist; they are simply not there any more. Only a brief reminder of all this is needed to clarify the influence of weather conditions on our experience of space.

A related phenomenon is that colours, too, make space narrower or wider. Light colours make space not only lighter, but also wider, while dark colours make it narrow. A black ceiling has something heavy, even oppressive, about it, but it can also convey a character of seclusion and cosy warmth. This is also true of the qualities of the individual colours. Goethe carefully examined this effect under the heading of the 'effect of colour with reference to moral associations.' 'Experience teaches us', he writes, 'that particular colours excite particular states of feeling.'[5] It will

5 Goethe, *Farbenlehre. Gedenkausagabe*, vol. 16, p. 207 ff. [*Theory of colours*, translated by Charles Lock Eastlake, London: 1840, p. 304 ff].

therefore be best to clarify this connection in terms of his own observations, restricting ourselves to the purely phenomenal, and as far as possible leaving Goethe's theory of colour aside.

The colour yellow, Goethe points out, 'has a serene, gay, softly exciting character ... We find from experience, that yellow excites a warm and agreeable impression ... This impression of warmth may be experienced in a very lively manner if we look at a landscape through a yellow glass, particularly on a grey winter's day. The eye is gladdened, the heart expanded and cheered, a glow seems at once to breathe towards us.' The stimulating effect of yellow is enhanced the more the colour changes to red. If red-yellow (in Goethe's diction) gives us an 'agreeable and gladdening feeling', the 'feeling of warmth and gladness', then in yellow-red colours (such as vermilion) this effect is enhanced up to a point of 'extreme excitement.' 'The active side is here at its highest energy ... In looking steadfastly at a perfectly yellow-red surface, the colour seems to actually penetrate the [eye].' This yellow-red is thus the most active colour; it comes closest to the individual, it narrows his space, but at the same time it has a stimulating effect. Perhaps, diverging somewhat from Goethe, we will shift this characterization to red itself, for what Goethe describes as red is a special crimson tone, conveying 'gravity and dignity', whose peculiar position is to be understood only in the context of his theory of colour.

Blue however has quite the opposite effect. While yellow-red intrudes on us and thus narrows our space, blue seems to retreat from us. We 'love to contemplate blue, not because it advances to us, but because it draws us after it.' So blue, as the colour of the distant skies and mountains, expands the space around us. But on the other hand it also gives us 'an impression of cold, and thus reminds us of shade.' This effect is also evident when blue appears as the colour of interior space. Goethe remarks: 'Rooms which are hung with pure blue [wallpaper], appear in some degree larger, but at the same time empty and cold.' So, if we may summarize the special spatial point of view, yellowish-red has an active effect on man, intruding upon us, enlivening us but at the same time narrowing our space, while the effect of blue is to retreat, expanding our space but at the same time emptying it and allowing it to become fixed.

Green, on the other hand, is the outstanding colour in which the opposing effects balance each other and which therefore neither narrows nor expands, but in its neutrality rests in itself. It is therefore commended as particularly restful and is preferred for people's living rooms. 'The eye experiences a distinctly graceful impression from this colour. If the two elementary colours are mixed in perfect equality so that neither predominates, the eye and the mind repose on the result of this junction as upon a simple colour. The beholder has neither the wish nor the power to imagine a state beyond it. Hence for rooms to live in constantly, the green colour is most generally selected.'

It should finally be mentioned in connection with Goethe that this 'sensual-moral effect' of colours does not primarily come from an association, that red-yellow does not appear warm to us because it reminds us of flames and warm sunshine, or that blue seems cold because it makes us think of cool shadows and frosty ice. Rather (even if with Goethe the two viewpoints seem to go together), these are qualities which attach purely phenomenally to colours and which one therefore experiences most purely in their complete saturation, when they are dissociated from a particular object, for example in the decoration of a room, or even better, in the graphic example so often chosen by Goethe, when one looks at the surrounding world through a coloured glass.

Interior spaces

What has been said here about the effect of colours, above all where they almost entirely saturate the character of our surroundings, is true in a differentiated sense of every space that surrounds us: each one has its own atmospheric character that impinges on us and takes hold of our feelings so that it falls into accord with this mood. We will for now restrict ourselves to some examples of such interior spaces that have been consciously constructed by their builders to create such a mood. If we merely cast a fleeting glance at art history, the most varied possibilities crowd in upon us.

The twilight space of a church puts us in a reverential mood, even if there is no religious service being held there at the moment. It is the special character of the space itself which creates this effect. Quite different, in contrast, are the buildings of the Reformed church of the eighteenth century, which are consciously intended to create a mood of enlightenment, brightness and at the same time sobriety. They were meant to put the visitor in the mood for clear reception of [religious] teaching, no longer for participation in a sacred event.

One can look at the whole of architectural history from the viewpoint of the different mood content of the interior spaces constructed in it. The early basilicas with their dark closed walls and golden mosaics dimly lit by candles convey the impression of a solemn, dark and enigmatic ceremony. And quite different are the free Gothic church buildings where the walls are almost entirely loosened up into a framework and a wealth of coloured light streams in through the great windows. Sedlmayer has placed this typical mood content of the Gothic cathedral at the centre of his book[6] and interpreted it as the heavens come down to earth. Be that as it may, in any case, here the heavy, gloomy vaults are opposed by a quite different lightness and expanse and freedom. The soul expands in this space and is drawn into the great upward movement.

Quite different again is the floating lightness of many late Baroque church buildings, so jubilant in their brightness that today they are no longer seen by many as a sacred space at all, which is what they undoubtedly are, in the spirit of their time. Here too the expanse of infinity reigns, taking hold of man, but it is no longer so much movement that tears him upwards away from himself, and away from here, but another movement which fills him entirely, putting him into a singing and floating mood, which comes over him with a sense of ceremony.

We will return to some of these examples in another connection. At this point they will merely be suggested, in order to make visible the multiplicity of possibilities that open up here.

The constricting space of the anxious heart

Such effects emanate not only from consciously designed interior spaces, but equally from the space of the open countryside. Like the dark vaults, the black rain clouds also have an oppressive and burdensome quality, even though 'in reality' they allow us ample room for movement. They throw us back upon ourselves and turn us inward. Eichendorff's 'Good-for-Nothing', for example, would never have left his mill on a dull rainy day, and not merely because rambling in the rain would be more arduous, but because it is only sunshine that tempts us out into the distance, while gloomy clouds draw the world much more narrowly together around us.[7]

This is the case in the reciprocal effect already mentioned, indeed in the indivisible unity of interior and exterior not only as the effect of the world on mankind, but also as seen from the human point of view. Space closes in around the tormented person, and everything becomes narrow to him, so that he painfully collides with everything around him. Even by lowering

6 Hans Sedlmayer, *Die Entstehung der Kathedrale*, Zurich: 1950.

7 Some overlapping with the earlier books *Das Wesen der Stimmungen* and *Neue Geborgenheit* was unavoidable, because what was discussed there has acquired new importance in the face of an altered point of view.

his gaze to the ground he loses sight of the horizon, and is constricted into a very narrow space. In this context Binswanger quotes a very apt statement by Goethe, in which the latter cries:

> O God, how world and heaven shrink
> when our hearts become anxious within their bounds.[8]

Anxiety – the German word 'Angst' in its original derivation literally denotes the oppressive sense of narrowness around the heart – at the same time narrows the whole world around us, narrows our room for movement in the world. And Binswanger adds, using this example to clarify the whole nature of mood space: 'By no means does Goethe envisage in this "if-then" relationship a causal connection, as though perhaps the anxiety of the heart were the "cause" of the shrinking of world and heaven ... In this relationship of personal mood and the space around us, nothing is generically primary or secondary, nothing is cause or effect, condition or conditioned, inducing or induced, indeed not even reason or consequence, but rather precisely that which we call anxiety of the heart also consists in a constriction of world and heaven, and conversely, the constriction of world and heaven consists in the anxiety of our hearts.'[9] Binswanger adds, determining the connection in the sense of our question in explicit terminology: 'These ontogenetic connections however are only possible on the basis of the phenomenological relationship to which we have given the name of mood space.'[10]

A similar direction is taken by the observations of H. Tellenbach on 'the spatiality of the melancholic.' In the alteration of experienced space described by him, the most striking aspect is the loss of the spatial dimension of depth. In this pathologically heightened condition, the surrounding world seems purely superficial, without a dimension of depth, and thus without three-dimensionality. 'It was all one flat surface',[11] 'everything is like a wall, everything is flat',[12] are typical recurrent statements relating to this condition. Combined with this is often the impression that things

---

8 'O Gott, wie schränkt sich Welt und Himmel ein, / wenn under Herz in seinen Schranken banget.' Goethe, *Die natürliche Tochter. Gedenkausagabe*, vol. 6, p. 375.

9 Binswanger, 'Das Raumproblem in der Psychopathologie', p. 200.

10 Binswanger, 'Das Raumproblem in der Psychopathologie', p. 201.

11 Hubertus Tellenbach, 'Die Räumlichkeit des Melancholischen', *Der Nervenarzt*, vol. 1, 1956, p. 12 ff. and p. 289 ff., p. 13.

12 Tellenbach, 'Die Räumlichkeit des Melancholischen', p. 14.

have moved away into the distance. 'Everything is so far away from me,' says one statement, 'I see everything so far away as if it were in another village.'[13] Tellenbach understands this condition in the context of Heidegger's analysis of 'Dasein' as the loss of the 'tendency towards nearness' that belongs to human nature: 'The melancholic has lost nearness in the sense of room made for equipment [Eingeräumtheit des Zeugs].'[14] 'The world-picture of the sick person consists of nameless backgrounds.'[15] This at the same time includes the emptying of all emotional participation in the individuals and objects around one.

'It was all empty and desolate,'[16] where it is significant in the sense of mood space that this condition of desolation pervades both interior and exterior. Tellenbach stresses, 'How inner deterioration and the deterioration of the world correspond to emptiness, how empty space is continued in an inner emptiness.'[17] Thus a sense of worldless lostness is created, which we can most clearly illustrate with the statement of one of the sick individuals: 'One has lost all connections. One is, or feels like, a single little stone lost in the endless grey of a dissolving landscape. The feeling of smallness, uncertainty and lostness can become so great that one has something like a sense of outer space, in which one is oneself a vulnerable point, like a last withered leaf being driven around by an autumnally dead world.'[18]

In this connection an observation from the declining Roman Empire, to which Jakob Burckhardt refers in his *The age of Constantine the Great*, also becomes comprehensible: 'To people in the Roman Empire it seemed as rivers began to grow sluggish and mountains to loose height; Aetna could not be seen so far at sea as normally, and the same phenomenon is reported of Parnassus and Olympus. Studious natural historians were of the opinion that the cosmos itself was going into general decline.'[19] This observation too may be based on the unity of soul and world which denotes the mood space. 'The feeling that everything in the present is trifling in comparison with the brilliantly conceived past'[20] the consciousness of their own meaninglessness that possessed the people of those days, had the direct effect of seeing

13 Tellenbach, 'Die Räumlichkeit des Melancholischen', p. 14.
14 Tellenbach, 'Die Räumlichkeit des Melancholischen', p. 292.
15 Tellenbach, 'Die Räumlichkeit des Melancholischen', p. 291.
16 Tellenbach, 'Die Räumlichkeit des Melancholischen', p. 13.
17 Tellenbach, 'Die Räumlichkeit des Melancholischen', p. 16.
18 Tellenbach, 'Die Räumlichkeit des Melancholischen', p. 290 ff.
19 Jakob Burckhardt, *Die Zeit Constantins des Großen. Gesammelte Werke*, vol. 1, Darmstadt: 1955, p. 198 [*The age of Constantine the Great*, translated by Moses Hadas, London: 1949, p. 219].
20 Burckhardt, *Die Zeit Constantins des Großen*, p. 195 [p. 216].

everything in nature apart from themselves as small. The flatness of the heart corresponds to the flatness of the world allotted to them.

Euphoric space

What has here been discussed on the aspect of oppressiveness is also true to an equivalent extent of the opposite mood. A sunny sky, with its impression of tempting distance, changes our whole inner state of mind. It opens it up, turns it outward, and even our movements gain a new character, of man reaching out into space. But here too the same reversibility of the relationship is found. When an individual in a cheerful mood raises his eyes again from the ground, then space widens for him. The sense of power of the state of happy fulfilment extends beyond itself and spans a far greater expanse.

In his work *Über Ideenflucht*[21] [On the flight of ideas] Binswanger discussed the connection between heightened mood and the corresponding form of human spatiality, at first in the psychopathological area, but what he brings out here in a highly intensified form with regard to the patient suffering from 'flight of ideas' in the detailed analysis of specific medical cases is to a great extent independent of this special point of departure and applies in an inclusive sense to optimists in general, in fact even more generally to every individual who is in a cheerful mood, even if only a temporary one. Taking as his starting-point the case of a particular patient he describes her form of movement, both physical and mental, as 'leaping.' He stresses here: 'A certain kind of leaping … comes from the fact that for the patient everything, thoughts, people, things "in space" have moved nearer, so that everything is for her much closer "to hand". Her living space, her world has become a different one, and it is from this change in her world that the change in her behaviour, her behaviour itself, is to be understood.'[22] The spatial character of this change, the easier availability of the things that have moved nearer, is expressed with direct clarity.

What has here become evident in terms of the pathological case proves to be generally valid in the world of the optimist. From the general characterization given by Binswanger to the mood of this optimistic world I will pick out only the sentences which are significant for the spatial structure assigned to it. 'The language', Binswanger summarizes,

21 Ludwig Binswanger, *Über Ideenflucht*, Zurich: 1933.
22 Binswanger, *Über Ideenflucht*, p. 19.

'describes the world of the optimist as rosy or cloudless, which means, at any rate, light, shining or bright. Since the optimist "knows no difficulties", his world is also described as easy; since he does not rub or wear himself out against it, it is clearly smooth; since he goes "easily through life", it is also even; since he "knows no obstacles", spatially wide or expanded, since he "always sees a way out" it is well lit, since even on a hard resting-place he feels "as though bedded on roses" it is soft, since he "makes the impossible possible" it is workable or malleable, … since he "thinks only the best" of people, it is, as a world of fellowmen, good.'[23] In this description of the cheerful world of the optimist we are struck, apart from the terms that refer directly to the spatial character of the expanse, by other descriptive terms such as easy, smooth, even, soft, workable, which indirectly contribute to the characterization of the spatial, by defining as softnesss, workability, etc., the ease of movement in this space, which simply retreats, 'gives space', when man tries to penetrate it.

This is even more clearly articulated by Binswanger in the following paragraph (and this is the passage on account of which, above all, I have taken up this whole train of thought): 'So we deceive ourselves if we believe that the statement "the world is narrow " and "things collide with each other in space" has a claim to universal validity. The world of the optimist is not narrow, but wide; therefore, things do not collide, but touch each other softly and smoothly, and one does not "collide" with them as with something hard, rather they retreat and "give space", so that one goes through them "almost untouched" and certainly uninjured. This ability to be transformed, changeability, solubility and fleetingness of the world of the optimist, in a word, its volatility, is the essential reason why it "does not weigh upon him", "does not force him to the ground".'[24]

So the general character of this optimistic world is that it does not constrict us, that things rather 'give us space', and that we can move freely in it. Binswanger describes this general character of reality with the concept of volatility, as related to the movement of flying. And thus we come again to the designations of floating, flying and swimming in this world, which we earlier encountered as 'leaping' in the analysis of a specific case; for the character of the world at the same time denotes a state of the individual moving in this world. Thus Binswanger stresses: 'On the other hand the fact of the volatility of this world also has an effect on the person who exists in it … The form of movement of the optimist [is] a

23 Binswanger, *Über Ideenflucht*, p. 58.
24 Binswanger, *Über Ideenflucht*, p. 59.

floating, flying or swimming in a milieu which everywhere and at all times "easily gives way".'[25] We will deal again later with this form of movement as a meaningful correlate of a specific experience of space.[26] If for the moment we relate this conclusion quite explicitly to our more specific one, we can summarize the connection between the form of movement and the form of space in Binswanger in the sentence: 'The leaping and gliding mode of human existence can be characterized in respect of the spatiality of being-in-the-world by means of the criterion of expanse.'[27]

A poetic confirmation

If one were to have misgivings about the fact that these characteristics of the joyfully fulfilled state have been gained from experiences of the pathological state of mind, it is of particular importance that the same characteristics are confirmed in the healthy individual. Only they are much more difficult to observe here, because in the happy moments of their lives people rarely reflect on their state and express themselves about it in tangible literary form. Thus, poetic testimony in which these experiences are convincingly expressed is of particular importance. A fine and appropriate passage is found in *Faust*, where Mephisto's spirits lull the hero into sweet dreams with 'beautiful images.' It is interesting in our context because it convincingly confirms the individual characteristics of the form of movement which Binswanger calls volatility.

Here the spirits sing:

Vanish, you darkling
Vaults there above us!
Now let the sweeter
Blue of the ether
Gaze in and love us!
Are not the darkling
Clouds disappearing?
Starlight is sparkling,
Suns of a gentler
Brightness appearing …
Birds drink their pleasure,
Soaring to sunlight,

25 Binswanger, *Über Ideenflucht*, p. 59.
26 See the present book, p. 277.
27 Binswanger, *Über Ideenflucht*, p. 192.

Flying to far bright
Islands that shimmer,
Trembling, enticing,
Where the waves glimmer,
Where echo answers
Songs of rejoicing
Shouted in chorus,
Where we see dancers
Leaping before us
Out over green fields …
Some of them hover;
All seeking life, each
Seeking a distant star
Where love and beauty are
Far beyond speech.[28]

Out of the larger context, I will draw attention to just a few points: the 'darkling vaults' refer to Faust's study, of which it has just been said:

This cursed, stifling prison-hole
Where even the heaven's dear light must pass
Dimly through pains of painted glass![29]

This constricting spatiality now widens into a splendid vision. That this is deceptive in this case does not detract from the truth of the content of what is seen here: the vaults disappear (we know not how), and even

28 'Schwindet, ihr dunkeln / Wölbungen droben! / Reizender schaue / freundlich der blaue / Äther herein! / Wären die dunkeln / Wolken zerronen! / Sternelein funkeln, / mildere Sonnen / scheinen darein ... /
Und das Geflügel / schlürfet sich Wonne, / flieget der Sonne, / flieget den hellen / Inseln entgegen, / die sich auf Wellen / gaukelnd bewegen, /
wo wir in Chören / Jauchzende hören, / über den Auen / Tanzende schauen, / die sich im Freien / alle zerstreuen ... / Andere schweben: / Alle zum Leben, / alle zur Ferne / liebender Sterne, / seliger Huld.'
And further: 'Geistige Schöne ... / schwebet vorüber. / Sehnende Neigung / folget hinüber. / Und der Gewänder / flatternde Bänder / decken die Länder, / decken die Laube, / wo sich furs Leben ... / Liebende geben ... / Stürzen in Bächen / schämende Weine, / rieseln durch reine, / edle Gesteine ... / Und das Geflügel / schlürfet sich Wonne, / flieget der Sonne / ... entgegen.'
Goethe, *Faust erster Teil. Gedenkausagabe*, vol. 5, p. 187 [*Faust part one*, translated by David Luke, Oxford: 1987, pp. 45-6].

29 'Weh! steck ich in dem Kerker noch? / Verfluchtes dumpfes Mauerloch, / wo selbst das liebe Himmelslicht / trüb durch gemalte Scheiben bricht.' Goethe, *Faust erster Teil*, p. 156 [p. 16].

the clouds melt away, the world opens up to the free ether, out of which gentler suns shine out. And everything expresses itself in a state of joyful fulfilment of life. I will now quote some lines, omitted from the previous passage for the sake of simplification, which are appropriate here:

> Children of light dance …
> Hovering, shining:
> Passionate yearning
> Follows them burning.
> And their loving vesture
> Streams out and flutters,
> Streams out and covers
> Arbour and pasture,
> Where lovers ponder
> As they surrender
> Each to each other …
> In streams descending,
> Through precious gleaming
> Stones they are streaming … Birds drink their pleasure,
> Soaring to sunlight …

The image is convincing, the joyful choruses, the dancing, the floating: it is all one exuberant, jubilant movement. And if we gather together all the verbs, the fluttering and flickering, the climbing and swimming, the plunging, trickling and foaming, the flying and dancing, and the hovering as the last word, fading away, then everything heaped up together is to be designated as the character of this free, light movement that glides over the severities of life. These are exactly the same characteristics of movement that Binswanger described under the name of volatility, only here they are lifted entirely out of the sphere of suspicious conditions, lifted up to the sphere of final fulfilment of existence. Everything here is pervaded by one single sense of jubilation: in cheering, dancing, floating, taken up into the movement towards the 'distant star, beauty beyond speech.' Liberation into the distance as the condition of this final blessedness. The decisive thesis on the problem of the mood space, the inner unity of the expansion of space and the gladdening of mankind is here overwhelmingly portrayed in the poetic image.

Finally, from the philosophical point of view, let us note some statements of Nietzsche's which aptly confirm this image. In *The birth of tragedy* he already writes of people in a state of Dionysiac intoxication: 'Singing and dancing, man expresses his sense of belonging to a higher community; he has forgotten how to walk and talk and is on the brink of flying and dancing.'[30] Here we also see singing and dancing as opposed to the walking and talking of everyday life, that is the raising above the state of earthly heaviness and the possibility of a new conquest of space.

This is finely confirmed in a statement by the later Nietzsche about the alteration of the experience of space in a state of intoxication: 'The sensations of space and time are altered: enormous distances are surveyed and can, as it were, be perceived for the first time.'[31] Intoxication as the final heightening of the euphoric state thus also allows its characteristics to appear with particular sharpness.

30 Nietzsche, *Groß- und Kleinoktavausgabe*, vol. 1, p. 24 [*The birth of tragedy and other writings*, edited by Raymond Geuss and Ronald Speirs, translated by Ronald Speirs, Cambridge: 1999, p. 18].

31 Nietzsche, *Groß- und Kleinoktavausgabe*, vol. 16, p. 234.

5. Presential Space

The spatial character of sound

'Singing and dancing', according to Nietzsche, man expresses his sense of belonging to a higher community; 'he has forgotten how to walk and talk and is on the brink of flying and dancing.' This directly links to what Binswanger reported as the form of movement of the euphoric human being. Dancing here appears as an extreme form of expression of joyful and liberated movement, and if we have become generally aware of the close connection between form of movement and experience of space, we will be able to expect from this case, even if it is a comparatively rare borderline case, some particular information which will also be important for the understanding of more normal conditions. For this reason, Straus, in his essay on 'Forms of the Spatial', which has become a classic work, when dealing with the question of the 'connection between quality of space, movement and perception',[1] placed at the centre the question of the structure of space experienced in dancing. Dancing appears to him to be the actual key phenomenon in researching these connections.

Straus starts from the assumption that there must clearly be a close relationship between music and dance. Attempts at an 'absolute' dance separated from music have not led to a convincing result, and Straus concludes from this that there must be an internally necessary connection between music and dance. 'Evidently, there is an essential connection that ties the movement of the dancer to the music and to the spatial structure of the music.'[2] This brings him back to the question of the spatial character of music, and this in turn is based on the more general spatial character of sound. Here Straus at first develops a more general analysis of sound space,

1 Erwin Straus, 'Formen des Räumlichen. Ihre Bedeutung für die Motorik und Wahrnehmung1 (1930), *Psychologie der menschlichen Welt. Gesammelte Schriften*, Berlin, Göttingen, Heidelberg: 1960, p. 141 ff. ['Forms of spatiality', *Phenomenological psychology. The selected papers of Erwin Straus*, translated by Erling Eng, London: 1966, p. 3 ff.].

2 Straus, 'Formen des Räumlichen', p. 141 [p. 3].

which we too must here adopt not only as a precondition of the following observations on dance, but also, beyond this, as an amplification of our earlier consideration of twilight space and night space; for the difference between day and night space is decisively determined by the different function of seeing and hearing in the structure of space.

Straus also starts out with a comparison between visual and acoustic space. He characterizes the world of coloured objects in the same way as we did earlier with the bright and visible space of daytime. Straus says: 'The direction in which we see colours themselves is precisely determinable ... We always see colours over *there*, i.e., in a direction and at a distance, somewhere vis-à-vis ourselves; [colours] confine space, differentiating it into partial spaces ordered sideways and in depth.'[3] 'Things stand out from one another with sharply defined boundaries.'[4]

Quite different, on the other hand, is the spatial character of sound. It has often been assumed that the acoustic area does not correspond at all to any original experience of space, that we rather only retrospectively inscribe acoustic perceptions into a space constructed by other means. It is pointed out in this connection how difficult it is to determine the direction from which the sound comes, and thus the point in space from which it originates. Straus however points out that a distinction must be made between the source of sound and the sound itself. The source of sound indeed is only to be determined with great uncertainty. The acoustic area, however, unlike the visual one, where the colour is indissolubly attached to its object, is characterized by the fact that the sound can be to a great extent detached from the source of sound, and it is to the sound itself that the question of its own spatial character is to be directed.

Straus also assumes from the start the doubleness of the acoustic, which is to a great extent linked to the difference between noise and pure sound: 'tone can simply point to or indicate something objective or it can attain a purely autonomous existence.'[5] The first is the case with noise. 'Noise retains the character of indicating and pointing to.'[6] This includes for example the noise of an approaching car. 'We hear this sort of noise outside, in a particular place, where we localize the source of the sound.'[7]

3 Straus, 'Formen des Räumlichen', p. 145 [p. 7].
4 Straus, 'Formen des Räumlichen', p. 156 [p. 16].
5 Straus, 'Formen des Räumlichen', p. 147 [p. 10].
6 Straus, 'Formen des Räumlichen', p. 147 [p. 10].
7 Straus, 'Formen des Räumlichen', p. 147 [p. 10]. We need not here give further attention to the difference, discussed by Straus, between noise, which merely indicates the source which causes it, and can be understood only in the context of

But sound has the potential of separating itself from this indicative character and operating only in its own nature as a sound. This happens, in contrast to indicative noise, with pure sound and in its most complete form in music. Straus therefore comments: 'The sound that detaches itself from the sound source can take on a pure and autonomous existence, but this possibility is fulfilled solely in the tones of music.'[8] But sound itself has no intrinisic direction from which it comes. Straus points out: 'But [sound] itself does not extend in a single direction; rather, it approaches us, penetrating, filling, and homogenizing space.'[9] But it is wrong to describe sound for this reason as unspatial; it is only another space that offers itself in it. It is, in relation to the directional space of the visual, as Straus expresses it, a 'homogenized' space. To have recognized this individual character of sound space is an enduring achievement of Straus.

But this spatial character is not present only with pure sound. From noises, there are individual and very interesting transitional forms. Straus clarifies this with a revealing and very well observed example: 'If we are not in familiar surroundings but in the hubbub of a foreign city with a strange language, customs, and ways, then noises already begin to loose their particular effects [of indicating something] and approach the phenomenal mode of the existence of tone, of which music is the perfect realization. Under these conditions, noise, too, penetrates and fills space; by homogenizing space, it makes orientation difficult and increases confusion and strangeness. A jumble of voices differs in its mode of spatial appearance from that of words and sentences overheard on the crowded street, words and sentences that we could understand. As noises grow increasingly confused and lose their ostensive function, they tend to approach the phenomenal mode of givenness of musical tones.'[10]

But we also find similar spatial characters everywhere in indistinct, confused noises, such as the humming that fills the air near an apiary, or the rustling of treetops in the forest. Eichendorff loved to conjure up these confused noises, which for him constituted an essential part of the specifically Romantic character of his poetry. But this spatial character appears in its purest form in music. While the singer is still there as an individual and also represents himself as an individual, in pure instrumental music the sound, if we surrender ourselves to it as such, completely separates itself

---

a more comprehensive understanding of the world, and seeing, in which the seen object is directly given.

8 Straus, 'Formen des Räumlichen', p. 147 [p. 8].

9 Straus, 'Formen des Räumlichen', p. 146 [p. 7].

10 Straus, 'Formen des Räumlichen', p. 147 [p. 8 ff.].

from the instrument. It fills and homogenizes the whole space. But in this filling of space it has an extraordinarily dynamic effect. '[Sound] presses in on us, surrounds, seizes, and embraces us … The acoustical pursues us; we are at its mercy, unable to get away.'[11] Straus points out that even purely linguistically, in the German language, hearing [Hören] is linked with belonging [Gehören] and obeying [Gehorchen].

Straus tries to define this characteristic terminologically, by referring to the condition of sound as 'presential' [präsentisch] and accordingly also speaking of sound space as a 'presential space.' 'All hearing is presential', is how he formulates it. 'In sound, we apprehend the happening presentially, while in colour we lay hold of Being at a distance.'[12] He also distinguishes the two sides by means of terminology derived from Klages as 'the gnostic and the pathic moment in perception',[13] where the pathic – derived from the Greek πάσχειν, to suffer – represents the peculiar experience of being carried away and emotionally affected by hearing sound. In this sense, gnostic and pathic are for Straus 'the modes of the spatial', which as 'basic forms' rule all 'experiences of perception.' 'The gnostic moment develps the "what" of the given in its object character, the pathic the "how" of its being as given.'[14]

For relevance in our context, one further thought is important, which is suggested by Straus: this pathic factor is not restricted to the acoustic area, but also exists to some extent in the visual area. In artistic representations, for example in the chiaroscuro of Rembrandt's paintings, the clear proximity of things disappears. But the same effect is also produced outside artistic representation in the direct perception in twilight and at night. Straus says: 'Twilight is called intimate [traulich] because here nature veils the boundaries separating things from one another as well as the distances that divide us from them. Still more, twilight, like night, fills space with effects like those of music, filling and homogenizing space, unifying and binding together everything that strives apart.'[15] Here it is important in our context that what Straus first perceived as sound goes beyond this area and also includes the visual world. This suggests that this property is not based as such in the nature of an area of the senses, but is rooted more deeply in the nature of space in general, and so in fact, in Merleau-Ponty's words, refers to an 'original spatiality' lying beyond the clarity of day.

11 Straus, 'Formen des Räumlichen', p. 155 [p. 16].

12 Straus, 'Formen des Räumlichen', p. 156 [p. 16; 'presentic' in the original English translation is given as 'presential'].

13 Straus, 'Formen des Räumlichen', p. 150 ff. [p. 11 ff.].

14 Straus, 'Formen des Räumlichen', p. 151 [p. 12].

15 Straus, 'Formen des Räumlichen', p. 157 [p. 16].

The purposeful freedom of dance

This connection between sound and space acquires a new, broader significance when one goes beyond mere perception and also includes movement. When music takes hold of us, it evokes an accompanying movement, and not just an arbitrary movement, but one which is possible only under the influence of music and sharply distinguished from that of everyday life. Straus states: 'Music founds the structure of the space within which the dancing movement can occur.'[16] Straus also mentions marching to music, but above all dance. The particular character of the movement of dancing distinguishes it sharply from all movement of purposeful behaviour in the world, according to our observations so far on the movements assigned to action space. From this viewpoint Straus formulates his basic thesis: 'Optical space is the space of the directed, measured, and purposive movement; acoustical space is the space of dance. Purposive movement and dance cannot be understood as different combinations of the same elements. They are two entirely different basic forms of movement, related to two different modes of the spatial.'[17]

For this reason Straus deals with a more precise analysis of dance movement, in order to work out from it the corresponding experience of space. I will try here to pinpoint only the most important aspects and at the same time, though I will repeatedly quote his highly accurate formulations verbatim, to simplify somewhat his train of thought. When, as a non-dancer, one regards dancing from the point of view of normal purposeful behaviour in the world, one is struck by the fact that it is characterized by an abundance of movements, by circular and backwards movement and so on, which must appear inappropriate, indeed positively foolish. According to the hodological principle, we seek to reach our destination by the 'distinguished' way, on even ground in a straight line. But the dancer, though constantly in motion, never gets anywhere. The dancer's movements, as Straus observes, 'do not serve towards progress in a specific straight line.'[18] Dance is therefore not to be understood from the point of view of sensible behaviour in action space. For this reason Weininger described it as a positively indecent movement and rejected it.[19] So it must be a question of something quite different. Straus explicitly stresses: 'We

16 Straus, 'Formen des Räumlichen', p. 160 [p. 20].
17 Straus, 'Formen des Räumlichen', p. 160 [p. 20].
18 Straus, 'Formen des Räumlichen', p. 164 [p. 23].
19 Otto Weininger, *Über die letzten Dinge*, Vienna and Leipzig: 1918.

do not dance to get from one point to another in space.'[20] He also refers to the dances of primitive peoples, where absolutely no alteration of place occurs.

A second point: in the space of everyday life – Straus calls it, for simplicity's sake, visual space – turning and backwards movements are not only pointless, but also uncomfortable, and people would not execute them without discomfort. The turning movement soon produces dizziness, and we fall over if we do not stop in time. And going backwards robs us of the opportunity to overlook the terrain with the 'oversight' of the eye and avoid possible obstacles; we can only, with a hesitant, groping foot, attempt to steady one's step and expect to encounter resistance at any moment. And here again the difference emerges: 'Like turning as a directed movement, walking backwards in visual space is unpleasant to us, and we try to avoid it. But the apparently similar type of movement in dance becomes something quite obvious, we notice none of the difficulties and resistance that we sense as soon as we are forced to walk backwards.' He summarizes the difference: 'Walking backwards is experienced as a compulsion, dancing backwards as a spontaneous action.'[21]

This is based ultimately on the fact that the space of purposeful action, also called historic space by Straus, is a directed space. Particularly in the case of walking, it has a clear forward direction, the direction of the path itself. Straus expresses it by means of the contrast of fighting space and flight space. Movement backwards, in this originally forward-oriented space, is reprehensible behaviour. 'In historic space,' he writes, 'backwards movement is therefore directed against the impulse actually released by the space',[22] that is, the impulse to move forward. 'In dancing', Straus continues, 'we clearly feel nothing of the dynamic of historic space.'[23] 'Dance is not related to any direction.'[24]

One final aspect is linked to these. The space of our action, historic space, has a specific central point, to which the individual movements in space are related. 'The space in which we live', he writes, 'is a historic space.' This space is 'related to a central point, a fixed, immovable "here".'[25] It is from this point of view that we go forth and return, as we have previously observed. We distinguish to a certain extent between 'a fixed and a movable

20 Straus, 'Formen des Räumlichen', p. 164 [p. 23].
21 Straus, 'Formen des Räumlichen', p. 174 [p. 33].
22 Straus, 'Formen des Räumlichen', p. 176 [p. 34].
23 Straus, 'Formen des Räumlichen', p. 176 [p. 34].
24 Straus, 'Formen des Räumlichen', p. 164 [p. 23].
25 Straus, 'Formen des Räumlichen', p. 175 [p. 34].

here', a 'home and a place to stay.' Nothing of this is to be found in dancing. Dancing knows nothing of this interplay of going forth and returning, which we have so far come to know as basic to the structure of movements in experienced space. 'When dancing, we no longer move in a limited section of space directed at a fixed "here", but in a homogeneous space free of differences of direction and values of location.'[26] One place is here like another, one direction the same as the other. The dancer moves in a space stripped of all these qualifications, unstructured and uniform in itself.

It is with these qualifications that we can describe the behaviour of the dancer within his space. It is best to start again from the contrast with walking as the simplest movement in historic space. 'In walking', says Straus, 'we cover a certain distance, in walking we measure space. Dance, however, is a non-directed movement.'[27] Beyond this, it is a 'non-bounded movement'; for with the falling away of a destination to be reached in space, there is also no natural conclusion of the movement. It can be continued endlessly and must therefore, if it is not to be lost in space, be a movement that cyclically returns to itself. 'It lacks, not only a connection with direction and distance, but also a connection with spatial dimension and spatial and temporal boundary.'[28] Spatially this is expressed in the fact that dancing is possible even on the smallest surface, and is not constrained by being limited to this area. 'The dance surface may take any form … It is precisely its arbitrary structure in terms of size and shape that allows us to recognize that the dance finds its limit, not its necessary boundary, at the ends of the dance surface.' The same is true of time. The dance movement does not find its necessary conclusion at a point in time to be attained. Here too Straus says: 'That the dance movement knows no temporal boundary, that it is ended only by exhaustion or ecstasy, is to be observed wherever dancing has not become a social or artificial dance.'[29] Dancing is thus a movement unlimited in both time and space, in a directionless and unstructured space.

The changed relationship with space

To the extent to which the processes have been described so far, both dancing as a movement and the space assigned to this movement with respect to the purposeful action and the action space belonging to it have

26 Straus, 'Formen des Räumlichen', p. 176 [p. 34].
27 Straus, 'Formen des Räumlichen', p. 164 [p. 23].
28 Straus, 'Formen des Räumlichen', p. 164 [p. 23].
29 Straus, 'Formen des Räumlichen', p. 164 [p. 23].

been identified in a purely negative manner. Essential characteristics of action and action space are missing. It is therefore, to the extent to which it has been understood so far, an impoverished happening in an impoverished space. And if dancing were nothing else but this, it would not be understandable why people like to dance, and why it is specifically primitive people who experience the urge to dance. So we are led to the question: What is it that makes people want to dance? And this is how Straus approaches this new question: 'But what is it that drives people to execute movements that would be highly repugnant to them if they had to use them as a technique to move forward?'[30] Because the dance movement serves no external purpose, it must be in itself something pleasant, something pleasurable, and not as a single movement – for we cannot separate it from its context – but in the totality of the dance.

The reason for this is seen by Straus as being that in dancing, we reach a fundamentally changed relationship with space, that we experience a new space, which as such fundamentally differs from that of our everyday lives, and the experience of which fills us with an unspeakable joy. For this, it is not a question of distinguishing dance space only negatively, that is in terms of deficiencies, from action space, but of understanding it in its own positive character.

In dancing, man enters a changed relationship with space. Straus expresses this in the sentence: 'In walking we move *through* space, from one place to another, but in dancing we move *in* space.'[31] In one case, space is a medium that remains external to us, through which we move, inwardly unaffected. In the other, we are taken up into this space, we ourselves, in a certain way, become part of this space. The decisive factor is that 'in the experience of dance the tension that exists between subject and object, the ego and the world, is removed.'[32] Man once again becomes one with space. And it is on this that the endless joyfulness of dance is based. The dance becomes a deep metaphysical experience, in which the split between man and his world is overcome and he experiences it again: 'to be one with everything that lives.'[33]

It is in this sense that Straus now emphasizes: 'When we turn while dancing, we move from the start in a space which is already totally altered in relation to purposeful space.'[34] The latter is now characterized in a positive

30 Straus, 'Formen des Räumlichen', p. 166 [p. 25].
31 Straus, 'Formen des Räumlichen', p. 164 [p. 23].
32 Straus, 'Formen des Räumlichen', p. 166 [p. 25].
33 'Eines zu sein mit allem, was lebt', Friedrich Hölderlin, *Hyperion. Große Stuttgarter Ausgabe*, edited by Friedrich Beißner, vol. 3, Stuttgart: 1943-85, p. 9.
34 Straus, 'Formen des Räumlichen', p. 172 [p. 31].

manner. It acquires qualities of its own that are foreign to the sober action space. In this sense it is now emphasized by Straus: 'Dance space is not a part of directed historic space, but a symbolic part of the world. It is not determined by distance, direction and size, but by expanse, height, depth and independent movement of space.'[35] This now brings out the individual qualities of this space, which as such still need a closer definition (and which we will encounter again from another aspect in the next section on loving coexistence). Straus does not go into further detail about its various positive qualities, but restricts himself to stressing the individuality of these qualities, which distinguishes them from those of action space, using the example of expanse: 'Expanse is neither here, nor is it at the horizon … it is in fact not to be determined quantitatively, but is a quality of space. We can therefore say with justification that the dance movement is assigned to the symbolic qualities of space.'[36] 'The system of reference of dance movement is formed by the symbolic qualities of space.'[37]

Presential movement

In this space which is no longer foreign to man, but benevolently receptive of him, dance movements can now be understood in their individual character. When, in contrast to purposeful behaviour, no aim beyond the actual behaviour is realized and so no lasting change takes place in the world, we can understand it only in the sense that movement, as pleasurable in itself, rests in itself and, without indicating an external aim beyond itself, fulfils its meaning in itself. Straus therefore calls it presential movement, namely the movement which fulfils itself purely in the present. He describes it as follows in his consideration of the process of dancing: 'Presential, non-directed and non-limited movement knows only a rising and falling, a heightening and an ebbing away. It produces no change, is not a historic process, so we call it presential.'[38] He thus also calls the space assigned to this presential movement, in which the dance takes place, 'presential space.'

Again it is a question of comprehending in its positive nature what at first was characterized only in a negative sense. The purposelessness of this movement signifies moving out of the purposefulness of active existence in

35 Straus, 'Formen des Räumlichen', p. 176 ff. [p. 35].
36 Straus, 'Formen des Räumlichen', p. 177 [p. 35].
37 Straus, 'Formen des Räumlichen', p. 165 [p. 24].
38 Straus, 'Formen des Räumlichen', p. 172 ff. [p. 31].

general. This is how Straus describes it: 'In dancing, the historic action does not progress: the dancer has moved out of the flow of historic action. His experience is a being in the present, which does not indicate any conclusion in the future.'[39] The dancer has grasped eternity in the movement of the moment.

This touches on what seemed from another viewpoint as a lifting of the tension between subject and object. From this viewpoint too, the urge to dance proves to be founded in a deep metaphysical experience. In dancing, we experience a breakthrough from the everyday practical world of purposeful action and structure. We are moved out of the 'flow of historic action.' This means at the same time that we are moved out of the world of fate and its constant threats. The dancer knows no fate. What Straus says about the other aspect of this metaphysical experience, about the abolition of the split between subject and object, applies here too: one does not dance in order to have this metaphysical experience, dance is not a means to an end, but this experience is always present in dancing. This lifting above historic action is 'not the aim of the dance, but rather it underpins the experience of dancing from the start.'[40]

The spatial experience of the dance thus leads us to a link with the return to the origin which we have already encountered at various points, but it modifies it in a manner peculiar to itself. And if, in what has been said here so far, we have come to be familiar with various forms of joyful mood space, these too are enriched, by an expanded space of dance, undisturbed by fate, by a further possibility leading to a new depth.

Critique of Straus's dualistic spatial schema

Because I have been solely concerned here with presenting Straus's outstanding clarification of the spatial experience of dance, I have refrained from dealing with the details of his account. But perhaps a word of explanation is necessary, which is why I have exercised a certain restraint in making use of his terminology. In his understandable pleasure in having discovered a totally new form of spatiality, previously disregarded, in the space of dance, Straus is driven to the view that there are two 'modes of spatiality', in polar opposition to each other. In different passages, he uses different but equivalent names for each of them: he calls one political

39 Straus, 'Formen des Räumlichen', p. 176 [p. 35].
40 Straus, 'Formen des Räumlichen', p. 173 [p. 31].

space, purposeful space and historic space, and the other acoustic space, pathic space and presential space of dance.

My reservations about this terminology move in two directions: first, that these two modes by no means exhaust the possibilities of experienced space (which is by no means something Straus maintains, but it is a conclusion to which his antithetical thinking is necessarily driven), that, rather, there is a wealth of possibilities which cannot even be understood as intermediate forms between the two modes, but which have a thoroughly individual character of their own; and secondly, that on both sides things are lumped together which do not belong on the same level. Some of my reservations may perhaps seem only terminological, but in themselves they affect the understanding of the question.

If it may already be an excessive simplification to equate action space with visual space, it must appear even more questionable to equate action space with historic space; for action as the systematic realization of aims is ruled by the law of purposeful rationality, while historicity breaks through into this clear rational world as something darkly fateful. To say that the dancer is raised above fate means more than to say that he places himself outside rational purposeful connections. And if we are looking for a space charged with fate, it is more likely to be found on the side of pathic spaces.

Even stronger are the reservations to be found on the other side. To equate this space with acoustic space seems, again, too abstract a simplification, particularly since Straus himself so convincingly stresses the doubleness of the indicative character and individual nature of sound. More important, however, are the reservations about his designation of 'pathic space.' Binswanger has already pointed out in his response, continuing the discussion,[41] that this concept, borrowed from Klages, can too easily be understood in the sense of passivity, and for his part has proposed the concept of mood space (a term which seems in fact to have been first coined in this context). But here again, the concept of mood space, as we too have developed it so far, is again much wider, and within it the space of dance is only an extreme borderline case among many other possibilities. However, this fundamentally explodes Straus's dualistic schema of modes of space. Within mood space we once again find the polarity of optimistic and pessimistic space, which both together stand in opposition to non-mood action space. But we will put aside these reservations for the time being, because we must explore a quite different possibility of experienced space.

41 Binswanger 'Das Raumproblem in der Psychopathologie', p. 174 ff.

6. The Space of Human Coexistence

Among the factors that constitute experienced space there remains a decisively important one which so far we have put aside, namely the manner of human coexistence. We have already been made urgently aware of these connections when we were discussing the protective power of the house and the atmosphere of homeliness [Wohnlichkeit] that pervades it. For at that point we had noticed that this homeliness does not emanate from the walls as such, and is not to be based on material things, and that, further, it cannot be produced by the individual person by means of careful domestic organization, but that it requires communal dwelling by a family. The house is necessarily the common dwelling-place of a family, and its coexistence is decisive for that which we have called in a deeper sense the homeliness of the dwelling. We must now again deal with this question, which earlier we were not able to pursue further. When I refer succinctly to a space of human coexistence, I do not mean this in a loose sense, as one often speaks of a political or economic space, but here I mean space in the sense of quite specific external space. The space of human coexistence means an aspect of this space, like the aspects of action space or mood space that we have already encountered. It means space to the extent that it can be modified by human coexistence. Binswanger was probably the first to recognize this problem and he developed it in impressive fashion as the 'spatiality of loving togetherness' [Räumlichkeit des liebenden Miteinanderseins]. So we will also refer to him at this point.

The struggle for living space

It will be best to start again from the definitions of narrowness and expanse of experienced space. We learnt that Schiller's phrase about things colliding with each other in space loses its validity in the world of the optimist, that the latter rather sees an expanse around him in which he moves freely and lightly and does not collide with anything. Something similar is also true of the forms of human coexistence. Here too we say that man needs a certain 'living space' in which to move (where for the time being we use the term 'living space' [Lebensraum] in a non-specific sense). The claim on living space is greater in one person and less in another, and as a result the 'objectively' identical living space will be wider for the one and narrower for the other, indeed the same person, according to his mental disposition, will perceive his identical living space sometimes as narrower and sometimes as wider.

But because in the narrowness of living together people must share the available living space, a relationship of rivalry arises between them. When one unscrupulously extends his space, it is at the expense of the other. The one can gain space only by taking it away from the other. In the context of the general struggle for existence a struggle for living space takes place, in which one can win only at the expense of the other.

> Where one sits fast, another must make room,
> And who would not be driven out must drive;
> Strife is the rule, and strength alone will conquer.[1]

This struggle for living space pervades life, from the smallest areas to the largest. In professional life only someone who edges out his rival can assert himself, the seller can increase the sales of his goods only at the expense of the 'competition', and so on in the most varied of professions. But the most menacing manifestation of this struggle for living space is in the coexistence of nations, because here it has led to the outbreak of more and more wars. The formula 'a nation without space' was so dangerous because it seemed to justify the extension by force of living space at the expense of other nations.

The space of loving togetherness

The justification of this soberly realistic point of view is indisputable. Free space which need only be occupied without infringing the rights of others does not exist. 'The world is given' and new space in it is

---

1 'Wo eines Platz nimmt, muß das andre rücken, / Wer nicht vertreiben sein will, muß vertreiben; / Da herrscht der Streit, und nur die Stärke siegt.' Friedrich Schiller, *Wallensteins Tod. Sämtliche Werke*, edited by Eduard v. d. Hellen, vol. 5, Stuttgart and Berlin: n.d., p. 219 [*Wallenstein*, translated by F. J. Lamport, London: 1979, p. 351].

fundamentally to be gained only at the expense of others. But at precisely this point Binswanger introduces a subtle new notion, with which he applies the conditions discovered in mood space to the living space of human coexistence. This thought seems to me to be quite simply of fundamental importance for the understanding of all human coexistence. Binswanger readily concedes that a competitive relationship over living space does exist, such that one seeks to move the other out of the way, but he stresses that this is not the only relationship, but that in addition there are other possibilities, and he develops such a possibility, in total opposition to rivalry, in the introductory parts of his great book on *Grundformen und Erkenntnis menschlichen Daseins* [The foundations and cognition of human existence], as the 'spatiality of loving togetherness.'

In loving togetherness, Binswanger tells us, things are quite different. 'Love and power or force are mutually exclusive.'[2] This is why the struggle for space is here impossible from the start. 'As a result,' Binswanger continues, 'we also find here no increase or diminution of "own space", and thus no contact at all between the spheres of mine and yours, in the sense of "worldly" property.'[3] In contrast there is rather another way, admittedly extremely difficult to grasp as a concept, which Binswanger at first describes as 'the continual and carefree creation of a limitless, singular and indivisible space of "each-other", the unending, inexhaustible and unfathomable togetherness of love.'[4]

How often, on the borders of the comprehensible, have we referred to the evidence of poets, who are able to capture in unreflective direct expression what constantly eludes our probing deliberations. In the same way, Binswanger chooses some words of Rilke's to support his further analysis. Among lovers, says Rilke, 'neither can do wrong to the other by restriction; on the contrary, they continually create space and expanse and freedom for each other',[5] they promise each other 'expanse, hunting ground and home.'[6] These formulations in their heightened power of imagery bring out something quite decisive. On the one hand there is the creation of a limitless expanse with space to hunt and freedom to roam. Neither here

2 Ludwig Binswanger, *Grundformen und Erkenntnis menschlichen Daseins*, Zurich: 1942, p. 25.

3 Ludwig Binswanger, *Grundformen und Erkenntnis menschlichen Daseins*, Zurich: 1942, p. 25.

4 Binswanger, *Grundformen und Erkenntnis*, p. 26.

5 Rainer Maria Rilke, *Briefe aus den Jahren 1907-1914*, edited by Ruth Sieber-Rilke and Carl Sieber, Leipzig: 1939, p. 84.

6 Rainer Maria Rilke, *Gesammelte Werke*, vol. 3, Leipzig: 1930, p. 274.

restricts the other. Binswanger interprets it thus: 'so, quite simply space and expanse, and freedom from any spatial restriction.'[7] But this expanse means on the other hand no lostness in empty space, but the creation of a space of freedom, home and closeness. But how these two things belong together, that is the question. Binswanger in fact immediately draws the conclusion from the quoted phrases of Rilke that they show us 'an entirely new kind of spatial problem', which is not to be overcome with the means used so far.

Binswanger explains this as follows: 'Instead of the space-clearing displacing of the "other" from a given place and the occupation of this place by the displacer, there is the peculiar phenomenon that exactly where you are, a place [for me] is created; instead of the ceding of a position "to the other" in the given spatiality of reason (!) and the corresponding loss of individual space, there is the peculiar phenomenon of "limitless" increase of individual space through the surrender of individual space! Instead of the given area as such and its spatial order, in which one disputes with the other "the place" or "the position", there is a peculiarly indefinite (but totally familiar to the lover) shimmering and shining, bottomless "depth" and "expanse", in which there are no places and positions at all, and therefore no dispute over them, but only the joy of incessant "deepening" and "widening".'[8]

I have quoted these sentences verbatim, although a certain indefiniteness of expression and a certain wavering in the phrasing of the questions is unmistakable in them. This is not accidental, but corresponds to the groping advance into a totally new terrain, in which there are still no firm points of reference. Only the tracks of predecessors allow the successor to move ahead somewhat more safely. It is in these terms that we refer to the text quoted above. For our purposes, we must try to translate it into as tangible, comprehensible a language as possible, even at the risk that not all its depths will be plumbed and these fragile things may appear somewhat trivialized.

Here we must bear in mind that the question of spatiality is not Binswanger's exclusive theme, but only part of a larger complex, that of the 'foundations of human existence' in general. It is influenced by the fact that the question of space constantly intertwines with other questions. One is the whole question to do with lovers. And if it is certainly methodologically correct for the understanding of the total context to begin with an extreme borderline case, the orientation on love means in a highly erotic sense the interplay of other points of view, which at first mask the particular

7 Binswanger, *Grundformen und Erkenntnis*, p. 72.
8 Binswanger, *Grundformen und Erkenntnis*, p. 31.

problematic of space. For this reason, what Binswanger discusses in a very profound way under the name of a 'spatiality of love' has at first glance only an indirect connection with our enquiry into experienced space. What Binswanger says about the 'love that increases itself', about 'limitless expanse', 'bottomless depth' and 'inexhaustible abundance' refers to a spatial use of metaphor to describe mental processes which is of the greatest interest in the context of the spatial 'schematism' on which we have already touched several times, but which for the time being contributes little to the understanding of space itself. In the passages quoted, this concept is expressed by the 'shimmering and shining, bottomless depth and width that is so familiar to the lover.'

The second point to consider is the orientation of the 'spatiality of loving togetherness' towards Heidegger's spatiality of circumspect concern, resulting from the methodological approach of the book; not in the sense of a critique of Heidegger, but as an extension, through a possibility not seen or not taken into account by Heidegger, although Binswanger assures us that he is taking over Heidegger's analysis of existence as a whole, and moving within its framework.[9] When Binswanger stresses that the spatiality of love is different from that of reason[10] or 'ratio',[11] this is influenced by Straus's approach of two (and only two) opposed modes of spatiality. But this simplification too can lead to ominous conclusions, for the relationship of the spatiality of circumspect concern and that of loving togetherness is not to be understood as conflicting. The opposite of rational space, which is here rightly designated the space of circumspect concern, and which furthermore corresponds to what in our terms is called action space, is the mood space as the space given in emotional terms. And this in turn has numerous modifications, according to the kind of emotion which fills it. On the other side, the opposite of the space of loving togetherness is that of envy, hate, resentment, and rivalry in general. But this has a totally individual structure of its own, and it is wrong to assign the struggle for living space that belongs to this space simply to the area of circumspect concern. 'Above' the emotionally neutral level of circumspect concern there is rather a separation between the space of resentful opposition and that of loving togetherness. Both, in the area of our previous formulations, would belong to mood space, but both, in the manner in which they directly creatively influence the outside world, go beyond the area of 'mere' moods.

---

9 See my review of Binswanger's book: *Die Sammlung*, vol. 1, 1945, p. 122 ff.

10 Binswanger, *Grundformen und Erkenntnis*, p. 223.

11 Binswanger, *Grundformen und Erkenntnis*, p. 31.

These two, the space of lovers and the space of the envious, in fact form a true antagonism. Their common relationship with the space of circumspect concern however is a case of superposition (in the sense of Hartmann's layers of complexity). To that extent the meshing together of these two aspects is no problem at all, and this removes Binswanger's reservation that the world of everyday concern should not be ignored in the world of lovers. The formulation that 'the world of concern is "resolved" in the "home" of love and vice versa' is extremely apt.[12]

The space-creating power of love

After these differentiations, intended to resolve in advance some conceptual difficulties, the actual content of Binswanger's theory becomes visible in its full significance. Here again several interlinked questions arise. Above all, it seems to me necessary for the sake of clarity to distinguish between the following two aspects. One is the assertion of the '"limitless" increase of individual space through the surrender of individual space.' While it is easy to understand the negative part of this statement, namely that lovers reciprocally do not dispute over each other's space, it is enormously difficult to comprehend the positive aspect as a concept with any clarity.

Perhaps it is best to start with the observation that in intellectual life there is a form of non-violent and quiet self-development, which is withdrawn from the struggle for living space from the outset in that it makes no effort at all to assert itself through external violence, and that, in its non-violence, it is effective through the irresistible power of persuasion that emanates from it.[13] This development presupposes a space which lies outside the space of competitive exclusivity. Rilke, whom Binswanger after all invokes in this context as his important witness, has tried to portray this phenomenon using the image of the delicate unfolding of a rose blossom. Here he speaks in reverential emotion of

> an endless opening out,
> space being used, but without space being taken
> from that space which the things around diminish[14]

12 Binswanger, *Grundformen und Erkenntnis*, p. 77.

13 See O. F. Bollnow, *Die Ehrfurcht*, Frankfurt a. M.: 1958.

14 'Aufgehn ohne Ende, / Raum-brechen, ohne Raum von jenem Raum / zu nehmen, den die Dinge rings verringen.' Rilke, *Gesammelte Werke*, vol. 3, p. 110.

The one space is that generally identified, 'which the things around diminish', that is where every space that is claimed by one thing for itself diminishes the other's space to manoeuvre. But another space is opposed to this, in which an 'opening out', an unfolding, takes place, without anything being taken away from the space of the other. Rilke says the same thing in another, much later poem, explicitly about the rose: 'You create your own space.'[15] And this space, which is therefore also qualitatively different from everyday space, Rilke also calls 'Rose-space, in roses secretly raised'[16] and also 'angelic space.'[17]

This is for the time being merely an imaginary reproduction. But if we remember that the rose is for Rilke, right up to his enigmatic epitaph, the symbol of human life, 'and to us the ultimate' [Äußerstes auch uns], we must, even at the risk of coarsening, ask what this 'rose space' can mean in the area of human life, and we will have to answer that it is the space of pure non-violence, in which pure intellectual existence unfolds. It creates its own space, without disputing it with anyone.

But now a further aspect is added: from this existence there emanates a power which also transforms the other who regards it with a reverent heart, which moves him into a corresponding state, where he no longer makes any claim on 'that space which the things around diminish', and where he too, filled with a joyful lightness, gains a corresponding new space. And to that extent one can say with total aptness that in this existence not only is no space taken away from the other, but on the contrary, even more space is created for him. However this 'increase' does not take place at all in the area of the previous space – which, regarded in a purely quantitative terms, cannot be increased – but on a new, higher level. This is the 'angelic space', in which this encounter takes place. In this context, angelic nature would characterize a being which realizes a purely intellectual existence without an egoistic claim to power. Because such an existence creates space beyond itself, the paradox once formulated by Swedenborg, 'The more angels, the more free space',[18] acquires a much deeper significance.

These connections admittedly are not yet those that Binswanger has in mind when he speaks of the 'spatiality of loving togetherness', but they create a necessary precondition for understanding this. What we have

15 Rainer Maria Rilke, *Gedichte in französischer Sprache*, Wiesbaden: 1949, p. 77.

16 'Rosenraum, geboren in den Rosen', Rainer Maria Rilke, *Gedichte 1906-1926*, Wiesbaden: 1953, p. 557.

17 Rainer Maria Rilke, *Briefe aus den Jahren 1914-1921*, edited by Ruth Sieber-Rilke and Carl Sieber, Leipzig: 1937, p. 94.

18 See O. F. Bollnow, *Neue Geborgenheit*, p. 242.

discussed here (using Rilke's image of the rose as an example) about the quiet, non-violent intellectual existence, which almost unintentionally radiates this space, is now also valid of the corresponding forms of human relationships, in particular of love, for this is characterized in its nature by the fact that here egoistic intelligence loses its meaning, that the lover, rather, does not become impoverished by giving, but is himself enriched, that therefore he gains through surrender. This is expressed very well by Binswanger's formulation of the love that increases itself.[19] And this too is what he means by the realization, which is central in his thinking, of the '"limitless" increase of individual space through the surrender of individual space.' Here he reaches a truly fundamental precondition of human coexistence.

And yet, once again we pause and ask in what specific sense we are here speaking of space, in particular of individual space. And once we become perplexed about this, we will have to answer that we can speak here only in a very general, transferred sense about a living space in which lovers do not place obstacles in each other's way, but live together in harmony, and in which, through the reciprocal enrichment of life, their common living space is indeed increased in an overwhelming manner. But this does not contribute much to the understanding of experienced space in a quite specific sense. So it is understandable that Binswanger here too loses sight of the specific spatial question, in order to turn to the more general unfathomability of love.

The foundation of the home

And yet, the theory of the space-creating power of love also has a quite specific spatial meaning, and this is where the decisive core of Binswanger's discovery appears to me to lie. This is not grasped in its actual nature as long as one is oriented in the quantitative sense on the idea of increase and decrease of space in the sense of a narrowing or widening. It is rather a question of working out the qualitative alteration of experienced space, by means of which the thought of a divisibility and calculability of space is finally overcome. And Binswanger does in fact take this step, referring again to Rilke, in his formulation: 'The space that they [lovers] reciprocally create for each other is their home.'[20] This designates the deeper starting

19 Binswanger, *Grundformen und Erkenntnis*, p. 79.
20 Binswanger, *Grundformen und Erkenntnis*, p. 72.

point from which the superficiality of the competitive struggle for space becomes visible. The great and continuing importance of Binswanger for the problem of space is to have seen this clearly.

The space of loving togetherness will therefore be designated here more precisely as the common home to be created in love. This at the same time alludes to the earlier formulation, paraphrasing Goethe, 'that exactly where you are, a place [for me] is created.'[21] With this, the present question again leads into the context of which we became aware earlier when we were discussing the house as the site of the family, which at the time we left open. Thus the question arises: What does home mean in this interpersonal sense? What does it mean to say that the space created by lovers is their home? And in any case, what is meant by creating a home?

Once again and finally, we must carefully examine Binswanger's progress from a critical distance. He understands the home created by lovers in the sense of an 'eternal home' raised above earthly matters. He stresses that although the lovers are physically bound to a particular place in the world, in a deeper sense they are raised above it, because they are at home 'everywhere and nowhere.' This seems to me to be seen a little too much from the perspective of the first encounter of lovers, when they indeed float in a 'seventh heaven' and in their state of being transported out of the world only too often have to endure the smiles of those around them. But what we mean by it is not only that each finds a refuge, and thus a home, in the other. It is rather a question of both first creating a home together. And if this home, in accordance with the unconditional nature of love, must also be rooted in the unconditional and eternal – in this respect Binswanger is quite right – then it is surely only a home to the extent that in this earthly reality it creates a common life space. And it is here that our actual problem sets in, which is too quickly abandoned by Binswanger with his distinction between the 'everywhere and nowhere' as the true home of love and the actual connection to a place.

Perhaps Binswanger, taking poetic evidence of an ultimate heightened experience of love as his starting point, did keep too closely to the 'simple mood atmosphere of the love-landscape of people in love';[22] for the actual problem that is rewarding for us to examine begins only at the point where it is a question of fulfilling the promises of love and really creating this home, which is a home only in so far as it is rooted in this finite space.

21 Binswanger, *Grundformen und Erkenntnis*, p. 31.
22 Binswanger, *Grundformen und Erkenntnis*, p. 256.

I will refer once more to Binswanger's formulation that 'exactly where you are, a place [for me] is created.' In the context in which this phrase occurs, it means, to begin with, that the claim on the specific space by one person does not withhold it from the other, but in fact makes it available to the other. Binswanger here alludes to Goethe's well-known lines:

> To me the field and the forest and the rock and the garden
> were always only a space, and you, beloved,
> make them into a place.[23]

For Goethe these lines clearly mean that the presence of the beloved makes the space which was previously meaningless, and therefore fleetingly hurried through, into a place charged with meaning, and therefore beloved by him, a place where he prefers to linger. So here it is not a matter of a claim on an area of space by the one or the other, but – as is already expressed by the change of designation from space to place – of the suitability of a place as somewhere to linger, to dwell. The question of spatial extension is insignificant here, for the place as a place can be neither narrow nor wide, but rather it designates the specific, assignable place on earth. With the link to this specific place there then begins the foundation of the home.

And now there is a repetition on the new level of togetherness of something we discussed earlier, as yet in too abstract a manner, from the particular point of view, and which we must now examine further from the point of view of the commonality of coexistence: that dwelling requires a specific dwelling place, a house as a place of seclusion. Here, in the case of lovers, it is a question of transition from the mere mood of being in love to enduring togetherness. If the love relationship is a serious one, the decision is made to create, beyond the 'eternal home', an earthly location, that is, to found a family and to build a house as a place to dwell together. Among primitive peoples it is a widespread custom that marriage necessarily coincides with building a house. But even if, in today's conditions, the newlyweds do not as a rule immediately build their own house, but rent and furnish an apartment, the task in principle still remains the same. Here, specifically and directly, the 'making-room of the limitless, singular and indivisible space' takes place. This is the space where space is directly created, and this is from the start a common space.

---

23 'Immer war mir das Feld und der Wald und der Fels und die Gärten / nur ein Raum, und du machst sie, Geliebte, zum Ort.' Goethe, 'Vier Jahreszeiten', *Gedenkausagabe*, vol. 1, p. 257.

For the sake of simplicity I will at first restrict myself to the simplest case, where a house is newly built, for here what is meant by creating space is directly observable. Certainly, in an abstract sense a space mass was already there: the number of cubic metres of air space, which is transformed by the walls of the houses into a 'built-up space.' But such a definition does not really convey the actual conditions. Space means here, quite directly, space to live and space to dwell: that space which is already expressed as a linguistic concept as being carved out like a hollow space for dwelling, out of surroundings no longer perceived as space, a thicket in the forest or the like. This is the place where in the most original sense space is created. And basically it is no different with a rented apartment in an already existing city house; here too, from a merely virtual space, the content in cubic metres of an empty part of the house, a real, that is, a human space is created.

But this creation of space does not take place in a single event of renting and acquiring furniture, but in the fact that this apartment becomes a home through common harmonious dwelling. In the gradually developed dwellability of the apartment the home eventually takes shape. If we look back from this point, it becomes clear how inappropriate it was to speak of a surrender or assertion of an individual space; for before the creation of this dwelling space there was no individual space there which could then be differently allocated. It was created from the outset as a common space and could only be created as this common space, and it is only a secondary process if later, perhaps when the children grow up, a (relatively) individual space is divided off in this common space.

Here, at the same time, the point is defined where this deeper problem is distinguished from the connections which we discussed earlier, based on the example of the sufferer from 'flight of ideas', with respect to a merely euphoric state. In a state of heightened emotion, space too expands, and in a mood of trustfulness one feels 'at home everywhere' and lifted above the cares of everyday life. But what here remains quite indefinite, and with a change in mood can at any time change suddenly into its opposite, can be permanently fixed here by space. And this is what happens in the building up of a concrete home, which the loving couple, as soon as their love has passed the stage of uncertainty, design as a common plan for living and make into a reality by concerted hard work.

Here the philosopher – who is used to learning from the works of poets, because they always open up new vistas and, at the limits of what is sayable, enlighten us by making further aspects visible – would also like to find help and continuing confirmation. But it is here that the poets abandon him. About the true creation of living space in the family, they are silent. It seems to suffice for them to describe the joy of being together – or indeed the pain of not being able to be together – but on real loving living-together they are silent. Inexplicable! For this reason, our portrayal must renounce the heightened brilliance of the poet's words and in our own, only too prosaic words we must try at least to suggest these important connection.

The common space of friendly co-operation

Binswanger certainly sees the problem of a common harmonious shaping of the specific living space in this world, but he discusses it in a somewhat different context, in a passage where he attempts to pursue the 'transition from the infinite home of love into the limited land of friendly sympathy.'[24] And certainly what is true here is that beside the love between man and woman, we must take into account the various other forms of sympathetic concern, because in them the common creation of space is transformed into respectively very different forms. But still the transition from the 'infinite home' to the 'limited land' is not to be traced back to the relationship of sexual love and male friendship, but must also be kept up within love itself which actually undertakes the creation of this home in the earthly world by the foundation of a family and the building of a house.

On the topic of friendship, Binswanger comments very aptly: 'It is by mutual sympathy that togetherness here "constitutes" itself, an actual community of the world, a world which can then "retrospectively" be divided again.'[25] But this applies not only to friendship as opposed to actual love, but it applies in exactly the same sense to friendship itself. This means, if we can try in our debate to translate it in as unpretentious terms as possible, that space in some abstract sense is not there at all in the first place, that rather it must be created by mutual human effort, which is here described as the creation of a home. So this space, created by mutual effort, is from the beginning a common space. It is only in this way that the gaining of a space for settlement by common land-clearing and cultivation can be understood. In this way it corresponds with the space of the house that is occupied in common by a family. But in a corresponding way it is also true in a transferred sense of the various living spaces. The space for professional work, a 'workshop' or a 'business', is from the start so much

24 Binswanger, *Grundformen und Erkenntnis*, p. 256.
25 Binswanger, *Grundformen und Erkenntnis*, p. 256.

a common space that the question of the division of this space, let alone a dispute over an adequate space, does not come up at all. In the reciprocal completion of work functions this common space is filled up to the extent that the demarcation of individual spaces has no meaning. Here too, with an appropriate variation, the phrase already quoted several times applies, 'that exactly where you are, a place [for me] is created.' Here this means that it is the achievement of one person that makes the other's work possible. This is most directly and clearly observed in the family, but it is correspondingly true of all professional organizations, and more generally of every form of human coexistence. On a larger scale it is also true of the lives of nations.

Only when this original order is disturbed – and it will necessarily become more vulnerable to such disturbances in the course of the differentiation of all relationships – when, that is, the original togetherness of the space is lost, then the competitive and often bitter struggle for one's own living space flares up. But this is always a later possibility and must not be placed unquestioningly at the beginning as a struggle of all against all.

But the reverse is also true: this battle for one's own living space, which places the interpretation presumed to be the only realistic one as the primary one, is not only the expression of a disturbance which sets in only later, but it is also not necessarily its final outcome and can be removed again by an appropriate elimination of this disturbance. And this is to a great extent a case of the correct inner attitude of the individual. I will clarify this with the use of a quite simple example: in every human working community, in every group or team (to use these words in their widest sense) this connection is valid: where the spirit of enmity, mistrust and competition reigns, everyone in fact stands in everyone else's way, and everyone fears that the other will put him in the shade, that he will take away his space, work, success or something else. But where coexistence is reasonably conducted – it need not even involve particular friendship or sympathy – not only is there no question of any reciprocal restriction of co-workers, but on the contrary the result is a reciprocal heightening. The success of one at the same time creates new possibilities of achievement for the other. Here it is really the case that collective work creates a living space that is greater than the sum of the individual living spaces. Working together really creates new life space.

But what has been said here of the emotionally comparatively neutral professional work community is true in a stronger and deeper sense of the life community of the family which is based on real internal love. And to that extent the house is the primeval phenomenon of such a communally created and communally inhabited living space, indivisible by its nature.

But furthermore, this is true, although we cannot pursue it in detail, of the life of nations. Where true co-operation and true coexistence take place, the struggle for living space is overcome, because in true co-operation no success is at the expense of another, but everyone gains from common success.

V
THE SPATIALITY OF HUMAN LIFE

1. Being-in-space and Having-space

Intentionality as a starting point

In our introduction we distinguished between the spatiality of human life and the corresponding lived and experienced space,[1] but at that point we temporarily put aside the question of spatiality as a determinant of human nature, in order to pursue, as spontaneously as possible, the objective side, experienced space in the richness of its defining characteristics. Admittedly these questions could not be entirely separated, and so we continually came up against the inner relationship of individuals with their space. But we paid no further attention to this 'subjective' side of the question, because we did not wish to interrupt prematurely the objectively directed course of our study. We must now make up for our earlier neglect. In doing so, we will not be able to avoid at various points returning to our earlier discussions from a new point of view.

To formulate it, for a start, as loosely as possible, it is a question of the relationship of man with space, or, in case this should already contain a misleading anticipation – where space might be understood as something objective to which man can react in one way or another – the question of how space belongs to the nature of man.

One commonly says, without giving it very much thought, that man is located in space. But this objectivizing statement already conceals the actual dubiousness of the state of affairs, and must be released from its apparent self-evidence. For this reason Heidegger pointed out emphatically that being-in-space means something different from what we mean when we say of an object that it is in a container. The difference lies in the fact that man is not a thing among other things, but a subject that reacts to its surroundings and which to that extent can be characterized by its intentionality. Man is, to the extent that he reacts to space – or, more cautiously, to the extent that he reacts to things in space – himself not

1 See the present book, p. 41 ff.

something inside space, but his relationship to things is characterized by his spatiality. Or, to express it differently, the way in which we are located in space is not a definition of the universe that surrounds us, but of an intentional space with reference to us as subjects.

We are located at a particular place in space, but this place is itself not within space as we perceive it and is very difficult to determine in its nature. We must think of this place as a point, and indeed we did earlier speak, in a preliminary mathematical terminology, of a natural zero point in a coordinate system. But this point cannot be inserted into the spatial, but remains the unfindable centre to which all spatial conditions are related by distance and direction. It is not a point that can be observed from the outside, but it is a 'here' in relation to one 'there' or another.[2]

The psychology of perception has researched in detail this intentional space as the space of the senses (subject-related by its nature), above all as a space of seeing. The way in which we builds up this space around ourselves can be schematically clarified with a system of polar coordinates, which relate to the perceiving individual as direction and distance. Heidegger then, as we briefly reported when discussing room for action, adopted these connections in the basic philosophical framework of his analysis of 'Dasein' [existence], and in relation to the space structured according to content represented the 'spatiality of existence' with the concepts of distance [Ent-fernung] and direction, no longer to be understood psychologically, but in terms of life. This interpretation of spatiality is basic to all further discussion.

Nevertheless, our discussion has repeatedly taken us beyond the concept of intentional space approached here, and has cast doubt on whether we can adequately grasp the nature of space from the concept of intentionality alone. But it is extraordinarily difficult to define this inadequacy positively. I can only attempt to isolate and draw attention to some of these approaches that are closely entwined with each other.

Space as a medium

On the one hand, just as intentional space is built up around the perceiving and moving individual, it is necessarily related to the individual's location as its centre at that time. The question as to where and how this individual is

2 In languages, adverbs of place and pronouns have a way of revealing the structure of these spatial relationships in a very subtle, precise and diverse manner; see above all K. Bühler, *Sprachtheorie* (Jena: 1934).

located in space cannot from this point of view be meaningfully answered at all, for man is the permanent centre of this space of his, and the space as the system of relationships with things travels with the individual when he moves. And yet, as we have already pointed out in the introduction, it makes good sense to say that man moves in space, treating space as something that is at rest. Man is located 'somewhere', at a particular point in space, while space, in particular quite specifically the surface of the earth, is perceived as fixed and basic to all human standing.

> Dear earth, this night has left you still unshaken,
> And at my feet you breathe refreshed[3]

This is a description of awakening from sleep in the feeling of self-assured security in this fixed space. A consciousness of this kind cannot be meaningfully explained from the viewpoint of the intentional concept of space. Here the change in space would be only the transition from one system of coordinates to another system relative to it, while rest and movement can only be conventionally determined.

But another point of view explores this more profoundly. The way we experience being in a place can be very different, according to whether we are lost in the fortuitousness of a 'somewhere' or feel bound to this one specific place as the one which belongs to us or has been granted to us. We can feel lost or sheltered in space, in unity with it or unfamiliar with it. There are therefore forms of being in space, variations of the relationship with space. Man is also always in space 'somehow.'

If we define space in terms of human intention only, such questions cannot even arise. This space is a mere system of relationships. But now space becomes a sort of medium in which I find myself, and only with such a medium can one speak meaningfully of being in a space. As such a medium, space becomes something quasi-material, in the sense that one can now really react in a certain way to space and not merely to the things in space, without objectivizing it (and also without subjectivizing it again). As a medium it is intermediate between an 'object' and a 'way of seeing', neither a 'container' independent of the viewer, nor a merely subjective design. With this way of talking about space as a medium we are not taking up again the old debate about the ideality or reality of space, it is by no means to be understood as a hypothesis about the 'nature of space', but

3 'Du, Erde, warst auch diese Nacht beständig / und atmest neu erquickt zu meinen Füßen', Johann Wolfgang von Goethe, *Faust zweiter Teil. Gedenkausagabe*, vol. 5, p. 293 [*Faust part two*, translated by David Luke, Oxford: 1994, p. 5].

we are using it merely as an aid, in order to express what is phenomenally given in direct experience of space: that I can actually react in different ways to space. In this sense, space and world, being-in-space and being-in-the-world can approach each other and sometimes even mean almost the same thing. Space is the commonest form of the world, if one disregards the individual things that fill it.

Forms of sensation of space

What is meant by the various ways of being located in space and reacting to space becomes clear from a specific experience, which we will in anticipation call the concept of space consciousness or the sensation of space. This is a certain mood which pervades our entire relationship with space and as such is to be distinguished from the emotional colouring of the relationship to an individual object in space.

That there are such different forms of sensation of space, and that these are very closely bound up with the entire human sensation of life, is made clear from a glance at the intellectual approach of our time, already touched on several times, which revolves around existentialist philosophy. Our best starting point is Heidegger, by whom these relationships are most powerfully worked out conceptually. Heidegger characterizes human 'being-in-the-world' as 'being-thrown.'[4] This includes the relationship with space, and we will need to understand this too as a 'being-thrown.' To say that man is thrown into something means more than that he is located there in a neutral sense. It means rather that, unintentionally, or even against his will, he is in a rather ungentle manner brought into a medium that is unfamiliar to him. We should also not ignore the emotional overtone that goes along with this; for this word has been chosen deliberately and has not appeared as though by accident. It is more than if he were placed or perhaps even planted into it. An element of carelessness and fortuitousness is contained in it. All throwing contains a note of aggression. Wild beasts have their food thrown to them, while humans are offered food in a rather more cautious manner. And so, man finds himself thrown into a medium that is strange to him, that is hostile and uncanny. And this too is how his location in space is to be understood. Space is such a strange and oppressive medium, in which man may find himself at any location. To use Sartre's term, he is 'de trop' in it, pointless and superfluous.

4 Martin Heidegger, *Sein und Zeit*, Halle a. d. Saale: 1927, pp. 135, 284, 345, 383, etc. [pp. 173, 329, 395, 434].

This is indeed an aptly envisaged image of the relationship with space, as it characterizes the man of our time, the individual who has become homeless and uprooted. Only one must take care not to apply it to humans in general; on the contrary, it characterizes man only in so far as something essential is missing in his relationship with space.

Bachelard sharply pinpointed this aspect: 'Before he is "cast into the world", … man is laid in the cradle of the house.' And he points out: 'Life begins well, it begins enclosed, protected, all warm in the bosom of the house.' Only afterwards is man 'thrown out', which in the imagery of the house means 'put outside the door.'[5] This is at first seen in genetic terms by Bachelard: at the beginning of human development the sensation of being in space cannot be characterized as being thrown. Where this is experienced, it is something that occurs later. But it can be assumed that behind this a natural connection is hidden, and that the state of being protected in the house takes precedence, also in objective terms. But if we leave this question aside for now, the point is for the time being that there is a way of being in space which cannot be characterized as being thrown, but rather stands in sharp contrast to it.

And this again entirely corresponds to the thinking of Heidegger, who points out in his text, already quoted earlier, on 'Building, dwelling, thinking', that man must first learn to dwell, phrasing it in this context as: 'To be a human being … means to dwell.'[6] By dwelling, he certainly means a way of being in space, which is fundamentally opposed to being thrown: for dwelling after all means no longer being abandoned to the arbitrary place of a foreign medium, but being sheltered in the protection of the house. But that man must first learn to dwell can only be understood as meaning that in the course of a perhaps unavoidable, but in any case ominous, development, he must by his own effort transform the state of being thrown into that of dwelling.

Dwelling

The concept of dwelling, which we have already encountered while considering the house as a central anthropological concept, thus again

5 Gaston Bachelard, *Poetik des Raumes*, translated by Kurt Leonhard, Munich: 1960, p. 39 [*The poetics of space*, translated by Maria Jolas, Boston, Mass.: 1969, p. 7].

6 Martin Heidegger, 'Bauen, Wohnen, Denken', *Vorträge und Aufsätze*, Pfullingen: 1954, p. 141 ['Building, dwelling, thinking', *Poetry, language, thought*, translated by Albert Hofstadter, New York: 1971, p. 147].

enters our field of attention in an altered version. While in the earlier passage[7] it was a question of what the possession of a house meant for the individual, it is now one of the disposition of the individual himself, which manifests itself in dwelling. And while at that time dwelling was understood with a certain self-evidence as dwelling in a house, it now acquires a more comprehensive and profound sense as genuine location in space appropriate to man. We must now examine the concept again in this sense and ask, what does 'dwelling' mean? In what way is the actual human relationship with space substantiated? And what does spatiality understood in this way tell us about human understanding of our nature?

In this context, let us first recall what emerged from our first, preliminary discussion of dwelling:

1. Dwelling, as we saw, stands in contrast to the accidental, merely transient stay at an arbitrary point in space. Dwelling means belonging to a certain place, being rooted and at home there.

2. Dwelling, as we further realized, means having a closed-off area of seclusion, an individual space of the house, in which man can withdraw from the threatening exterior world.

But now, in accordance with the new question, we must focus on what this dwelling, this staying in a lasting dwelling-place separated from the outside world, means for the inner disposition of man, for the understanding of his spatiality. Here we notice that the word 'dwelling' has recently acquired a more general meaning, which is not restricted to living in a house, but also characterizes the relationship of man to space – location in space as a whole. Human spatiality as a whole is understood as dwelling. We must now try to examine this question. We will approach it by first taking a comprehensive overview of this linguistic usage and then trying to work out what is meant by it.

In defining the linguistic usage we will make use of an example which is admittedly taken from the French language (which is no disadvantage at this point, since there is no essential difference between the equivalent words that concerns our problem), but which has the advantage that it stands in immediate connection with our present problem area. I am referring to the very extended use that has been given to the word 'dwell' [habiter] by Merleau-Ponty, and which seems to be typical of the way in which his own position, quietly and without explicit disagreement, is distinguished from the existentialist position of Sartre.

7 See the present book, p. 147 ff.

Earlier[8] we pointed out that for Merleau-Ponty the word 'dwell' [habiter] has become practically a key word in describing our relationship with the world and with life. And precisely the fact that he gives no definition of the word, that he seems not to have reflected at all about the nature of dwelling, but that the word seems to have appeared as if of its own accord exactly at the point where he is trying to express a relationship with being which is not to be grasped by means of existing terms, makes it seem particularly appropriate to clarify this new expression for a sense of space by using his example.

Merleau-Ponty uses the word 'habiter' in such a general sense that, in one of his last works, he is almost able to say that man dwells in being[9] (while there is a certain difficulty in translation caused by the fact that the French 'habiter' is also used as a transitive verb [like the English 'inhabit']; whereas in German we can use 'bewohnen' [inhabit] only with some difficulty, because to dwell in something and to inhabit something are distinguished by a small nuance). This phrase, 'dwelling in being', in fact felicitously describes the new relationship with being. Merleau-Ponty seems to have been entirely aware of the fundamentally different character of this new relationship, for he begins his last work, 'L'oeil et l'esprit', with the programmatic sentence: 'Science manipulates things and gives up [dwelling] in them.'[10] This clearly distinguishes scientific objectivity with its confrontation of the object[11] from the intimacy of dwelling. Thus he speaks generally of our dwelling in the world.[12]

In order to understand what is meant by this word, we must look a little more closely at Merleau-Ponty's various linguistic usages, and how a comparison between them can shed more light on them individually.

1. The basic meaning is of course the one which we have exclusively focused on up to now, the dwelling in a house. The other meanings derive

---

8 See the present book, p. 151.

9 Maurice Merleau-Ponty, *Signes*, Paris: 1960, p. 20 [*Signs*, translated by Richard McCleary, Evanston: 1964, p. 15]. Regarding the numerous references to Merleau-Ponty, I am especially indebted to the dissertation in progress by W. Maier (Tübingen, 1963), 'Das Problem des Leibes bei Sartre und Merleau-Ponty'.

10 Maurice Merleau-Ponty, 'L'œil et l'esprit', *Les Temps Modernes*, vol. 184-5, 1961, p. 193 ['Eye and mind', translated by Carleton Dallery, *The primacy of perception*, Evanston: 1964, p. 159 ff.; translation modified].

11 See Maurice Merleau-Ponty, *Phénoménologie de la perception*, Paris: 1945, p. 382 ff. [*The phenomenology of perception*, translated by Colin Smith, London: 1962, p. 332 ff.].

12 Merleau-Ponty, *Phénoménologie de la perception*, pp. 462, 491 [pp. 403, 429] and Merleau-Ponty, *Signes*, p. 69 [p. 59 ff.] etc.

from this one. The other kind of dwelling takes place 'as man dwells in his house.'[13] But conversely, this dwelling in the house must then be understood retroactively from the point of view of the other, extended and transferred meanings of the term.

2. The concept of dwelling is then also used to define the relationship of the soul to the body. 'The soul dwells in the body'[14] is a phrase that Merleau-Ponty likes to use. By this he means the close relationship of the 'incarnation' of the soul in a spatial shape. If this relationship is called dwelling, it is certainly a dwelling of a particular kind, for the soul cannot leave this 'dwelling' in the body, as man can leave his house, it cannot 'move out', without completely abandoning this life. Therefore, we will rather have to read this linguistic 'equation' in the reverse direction: that the relationship of man to his house is to be understood in the intimacy of his relationship with his body. Dwelling in a house is also a kind of incarnation.

3. This close relationship is expressed even more clearly in a different linguistic usage. Merleau-Ponty also speaks of the sense or meaning dwelling in a word. 'The link between the word and its living meaning is not an external link of association, the meaning inhabits the word, and language is not an external accompaniment to intellectual processes.'[15] Similarly he also suggests that the meaning is directly contained in the moment of expressive realization in the way that empathy seems to allow us to dwell in the body of another individual.[16] If the unity of word and meaning and, with the example of empathetic understanding, that of mimic expression and the psychological state expressed in it, are defined by the word 'dwell', it becomes clear that, conversely, the word 'dwell' means such an indissoluble unity of dwelling and dweller.

4. The word can also be used in the sense of humans dwelling in the world.[17] This means that they do not appear arbitrarily in the world, but are bound to it in a relationship of trust like that of the soul with its body, that of the signified to its sign. He remarks that individuals dwell in the world in different ways, which can then be made visible by the painter in artistic representations.[18] He stresses that 'the eye dwells in being as man dwells

13 Merleau-Ponty, 'L'œil et l'esprit', p. 200 [p. 166; translation modified].

14 Merleau-Ponty, *Phénoménologie de la perception*, p. 369 etc. [p. 319, translation modified].

15 Merleau-Ponty, *Phénoménologie de la perception*, p. 225 [p. 193].

16 Merleau-Ponty, *Phénoménologie de la perception*, p. 215 [p. 184].

17 Merleau-Ponty, *Phénoménologie de la perception*, pp. 462, 491 [pp. 403, 429].

18 Merleau-Ponty, *Signes*, p. 68 [p. 59 ff.].

in his house.'[19] Dwelling here means the form of a trusting-understanding bond. This is true of the world as a whole, as well as of individual things. 'Man dwells in things', as the phrase already quoted says; this means that he is inwardly so bound up with them that they are no longer outward objects to him, but have become part of his life as the agents of a deeper being.

To summarize the linguistic understanding developed so far, the concept of dwelling serves to denote the indissoluble unity with which something psychological is embodied 'in' something physical. And so it can also be used to denote in a general way the relationship of man with space. For Merleau-Ponty, man dwells in space. And we will have to try to identify the understanding of space contained here.

We need not be detained by the idea that man dwells in all areas of the world by means of his body;[20] for here the body appears as a mere instrument, with whose help he can react to the world (similarly, Schopenhauer saw the body as the 'direct object'). So this tells us nothing about the nature of dwelling. What is more important is that Merleau-Ponty seeks to understand our body itself in its spatiality as the primeval form of all other experience of space. 'The body', he says at one point, 'is both natal space and matrix of every other existing space.'[21] The body is here not just a tool, through which space is experienced, but is itself an experienced space, and moreover the most originally experienced space, according to whose model all other spaces are understood. So, not as a spaceless subject, but through the body as a spatial form in its own right, we are sunk into the greater surrounding space. We will have to come back to this when considering the body.

5. From this point we can understand that the concept of dwelling is also applied to the relationship with space and time. 'The body dwells in space and time.'[22] Even though at the specific place where Merleau-Ponty deals with this, he is thinking more of the indissoluble interconnection with space and time, and so dwelling is used in the same breath as being-committed, with being-involved in the situation, in order to reject the idea of a worldless subject, we must pay particular attention to the implicit interpretation of the relationship with space, which is given with the concept of dwelling that is pregnant with the different linguistic usage. From this point we will

19 Merleau-Ponty, 'L'œil et l'esprit', p. 200 [p. 166].
20 Merleau-Ponty, *Phénoménologie de la perception*, p. 359 [p. 311].
21 Merleau-Ponty, 'L'œil et l'esprit', p. 211 [p. 176].
22 Merleau-Ponty, *Phénoménologie de la perception*, p. 162 [p. 139, translation modified], see p. 118 ff. [p. 101 ff.], p. 164 [p. 140].

perhaps have to report misgivings about extending the concept of dwelling to the relationship with time, and say rather that man dwells in space, but not in time, thus expressing a significant difference between space and time. But for now we must simply accept Merleau-Ponty's linguistic usage for what it is.

To summarize: man, or the ego, dwells in the body, in the house, in things, in the world, in space and time. But the meaning also dwells in the word and the sign, the expressed mental state dwells in the expression. If, in retrospect, we once more observe the passing before our eyes of the wide field of these possible usages, it becomes clear that in enumerating examples, certain basic features of understanding have at the same time emerged, which allow us to gather together various relationships within the common concept of dwelling. Everywhere it is a question of designating a particular intimacy of the relationship, with which something mental or intellectual is to some extent merged into something spatial. This is a relationship which is difficult to express with the usual conceptual means. Thus, at one point, dwelling was positively made to contrast with the scientific attitude. And only, as it were, by circumscribing, only as indirect indications, expressions then appear such as being-incarnated, being-committed and the like. We must now try to focus more sharply on the relationship with space which is described in this way.

Having-space

So we will take up the earlier thread again, when we spoke of the difficulties that arise when one tries to clarify the given nature of space from the viewpoint of intentional relatedness. Perhaps it was from the beginning too narrowly expressed, or at least too one-sidedly when with reference to the relationship of man with space we spoke of 'being-in-space.' We must ask ourselves if it is an original statement, meaningful in the sense of naïve linguistic usage, if we say 'humans are in space', or 'they are located in space', or whether the relationships are not already neutralized in the sense of the abstract mathematical concept of space. We can certainly say 'the individual is at home' or 'he is in his workroom.' This is no different from when we speak of a container, such as the cup in the cupboard. It designates the specific inner space in which one can seek and find the individual. Here one is always in a specific space, and the statement remains in the area of objective observation. The individual is regarded as no different from a thing which is located in the space in question.

But outside the house, man is no longer in a space, but in a particular place or in a particular area. The statement that he is then still in an abstract sense 'in space', 'simply in space', has no specifically assignable meaning for the sense of language that is still unspoilt by scientific usage. And we must be very cautious about such carelessly expressed abstract formulations, which cannot be verified with reference to the specific life situation.

If we go back to the unreflective linguistic usage, in order to gauge from it the original way in which man is given something like space, we will find the connections understood here in a completely different way. In addition we must go back once again to our introductory references to linguistic usage and linguistic history. Space, we said at that time, is something which is to hand, which is more or less available and which is also sometimes lacking.[23] We speak of a need for space, of a lack of space or excess of space and in some cases also of a waste of space. Man needs space. We can make a claim to more or less space. Space, in any case, is something that one can have or not have. And this is something completely different from what we mean when we say that man is located in space. We can perhaps make the statement more pointed by saying that man is located or 'is' in a specific and limited space, but he has space in general. In the first case, always with the article included, it is a question of a specific, quantitatively determinable space, while in the second case, always without the article, it is a space that is so closely bound up with man that it defies all quantitative determination. This space, which man has in an initially still unspecific way, is more original than the space in which he 'is' in a particular place, and only with this kind of space do we find the actual basis of human spatiality.

So there are three concepts of space that are so different that one should really distinguish linguistically between them. But in order not to introduce any new, excessively barbaric coinages, we will for the time being refer to the new space, rather awkwardly, as the 'space that one has.' To speak of a 'had' or 'possessed' space would be impractical, because it could then be understood as a space that one once had or possessed in the past, and just does not have any more. So in addition to the objective space of the interior world, in which things and individuals are to be found, and intentional space, which is built up in distance and directions around the human subject, we now have a third concept of space, the 'space that one has.'

This is not the place to pursue further the more general problem of having, which opens up with particular insistence from the question

23 See the present book, p. 54 ff.

of human spatiality, and which proves to be more deeply searching and considerably more complicated than the problem of being, which so far has been so unilaterally preferred by philosophy. The original definitions of human life are those of having and not of being (while having is itself a very diversely modified concept), and it is only from the point of view of having that we can ask at all what 'being' means in the human context. We must here restrict ourselves to the one aspect, arising from space, and in these terms we can refine our considerations to the question: What does the statement that 'man has space' mean? In what sense can one have 'space' or 'a space'? And indeed how can one determine the amount of space that man 'needs'?

Individual space

At first everything seems quite simple, and only sophistry seems to have produced such a question. We need not even refer to the trivial fact that man takes up a certain volume of space with his body. This is not what is meant here, but that man needs as much free space around him as is necessary for him to move without colliding with things, and thus being hindered in his movement. Narrowness and width are the basic determinants of this space that is needed by man. If man were alone in the world, or, for example, in a desert, he would have the most space. But he would have so much that space would never be a problem for him. It becomes a problem only when an individual with his need for space collides with another individual. And this again does not mean that he collides with the body of the other, but that he collides with the space for movement claimed by the other, where movement is again used in a general sense, beyond the sense of merely spatial-physical movement. The space that man needs, and that in a specific case he has or does not have, is thus that which we call in a general sense his space for movement or, perhaps better (if the word had not been outworn through careless linguistic usage) his 'Lebensraum' [space to live].

But because the ability to move is constantly endangered by external disturbances, by the intrusion of other people, by weather conditions, and so on, man must secure his freedom to move, that is, he must defend his space and protect himself against the intrusion of disturbing influences. This can happen without visible change by means of his constant alertness and readiness to defend himself. But it can also happen in a lasting manner, by his demarcating his space from the outside world by means of hedges and fences, walls and ramparts, and securing it against the intrusion of foreign forces by enclosing his space (to use a concept we employed earlier). And if, earlier, the mere spaces for movement (as in road traffic) intersected without hindering each other, now spaces exclusively belonging to individuals are created. The open space for movement becomes a separate, occupied space. We speak in a general sense of an individual space, a term which can now be used to denote the concept left open earlier, of the 'space that man has.'

This changes the relationship of man with space. The individual no longer 'has' the space in an uncertain sense of availability, only momentarily and accidentally, while this could change again at any minute; instead, 'having' now acquires the more succinct sense of possession. It is his space, which belongs to him exclusively, which he possesses as his space and defends as his possession. At the same time, the generally understood, not precisely definable quantity description 'space' becomes the specific, delimited space that the individual calls his own.

How large is the individual space claimed and possessed by the individual, remains very variable in specific cases. The daemonic power of immoderate striving for possession of space is very graphically portrayed by Tolstoy in his novella *The death of Ivan Ilyich.*[24] And yet the reference to the meagre space that man will one day occupy in his coffin is to be taken only as a warning, not as an answer to our question; for, strictly speaking, death causes the total breakdown of individual space, because the question of necessary space for manoeuvre loses its meaning. But even within this space for manoeuvre there are evidently still very different ways in which man can have an individual space, and the Tolstoyan example illustrates only an extreme borderline case, where the 'alienated' space has become a disposable possession. On the other hand, there then emerges the task of 'appropriation', that is, inclusion of the possessed space into living life, and we observe the danger of the phraseology that unthinkingly equates having with possession, because the latter can too easily be taken to mean disposability.

24 Leo Tolstoy, *Sämtliche Erzählungen*, edited by Gisela Drohla, Frankfurt a. M.: 1961, p. 603 ff.

2. Forms of Individual Space

Three areas of dwelling

So in what sense can we say that we 'own' a space, that an individual space 'belongs' to us? For in the direct sense of the word we can only own things, and space evades the grasp which we exert over things. The answer to this question is inseparable from the specific determination of the space possessed by man.

The way in which we own an individual space in our lives is called 'dwelling', and thus we adopt the concept of dwelling in a more general sense. In the present context we do not distinguish between 'dwelling' and 'inhabiting.' Man dwells in the space that belongs to him, or he inhabits his space, two things that we take as equivalent, although in the first case the aspect of having and in the second case that of being-inside is more strongly stressed. Being and having here become inseparably intertwined.

In our overview of the range of the word 'dwell', three forms of such an individual space emerged:

1. the space of one's own body
2. the space of one's own house
3. enclosing space in general.

Here the term 'house' is to be understood in a general sense as any closed individual area beyond the body, in which man can remain and move with safety. Furthermore, 'space in general' implies any enclosing space which is no longer distinguished by a recognizable boundary as an interior space from an exterior space. It will become clear in what follows why we must include this space too in one's individual space.

In each of the three cases the form of having or possessing individual space will be different, and therefore we must hope to be able, by means of a comparative examination of the three possibilities, to penetrate more deeply into the relationship with space and thus into the nature of human spatiality.

The body

The body needs to be discussed here only in so far as we can derive from it some general understanding of space. But here once again we must distinguish between two questions:

1. The body is the tool by whose help, that is, by means of its sense organs and ability to move, space is given to us. To that extent it belongs to the organization of the subject experiencing space.

2. The body is itself a space, an individual space, and thus a part of the space that surrounds us. To that extent it also belongs to the area of the experienced object.

And the peculiar difficulty here is based on the fact that both, again, are connected in the closest possible way.

a. Body and exterior space

In the first line of thought, we will once again go back to the structure of intentional space. Man, as we have seen, is at the centre of his space, at a 'here' in relation to one 'there' or another. But when one tries to define this 'here' more precisely, one soon gets into difficulties. Of course, one says, I am 'here', that is, at this place in space. That is quite obvious in everyday life too. When, for example, I am not to be seen in the dark, I can call out to announce 'where' I am, and then the other person knows where to find me. But when I inquire more precisely, then this 'where', this place where I am in space, has a peculiar uncertainty and is difficult to fix to the exact centimetre. For example, if I reach for someone in the dark and grab him by the arm, is he then there where I grab his arm? Or is this 'where' to be equated with the area taken up by his body? But then we would be identifying the individual with his body and missing the intentionality of his spatial condition. So I would have to try to determine a point in my body that denotes my position in space.

For seeing with only one eye, this point is fairly precisely determined in the interior of my eyeball. But as soon as I see stereoscopically with both eyes, this certainty quickly disappears. The 'where' would be located at some imprecise point between my eyes. But it would be a pointless precision to want to determine it more accurately. It is simply not possible to localize it further. And the uncertainty grows when one takes into account the other senses or even movement in space. Thus, for example, it has been pointed out that the seat of sensation for instinctive consciousness lies deeper, in the area of the heart, and that in dancing this centre moves further into the area of the body's centre of gravity.[1] We have to say that the 'here' in space is found only with the uncertainty conditioned by the dimensions of my body. It would be a senseless pastime to go beyond this.

Thus the body as a whole acquires a distinct meaning for the understanding of human spatiality. Admittedly we can easily say that the ego that exists in space is not identical with the physical thing, the body. But the body again is not just a physical thing. It becomes so only as a corpse. The body is in a direct sense the 'seat' of my ego, and the whole spatial world is transmitted to me only though my body, or rather, perhaps, I am admitted to the spatial world by my body. Sartre and Merleau-Ponty have worked this out very clearly: the world is given to me *à travers mon corps*, in a sense right through my body, which itself is something spatially extended and whose various sense organs are already separated from each other by spatial distances. So *à travers mon corps* means more than by means of my senses; for I can still see the senses as spatially unextended subjective points, but the body is itself a spatially extended formation, through which I am in a sense admitted to space, with a spatial mass of its own, and delimited outwards by a surface, and thus actually a sort of interior space, which is distinct from an exterior space. This body, as a spatial formation of this kind, is no longer a pure subject, but also not yet a pure object, but strangely in between.

b. The unobtrusiveness of the body

Thus, without a sharp distinction, we have already passed from the first to the second interpretation. But this gives rise to the question: in what way is man's body given to him as a spatial formation of this kind? In what sense does he 'have' his body? And how is his relationship with his body to be determined at all?

This question is surprising; for the naïve person does not ask it and cannot ask it at all. His body simply does not enter the sphere of his attention, but he is in a sense, beyond his own body, already directly among the things of his world. Sartre expresses this very acutely when he says: 'The body is the

---

1 See Karl Bühler, *Sprachtheorie*, Jena: 1934, p. 131, and Erwin Straus, 'Formen des Räumlichen. Ihre Bedeutung für die Motorik und Wahrnehmung' (1930), *Psychologie der menschlichen Welt. Gesammelte Schriften*, Berlin, Göttingen, Heidelberg: 1960, p. 167 ff. ['Forms of spatiality', *Phenomenological psychology. The selected papers of Erwin Straus*, translated by Erling Eng, London: 1966, p. 21 ff.].

passed-over, what has "silently happened".'[2] He compares the body with a sign. Like the sign, the body too is 'what is being transcended through meaning.' So I am not with my body, but always beyond my body with the things with which I occupy myself.

For this reason, for the naïve consciousness the body does not take up any individual space at all, but space only begins beyond the body, only outside the skin. The body is in a sense a 'non-space', as if not there at all, only the beginning of all spatial distances. For the system of all distances in space the body has only the function of a point, a zero point. It has itself, as it were, shrunk into a point.

It is only certain borderline experiences through which my body enters my explicit consciousness as a spatial formation. These include, for example, when it gets in our way in moving through space through its 'bulkiness' and to that extent obtrusively makes us aware of it (for example when, as children, we are no longer able to get through a hole in the fence). These include above all the obtrusiveness of pain, when we are ill and suddenly acquire the experience, until then totally lacking, of our own organs and their position in the body. Plügge has discussed this in a very convincing manner.[3] But here we always have to note that it is only the body alienated from us by illness that thus enters the field of vision of our attention. But behind this there emerges the further and deeper question: how is the space of our own body given to us when we still have a healthy relationship with it, and it is not yet objectivized by pain or other disturbances? In this sense, we will now look into the direct givenness of the body.

c. Incarnation as a mode of having-a-body

If we start from the concept of having, we can of course make the statement that the individual has his body. But this soon leads to difficulties, which Marcel, above all, has analysed in detail: for man does not 'have' his body in the way in which he has his other possessions. He cannot have his body at his disposal in the same way. He is somehow more closely connected with his body. According to Marcel, it is a question of

---

2 Jean-Paul Sartre, *Das Sein und das Nichts* [*L'être et le néant*, Paris: 1943], translated by v. J. Streller, K. A. Ott and A. Wagner, Hamburg: 1962, p. 429 [*Being and nothingness*, translated by Hazel E. Barnes, London: 1957, p. 330].

3 See Herbert Plügge, *Der Mensch und sein Leib*, Tübingen: 1967, and *Wohlbefinden und Mißbefinden*, Tübingen: 1962.

an 'enigmatic and intimate connection between me and my body.'[4] One cannot distance oneself from one's body. Therefore there is not here, as there is for other kinds of having, a problem of appropriation, that is, of the inner inclusion of what was outwardly already possessed, as, for example, a work of art which has only been outwardly possessed, can be inwardly appropriated. The body in living use is always already appropriated, it is already included in the person.

Man somehow already 'is' his body. Thus it also directly corresponds to the naïve consciousness that does not distinguish between person and body. Let us merely recall the beginning of the *Iliad*, where the wrath of Achilles

> sent the gallant souls of many noblemen to Hades, leaving
> their bodies as carrion for the dogs and passing birds.[5]

So here too the individual 'himself' is still quite naïvely equated with his body as distinct from his soul. In the same way today the naïve living person identifies himself with his body. For this reason he experiences the touching of his body directly as an attack on his person. He feels injured in his own person if he is taken hold of by another, for example tugged by the sleeve, held fast or even attacked with a blow. He feels this as an injury, not only outwardly, to his mere body, but actually inwardly, to the honour that is attached to his person.

To that extent a relationship emerges that one could describe almost as one of identification with one's body, even if it is perhaps only a partial identification, which on a higher level at the same time admits a certain measure of at least intellectual distance from what happens to one's body. So it would be false to say that we have our body, because we cannot do what we want with it as with a disposable possession. The body is somehow closer to us than anything else we have. But to say that we are our bodies is equally impossible, and the linguistic contradiction of the phrase already expresses the difficulty of the relationship. Here Sartre finds himself forced into the formulation: I 'exist my body.'[6] But this expression must be as linguistically contradictory in French as in translation. So it is to be taken only as a consciously paradoxical indication of the intermediate position,

---

4 Gabriel Marcel, *Être et Avoir*, Paris: 1935, p. 9 [*Being and having*, translated by Katharine Farrer, Glasgow: 1949, p. 11]. See also O.F. Bollnow, 'Gabriel Marcel, Christlicher Existentialismus', *Die Sammlung*, vol. 3, 1948, pp. 401 ff., 481 ff., 549 ff.

5 *Iliad*, book 1, verses 3-5.

6 *Sartre, Das Sein und das Nichts*, p. 454.

not expressible by means of normal language, that I am my body, and yet I am not, because it remains external to me; I have my body, and yet I do not have it, because it still inwardly belongs to me.

Again, it is only another formulation of this partial identification when I say, in Marcel's phrase, that I am incarnated in my body. For 'incarnation', as Marcel formulates it, is the 'situation of a being who appears to himself to be, as it were, bound to a body.'[7]

This is basically only a different description of the same enigmatic relationship with space by which I have become corporeal and thus spatial in my body, that, therefore, I am rooted in space by my body. But it is thoroughly justifiable to invoke this theologically predetermined concept (even though in a slightly altered sense) to describe the general anthropological nature of man. Admittedly it explains nothing, but it draws our attention to the secret that is at work here. And it should here be taken only in terms of this indication.

And once again, it is nothing but this mysterious unity, which cannot be traced back any further, that Merleau-Ponty too has in mind when he says that I dwell in my body. To dwell in something means to be incarnated in something. And if we drew attention to the fact that with the body it is a case of a special kind of dwelling, that is, of an indissoluble connection with the dwelling, on the other hand we must be able to derive from the common ground between the linguistic usages the presumption that something of the relationship that has been described as incarnation in the body is perhaps also found in dwelling in the house, and perhaps in dwelling in space in general, and that to this extent the concept of incarnation proves to be productive for the general understanding of the spatiality of human life.

The house

a. Incarnation in the house

The second form of the individual space possessed by man is the house or the dwelling, and this is the form to which we apply the concept of dwelling in its actual sense. We can be brief here, because earlier we discussed in detail the anthropological function of the house as a place of peace and security, so that here we only need to bring out in a more exhaustive manner the inner relationship of man with his dwelling space. In

---

7 Marcel, *Être et Avoir*, p. 11.

this connection it is important that the relationship of man with his dwelling is similar in some way to his relationship with his body. Without wanting to exaggerate the analogy artificially, we can still regard the house to a certain extent as an extended body, with which man identifies himself in a similar way and through which he correspondingly integrates himself in a greater surrounding space. In each case there is a clearly recognizable limit which separates the individual space with which I identify myself, which in a certain sense I therefore 'am', from the other space, which I no longer am, which does not belong to me and which is foreign to me. But the difference here is that I am indissolubly bound up with my bodily individual space and carry it around with me wherever I go, but my domestic individual space is fixed, so that I can leave it and return to it again.

Here both interior space and exterior space also have a completely different character. As with the body, here too we can say that space, in the sense of a connection structured by distance and directions, begins only outside the house. It is only at the door of the house that the paths begin that open up the world to us. But it would be inappropriate to apply the concept of the path within the house as well. The steps that we take in the house cannot be added to those taken in the street to make a common distance. The spaces that open up inside and outside the house, and that cannot be directly gathered together to form an overriding total space, are different, while domestic inner space (like that of the body), precisely because of its intimacy, opens up only with difficulty to scientific observation.

Thus there is a direct identification with the house, even though it is perhaps not as marked as with the body. Man identifies himself with his house. He merges into it. In dwelling in his house, he is directly present in it and feels almost physically injured if a stranger intrudes against his will in the sphere of his house. But this domain goes further and is also applied, though to a lesser extent, to all space which is part of our sphere of possession. Thus the farmer, in an equivalent way, identifies himself with his farmland, and his anger at unauthorized entry to his land does not arise from concern about the possibility of damage being inflicted on it, perhaps by trampling on his corn, but quite directly from resistance to intrusion on 'his' space, which causes him to feel directly injured and offended in himself. A similar case is the anxiety with which a state defends itself against injury to its territory. It feels that its honour is attacked by an intrusion, in itself insignificant, across its borders.

Having been able to transfer the concept of dwelling, arising from the house, to the body, we can now also, conversely, transfer the concept of incarnation from the bodily sphere, in an extended sense, to the house, and express the relationship between man and house by saying that man is incarnated in his house. Through this close connection, the house becomes an expression of his nature. And since we earlier pursued the way in which man can impress the character of his personality on his dwelling space to such an extent that the latter can then be understood from the former, this again takes us back to the intimate relationship between man and space that we are seeking to describe with the concept of incarnation.

How strongly man is bound up with his house also emerges from some notions of a primeval consciousness that have been to a great extent preserved until now in popular belief. Bilz, who first became aware of these relationships in a psychopathological context, speaks of an 'archaic binary relationship between subject and house.'[8] One could furthermore almost speak of an identification of man and house, which still has a lasting effect today when one jokingly addresses another person in German as 'altes Haus' [old house]. What Bilz gathers from a report on Norwegian conditions, namely that people are called after the houses in which they dwell, has also survived in many cases in Germany. So for example one says of a family in the Westerwald region of Germany that their name is Langhans, but they are known as Schneider. One is the name that is applied to the house and that is inherited by every new owner, the other is the family name inherited from the father, as it is recorded at the register office. But the phrase 'he is known as …' expresses the idea that the first name is the actual one by which the person is known in everyday usage, while the other is considered only as something secondary, only as a formal matter of bureaucracy. This shows that here the spatial connection with the house is stronger than temporal rootedness in family succession.

Another linguistic usage is interesting in the context of the identification of man and house. The house is also an economic unit and in another sense the word refers to everything that belongs to the 'household.' Beyond this, the house is also important in its legal meaning, for it designates a sphere of power which frequently extends beyond the walls up to the roof guttering. The German phrase 'Ich aber und mein Haus' [I and my house] in patriarchal usage includes the whole circle of individuals who belong to a household. In particular, in the case of royal houses, such as the house of Habsburg, it is used to designate the genealogical connection.

8 Rudolf Bilz, 'Pole der Geborgenheit. Eine anthropologische Untersuchung über raumbezogene Erlebnis- und Verhaltensbereitschaften', *Studium Generale*, vol. 10, 1957, p. 552 ff.

b. The transformation of man in his house

The intimate relationship of humans and their house is however shown not only in the fact that we are able to impress the character of our own nature on our dwelling space, and conversely the latter has its effect on us, but equally in the way in which we in our nature are determined by our environment, and our nature is transformed according to the nature of our environment. Saint-Exupéry says very aptly in one passage: 'The women themselves became quiet or demanding or timid, according to the part of the house in which they happened to be.'[9] What is said here about women in a poetic context is of course true in an extended sense of humans in general, and not only of the place in the house, but generally of the place in space. In a similar sense, Bachelard points out: 'For we do not change place, we change our nature',[10] and he speaks explicitly of a 'fusion of being in … a concrete space.'[11] This link means not only that space has a modifying effect on us, because this would still be a reciprocal effect between things previously separated, but that we acquire a particular nature only in unity with a specific space. We do not have nature 'in itself' and independently of the space in question, but only acquire it in the specific space.

This is true to a particular extent, according to whether we are inside or outside our house. Fischart says in one passage:

> Each man is free in his own house,
> outside it he is lost, anxious, timid.[12]

The relationship with space is basically different in the two cases, inside and outside the house. The external world is the space of our work, our business, our tasks in the world in general. Here we need total attentiveness in order to have control of the situation and react quickly to surprises. We need to have active consciousness of what we are doing at all times. This is therefore the area of total division between subject and object. It is a space that is foreign to us, even uncanny and threatening, into which we are 'thrown.'

---

9 Antoine de Saint-Exupéry, *Citadelle*, Paris: 1948; *Die Stadt in der Wüste*, Bad Salzig and Düsseldorf: 1951, p. 39 [*The wisdom of the sands*, translated by Stuart Gilbert, London: 1952, p. 17].

10 Bachelard, *Poetik des Raumes*, p. 236 [p. 206].

11 Bachelard, *Poetik des Raumes*, p. 236 [p. 206].

12 'In seinem Haus ist jeder frei / auswendig verlassen, furchtsam, scheu', Fischart, quoted in Grimm, *Deutsches Wörterbuch*.

In the peace of the house, on the other hand, man has no need of this tense attentiveness. Therefore, the tension between subject and object is immediately relaxed, and with it the intentional character of spatial relationships. And this again is the precondition for man's merging with his space, for his being admitted, surrounded and held by it.

The same conditions of course also apply to the various other forms of limited individual space, for which we have taken the house representatively as the simplest example. This applies on a larger scale in an equivalent fashion to the space of the home, the space of the foreign, and the various ways in which larger (and then always at the same time collective) individual spaces are delimited from foreign spaces. But it also applies on a smaller scale to the various areas within the house, and our earlier discussions of the space of the bed and the process of falling asleep become productive for the understanding of the modifications of spatiality.

c. The territory of animals

The concept that human life can develop only in connection with a specific residence and a specific home area finds a welcome confirmation by equivalent experiences of the behaviour of animals, of which the more recent researchers into animal psychology have become aware. After Uexküll had drawn attention to the perfection of the way animals are suited to their environment, biologists occupied themselves more intensively with the development of such animal environments and thus became aware of the inner unity between the animal and the space in which it lives, a result that exactly corresponds with what we have been saying so far about humans. In this context, the Swiss biologist Hediger explicitly points out: 'The animal and the space that surrounds it form a unity, a totality; plan and organization are continuous. Plan and organization encompass bodily structure, behaviour and space.'[13] From the more general biological question we will deal only with the point with which we are here specially concerned. That is the link to a particular place or area.

Ornithologists were probably the first to observe that birds do not live in the forests with the freedom of movement that is so easily imagined, but are bound to a certain area throughout their lives that they do not voluntarily depart from. The same is true of countless other creatures. The concept of territory was introduced by biologists to designate the specific living space of an animal or a pair of animals or even a group of animals.

13 H. Hediger, cited by H. Peters (see note 37 below).

Peters published a very fine report on these connections in the journal *Studium Generale.*[14] These territories are divided externally from those of others, and each animal defends its territory against the intrusion of other members of its species. Biologists speak of a kind of possession in order to describe the relationship between an animal and its territory. Peters, citing Meyer-Holzapfel, refers to a 'Be-sitzen' [possession], of which one speaks with a certain justification with reference to territorial animals, who have to wrest their domains with great effort from the world around them.'[15] This is fundamentally a very anthropomorphic concept, which makes its application to the animal kingdom all the more striking.

The claim to possession of such territories is frequently announced by their inhabitants by means of various signs. In a sense they affix their stamps of possession to them. In the case of birds, these can be acoustic signals, their calls and songs. With mammals they are frequently signals by smell. We are most familiar with the habits of dogs, who mark out the limits of their zones by these signals which are recognizable to the members of their species. Of course there are conflicts, particularly in the case of a lack of food. Then their own domains must be defended. And so the various territories are delimited. 'Owners of territories', writes Peters, 'tend to keep within their limits. When these are crossed, this leads to battle, where as a rule the established occupier retains the superior position, even if he is weaker than the intruder. But in general attacks do not take place.'[16]

But the territories are delimited not only outwardly from other territories, but also subdivided in themselves according to the needs of their inhabitants. Not every vital function can be satisfied in any arbitrary part of the space; there are certain areas for sleeping, eating and drinking, urination and defecation. Even movement from one part of the domain to another is not arbitrary, but the animal constructs particular 'roads' for this purpose, such as the 'runs' of game animals. 'Even the traffic from one point to another is not arbitrary. Their "runs" serve a purpose; they signify a self-imposed limitation in the face of the available possibilities.'[17] So we find in the organization of the living space of animals according to vital

---

14 H. Peters, 'Über die Beziehungen der Tiere zu ihrem Lebensraum', *Studium Generale*, vol. 10, 1957, p. 523 ff.

15 Peters, 'Über die Beziehungen der Tiere zu ihrem Lebensraum', p. 525, see Monika Meyer-Holzapfel, *Die Bedeutung des Besitzes bei Tier und Mensch. Arbeiten zur Psycho-Hygiene*, Biel: 1952.

16 Peters, 'Über die Beziehungen der Tiere zu ihrem Lebensraum', p. 523 ff.

17 Peters, 'Über die Beziehungen der Tiere zu ihrem Lebensraum', p. 524, following Hediger.

functions a characteristic which already reminds us of human structuring of space.

But among their various vital functions, one is particularly striking, which appears quite particularly 'human' through the parallels with the human relationship with the house: the home, of which one also speaks within the animal territory. The home is the place where the animal rests and sleeps, just as does the human in his bed – and in certain circumstances there may even be several homes within the same territory, of varying importance, a main home with subsidiary homes as retreats. The home in the centre of the animal territory, therefore, is determined as a 'place of maximum seclusion.'[18] In this context Portmann points out: 'Home is a place where through peace and security essential moods of every higher animal find most satisfaction.'[19] It is certainly not just by chance that here, with animals, exactly the same concept of security arises that was decisive for us in discussing the anthropological function of the house. It is all the more evident in the discussion of existentialism that the concept of security already appears here as a necessary precondition of life.

In this connection, a further thought assumes greater importance for our question. Just as Saint-Exupéry at one point remarks that man becomes different according to the point in space that he occupies, the same is true of the animal: its nature changes according to whether it is within or outside its home or territory. The rightful owner of the territory tends to be superior to the intruder, even if it were to be the weaker outside that territory. From the wealth of literature on this subject I can give only a few particularly impressive examples.

Lorenz for example reports about jackdaws: 'As with all creatures that delimit their domains, with the jackdaw too the "possession" of a "territory" is based on the fact that the bird "at home" fights much more intensively than on foreign terrain. The jackdaw chattering in its own established nesting place [making itself heard by means of a certain call] therefore has a huge advantage from the start against any intruder; the latter generally weighs up even the greatest differences in rank that exist between the individual members of the colony.'[20] I will make two observations here for our purposes: one, that the bird is significantly stronger within its own

18 H. Hediger, cited by H. Peters, p. 524.

19 Adolf Portmann, *Das Tier als soziales Wesen*, Zurich: 1953, p. 273 [*Animals as social beings*, translated by Oliver Coburn, London: 1961, p. 177].

20 Konrad Lorenz, *Er redete mit dem Vieh, den Vögeln und den Fischen* Vienna: 1949, p. 101 [*King Solomon's ring* (1952), translated by Marjorie Kerr Wilson, London: 2002].

domain than outside it, and the other, that its home nevertheless remains under threat and must be defended, so that the territories are delimited from each other in an equilibrium of strength which must be constantly reassessed.

A description by Portmann of a sparrow which he calls Clarence is very relevant here: 'He has familiar places which have the emotive value of a home for him. He defends them; he is a different sparrow from outside in the strange world; he is the owner, gives evidence of a sense of possession. The defence of various homes is evidence that Clarence's living space has its own structure, that it has zones with different emotive values.'[21]

A very good further example refers to a quite different species, to the behaviour of sticklebacks, and I can do no better than quote the entire relevant text from Lorenz: 'It is only when he has founded his home that the stickleback becomes physically capable of reaching a state of full sexual excitement; therefore, a real stickleback fight can only be seen when two males are kept together in a large tank where they are both building their nests. The fighting inclinations of a stickleback, at any given moment, are in direct proportion to his proximity to his nest. At the nest itself, he is a raging fury and with a fine contempt of death will recklessly ram the strongest opponent, or even the human hand. The further he strays from his headquarters in the course of his swimming, the more his courage wanes. When two sticklebacks meet in battle, it is possible to predict with a high degree of certainty how the fight will end: the one which is further from his nest will lose the match. In the immediate neighbourhood of his nest, even the smallest male will defeat the largest one, and the relative fighting potential of the individual is shown by the size of the territory which he can keep clear of rivals. The vanquished fish invariably flees homeward and the victor, carried away by his successes, chases the other furiously, far into its domain. The further the victor goes from home, the more his courage ebbs, while that of the vanquished rises in proportion. Arrived in the precincts of his nest, the fugitive gains new strength, turns right about and dashes with gathering fury at his pursuer. A new battle begins, which ends with absolute certainty with the defeat of the former victor, and off goes the chase again in the opposite direction.'[22] This incorporates the processes described with total purity, the alteration of nature through location at a particular point in space is here almost reduced to a mathematical formula. In unfamiliar

21 Adolf Portmann, 'Vom Wunderspatzen zum Spatzenwunder', *Die Weltwoche* (11. 5. 1956).

22 Lorenz, *Er redete mit dem Vieh, den Vögeln und den Fischen*, p. 44 ff. [p. 25].

areas, that is, without a link to the nest to be defended, the stickleback loses his courage. 'Take his nest from a stickleback or remove him from the tank where he built it and put him with another male and he will not dream of fighting but, on the contrary, will make himself small and ugly.'

What has been described here can be transferred in an equivalent way to the human world. In the animal territory, human individual space too is delineated. But here we also see immediately the basic difference between man and animal. While the animal (as far as we can understand it) is firmly linked to its space, man has the possibility of withdrawing into himself by inwardly freeing himself from his individual space, and he gains inner freedom only by freeing himself in this way from his direct spatial connection. Thus man as wanderer becomes the symbol of this inner freedom.

> We should cheerfully traverse space by space,
> and not cling to any as to a home,[23]

writes Hermann Hesse, and the hero of *The glass bead game* formulates the resolution 'to make his actions and life ... into a transcendent, a resolutely cheerful striding, fulfilling and leaving behind of all space.'[24] How these two aspects, dwelling and wandering, resting in oneself and transcending, are more deeply bound up in man can only be touched upon here. At any rate, it is only after man has freed himself from this direct link with space that dwelling can become a task won in freedom and decisive for the fulfilment of human nature.

Free space

a. The protective character of space

The third space, of which it can be said that man dwells in it, is what we have called in a broad and general sense free space. We must try to clarify for ourselves the meaning of this statement. The statement that man dwells

---

23 'Wir sollen heiter Raum um Raum durchschreiten, / an keinem wie an einer Heimat hängen,' Hermann Hesse, *Das Glasperlenspiel. Gesammelte Dichtungen*, vol. 6, Frankfurt a. M.: 1952, p. 556.

24 'sein Tun und Leben ... zu einem Transzendieren, einem entschlossenheitern Durchschreiten, Erfüllen und Hintersichlassen jedes Raumes ... zu machen', Hesse, *Das Glasperlenspiel*, p. 483.

not only in a certain dwelling, but in space generally, means that he also lives in the sense of security and support that is based, in the house, on the material protection of the exterior and interior walls. But how is this possible where such material protection is no longer present?

Now, earlier we noticed that all sense of security in a house that is ultimately fragile, and all courage to rebuild a house over and over again, rests on the fact that this sense is supported by an ultimate and comprehensive trust in the world and in life that goes beyond all human activity. The mystery of this trust is the ultimate secret of human existence. And this again is most closely connected with our relationship with space, for the world is the most comprehensive space in which we live and with which we can also identify as with an individual space. Independently of all human protection, space itself now acquires a protective character.

In this respect, space differs significantly from time. Time makes us vulnerable to difficulties, for time is for the most part 'the time that tears' [reissende Zeit] (Hölderlin). Time signifies the transitory nature of all earthly things. 'For time is decay.'[25] This is how it has always been since the days of the Old Testament. Temporality means nothingness. This does not change even when, in Heideggerian terms, we confront it with the actual, deep temporality that is identical with man's own nature; for this is gained precisely in the decisive counter-movement against temporal threat, and does not remove the final isolation of man, but actually forces him into it. Man remains unsheltered in time. (Here I will disregard the experiences of a happily fulfilled present, because these, experienced as timelessness, are again indirectly based on the destructive character of time.)

But with space it is different. In space we are protected. Bachelard says: 'Space, vast space, is the friend of being',[26] where 'existence' in his terminology means human existence. So this sentence means that space is the friend of man. What is implied by this statement? Here Bachelard does not mean a special space in the house or in the nest. In the sentence quoted he speaks specifically of 'vast space', indeed it occurs in the context of his observation that man in the power of imagination can escape from the narrowness of 'here' to an 'elsewhere.' But I believe that this sentence can be taken in a more general sense. A friend is a person who is familiar to us, who is well-meaning towards us and in whose company we feel safe. If we transfer this to space, that is, not to a specific interior space, but to space in

25 Rainer Maria Rilke, *Briefe und Tagebücher aus der Frühzeit*, Leipzig: 1931, p. 248.

26 Bachelard, *Poetik des Raumes*, p. 238 [p. 208].

general, this would mean that man also finds an equivalent relationship of trust with space.

But how can space, the space that continues into infinity, transmit such a sense of security? This suggests that the concretely experienced space in which we live has by no means the character of infinity, but still retains that of a sheltering interior or hollow space, that is, the character that we found in the mythological view of the world and even in the space of classical antiquity. This space is indeed an extended hollow space, a house on a larger scale, so that we can transfer the characteristics of dwelling gained from the house to the world-space as well. So there is a gradation of dwellings: 'egg, nest, house, country and universe',[27] as Bachelard enumerates them with reference to Victor Hugo's *Hunchback of Notre-Dame*. And we can say, even of the last of these, 'the world is a nest',[28] a sheltering nest in which we can feel safe.

And just as the sun rises anew for us every morning in the east above the fixed earth, although we have long known 'better' from the Copernican system, so, despite all our knowledge about the infinity of the universe, space, as we concretely experience it, whether in a particular case it is narrower or wide, has always remained for us finite in its nature. We sense this particularly clearly in the experiences described in more detail earlier, in which space draws itself more closely around us in fog or in the night.[29] And however much distances may expand in the clear light of day, if it is to be protective, in principle the same character needs to be transferred to it.

b. Dwelling in free space

At this point we may be taken further by the concept of *retentissement*, of the echo in space, introduced by Minkowski in his book *Vers une cosmologie*. The literal meaning of echo is an acoustic phenomenon: how a space is filled with sound, when the sound waves are thrown back from the enclosing walls. But Minkowski adopts the concept to characterize, beyond the realm of acoustics, a general feature of experienced space. Space itself has an echoic character, through which it prevents the feeling of being diffused into the limitless. But how can infinitely open space prevent the diffusion of human consciousness? With the acoustic phenomenon walls were necessary to reflect the sound, which would otherwise vanish into

27 Bachelard, *Poetik des Raumes*, p. 119 [p. 90].
28 Bachelard, *Poetik des Raumes*, p. 132 [p. 103].
29 See the present book, pp. 244 ff., 249 ff.

infinity. But if this concept is to be transferred to space in general, this means that open space operates as though it had walls, so that we can be sheltered in it as though in a closed space.

Space can fulfil this task only because man does not originally find himself as a stranger in space, as a foreign element in it, but feels bound into it, merged with space and supported by it. It is this basic experience, immensely difficult to grasp, that Minkowski has in mind with the concept of echo, with which he seeks to express a 'fundamental property of life.'[30] Life can live in sympathy and harmony with its surroundings, because echo denotes a primeval state which is 'more original than the contrast of I and world.'[31] Because the split between subject and object is here removed or, rather, has not yet formed, this space can never become objective, but rather we can identify with it. Space belongs to us as does our body, and indeed we also have that singularly floating relationship with it that stands in the centre between having and being. In a certain sense we can say that we are our space. Bachelard stresses this too, when he particularly refers to the 'great' poetic line: 'Je suis l'espace où je suis.' [I am the space where I am.]'[32] Man is part of space and in that sense supported in the great encompassing space. In this way, man dwells in space. What we earlier anticipated as a statement, guided by linguistic usage, now receives its confirmation at this point. As a result of this merging, we may also extend the concept of dwelling to being in space. Man dwells in space in a way analogous to the way in which he dwells in his house, and dwelling in a house can give us protection, to the extent that man at the same time dwells more comprehensively in space.

For this reason we can now extend the concept of incarnation, which we at first transferred from the body to the house, to space in general, and cast new light on the concept of dwelling, often too carelessly understood, by saying that man is incarnated in space. That man is incarnated in space or that he dwells in space means more that he finds himself in a situation there. It says not only that he finds himself in a medium and can move in this medium, but also that he himself is part of this medium, separated from the rest of the medium by a boundary, and yet, beyond this, bound into it and supported by it. Because we are not 'thrown' into space, but embedded in it, no outer wall is necessary to hold it together. Admitted to it in this way, we are supported and sheltered by it.

30 Eugène Minkowski, *Vers une cosmologie*, Paris: 1936, p. 106.
31 Minkowski, *Vers une cosmologie*, p. 106.
32 Bachelard, *Poetik des Raumes*, p. 166 [p. 137].

So the original relationship with space is that of dwelling and not of intentionality. Here the forms considered earlier of an intentionally structured space of action are not cancelled, but they appear as something derivative, something later, and refer back to dwelling.

c. Other forms of becoming one with space

With these formulations, with the statement of a merging, of humans and space becoming one, we hesitate; for the suspicion impinges on us that perhaps we have been making high-flown statements that will not stand up to sober critical scrutiny. And yet it is the necessity of the thing itself that of its own accord constantly urges us to such formulations. But perhaps the statement of such a merging of man with his space loses some of its disconcerting nature when we remember that in the course of our investigations we have already encountered various phenomena of merging, and that these were not recounted by ourselves, but attested by the various authors that have been quoted.

We find this most clearly in the 'presential space' of dancing, as discussed by Straus; for when he points out that in dancing we do not move 'through space' but 'in space', this suggests a fundamentally altered relationship with space, where, as Straus himself explicitly stresses, the tension between subject and object is removed. Even when he points out that this 'totally altered space' is no longer determined by direction and distance, but by other qualities such as depth and width, this would entirely agree with our definition of individual space, not to be intentionally grasped. In general it was similar with the problem of mood space, most clearly with that of the optimist, as described by Binswanger. If objects here lose their sharp edges, so that man can glide freely and easily through them, this too is to be understood as a lessening of the tension between subject and object.

Furthermore, we should here accept nocturnal space, as we have tried to depict it with reference to Minkowski. With the unavoidability of the formulation that nocturnal space, as it were, lies upon the skin and encroaches without a sharp boundary on my interior or draws us into itself, the experience, difficult to grasp, is expressed that this space is so much more closely bound up with us that it appears to be an almost physically tangible medium into which we are admitted. And when Novalis says that the night supports us in a motherly way, this equally characterizes nocturnal space in the sense of such an active pervasiveness. Finally, we must remember how Merleau-Ponty had to invoke the 'mythological unity of the *mana*' to clarify the way in which night pervades us and positively extinguishes our 'personal identity.' And this again would be linked to the way in which, in acoustic space, sounds directly stream through us. Minkowski describes it thus: 'A melody, a symphony, even a single note, above all if it is heavy and deep, prolong themselves in us, pervade us to the basis of our existence, actually resonate in us.'[33]

All these connections are so difficult to understand because they belong to a realm which still lies before the foundation of our objective consciousness. And yet it forms the supportive basic layer, from which we live even after the formation of our consciousness, even though in general we are not aware of it, indeed it seeks by its own nature to withdraw itself from our cognition; for because our conceptual cognition assumes the connection between the formation of consciousness and the division between subject and object, it is incapable of adequately understanding this quite different area. There is no other choice but at least to describe it by necessarily inappropriate means, in order to view the experiences that it is based on. Nevertheless, it would be an unacceptable simplification of these relationships if, out of fear of possible misunderstanding, we were to come to a halt here, without attempting a further suggestion possibly going beyond the boundary of what can be adequately expressed.

33 Minkowski, *Vers une cosmologie*, p. 106.

3. Summary and Prospects

Modes of human space

Concerning the question of the relationship of man with space or his attitude to space, in the course of discussion various successive forms have emerged, which are not mutually exclusive, but rather overlap each other and are possible in combination with each other, and which one can thus designate as modifications of human spatiality. It therefore seems appropriate, in conclusion, to put them together once more in a schematic simplification.

1. First there is a naïve trust in space, a childish sense of shelter, which can then continue in later life as a natural or thoughtless sense of shelter in one's house and home. Here we are merged with our space, directly incarnated in it.

2. Secondly there is a state of homelessness or houselessness. Here space manifests itself in its uncanniness and strangeness. We feel lost in this space.

3. This results in, third, the task of reconstructing security by building a house, as discussed in detail in the third part of this book. Through this a sheltering inner space is created, separated from the outside world. Menacing space does not disappear as a result, it is only pushed out of the centre and to the side.

4. But because every house created by humans proves to be tangible (and because, further, menacing space still continues to lurk, hidden, even within the house), a further final task arises, to overcome once more the withdrawal into a fixed housing and to regain a final security in a space which is no longer the individual space of the house, based on man, but overall space in general. We must therefore, beyond the rigid appearance of an artificially created and always deceptive security, reach the other, open security in which naïve spatiality is reconstructed on a higher level. But to reach this is not easy, and demands from us the special effort of freeing ourselves from the deceptive security.

The precedence of protective space

At this point the obvious objection to Bachelard's *Poetics of space* seems to have been resolved: namely that in his 'topophilia' (as he himself calls his viewpoint), his love of space, he restricts himself to 'images of *felicitous space*', while totally neglecting 'hostile space.'[1] This restriction, which he himself explicitly stresses, at first indeed seems to be a dubious one-sidedness, which substantially limits his book's claim to insight, and nothing seems more urgent than to extend and examine his findings by means of a complementary investigation of the 'spaces of hate and battle', as indeed has already been done in the excellent lecture by Pabst.[2] But as important as this extension to hostile and threatening space is, it can be tackled only *after* the completed analysis of happy spaces. For Bachelard's decisive and objectively totally justified approach means that these two modifications of spatiality, the happy and the hostile spaces, do not oppose each other on the same level as spaces of equal value, but the happy space is the original space, and it is only retrospectively and arising from its preconditions that the experience of hostile space is formed, which must then be overcome again on a new level.

The sentences already quoted in part above[3] must be seen, with explicit acuteness, in this context: 'The house … is the human being's first world. Before he is "cast into the world", as claimed by certain hasty metaphysics, man is laid in the cradle of the house.'[4] 'The experience of the hostility of the world … comes much later. In its germinal form, therefore, all of life is well-being.'[5] This clearly implies a sequence: '[F]rom the phenomenologist's viewpoint [who sees origins], the conscious metaphysics that start from the moment when the being is "cast into the world" is a secondary metaphysics. It passes over the preliminaries, when being is being-well, when the human being is deposited in a being-well, in the well-being originally associated with being.'[6] When he mentions 'conscious metaphysics' or a 'metaphysics of consciousness', where he probably specifically has Sartre in mind, we must understand this as a philosophical position which takes its beginnings from the developed consciousness. Bachelard opposes this

1 Bachelard, *Poetik des Raumes*, p. 29 ff. [p. XXXI ff.].

2 W. Pabst, 'Funktionen des Raumes in der modernen französischen Literatur', *Universitätstag 1960. Veröffentlichung der Freien Universität Berlin*, 1960.

3 See the present book, p. 300.

4 Bachelard, *Poetik des Raumes*, p. 39 [p. 7].

5 Bachelard, *Poetik des Raumes*, p. 132 [p. 103].

6 Bachelard, *Poetik des Raumes*, p. 39 [p. 7].

to the phenomenological position, which sees 'origins', 'preliminaries, when being is being-well.' In contrast with 'conscious metaphysics' this can only mean a position which refers back to an original stratum of human existence, which lies even further back than the formation of objective consciousness, as has indeed always seemed to us necessary for the description of an original oneness with space.

In contrast to this, the area of experience of the 'metaphysics of consciousness' only comes second: 'To illustrate the metaphysics of consciousness we should have to wait for the experiences during which being is cast out, that is to say, thrown out, outside the being if the house, a circumstance in which the hostility of men and of the universe accumulates.'[7] Bachelard also recognizes the justification of this aspect. A 'complete metaphysics' for him is one that '[encompasses] both the conscious and the unconscious.' But it is bound not only to the temporal, but also to the objective fundamental order of things, it 'would leave the privilege of its values within [that is, within the world of the house].'[8] This is a view which is in total agreement with the structure of the modes of human space that we have sketched out here.

Requirements for true dwelling

These four modes of the human relationship with space not only develop separately in a temporal sequence, but they are also preserved throughout the course of life and overlap each other in a richly structured system of strata. But just as in a temporal sense the realization of actual temporality (as developed by Heidegger) does not happen of its own accord, but demands of us the entire effort of our existence, so it is in relation to space. If we have designated the true form of human life in space as dwelling, this dwelling again is something that we can grasp and realize only in the full effort of our being. This is why Heidegger has stressed with profound justification that man must first learn to dwell.

At the same time, conditions in the spatial constitution of humans are yet again more complicated than with temporality, to the extent that there are two opposites to true dwelling: not-dwelling in the sense of homeless thrown-ness into a hostile space, and false dwelling in the sense of fearful withdrawal into one's housing. Only, the place of true dwelling cannot be

7 Bachelard, *Poetik des Raumes*, p. 40 [p. 7].
8 Bachelard, *Poetik des Raumes*, p. 40 [p. 7].

found in the Aristotelian centre between these two opposites, but rather there are several different strata which are determined by this opposition.

The task of true dwelling is thus structured in a threefold manner and can be summarized schematically into three requirements:

The first requirement is directed against the homelessness of the refugee and adventurer wandering adrift in space. This means the necessity of settling in a particular place in space, firmly establishing oneself there and creating an individual space of security.

The two other requirements are based on the danger of missing the true mode of dwelling in this individual space. That is, one requirement (the second in the overall scheme) is directed against the danger of becoming isolated in one's inner space. It thus demands the total inclusion in life even of menacing and dangerous exterior space, and the toleration of the whole tension between the two spaces in which alone human life can be fulfilled.

On the other hand it is also a question, in spite of a tension with menacing exterior space, of overcoming one's naïve faith in the strength of one's own house and allowing oneself to be supported in a general trust of that greater space. As a result that 'great space' loses its dangerous character, and itself once more becomes a sheltering space, as we have tried to depict it in this last section.[9] Thus the third requirement consists in being able, while dwelling in one's house, to entrust oneself at the same time to the greater totality of space.

It is from the threefold demand of these requirements that man realizes his human nature through true dwelling in space.

---

9 Following the present publication, I have further developed the concept of a supporting and giving nature in my lecture 'Die Stadt, das Grün und der Mensch' ['The city, nature and humans'] at the International Green Forum, Osaka 1986, now in my book *Zwischen Philosophie und Pädagogik*, Aachen: 1988, pp. 44-62.

MIMESIS GROUP
www.mimesis-group.com

MIMESIS INTERNATIONAL
www.mimesisinternational.com
info@mimesisinternational.com

MIMESIS EDIZIONI
www.mimesisedizioni.it
mimesis@mimesisedizioni.it

ÉDITIONS MIMÉSIS
www.editionsmimesis.fr
info@editionsmimesis.fr

MIMESIS COMMUNICATION
www.mim-c.net

MIMESIS EU
www.mim-eu.com

Printed in Great Britain
by Amazon